OUTLANDER AND THE REAL JACOBITES

To/ Nadya.
Thank you so much for buying!
I hope you enjoy it!

Sharon.

For Diana Gabaldon, who gave us Outlander and sparked an interest in the Jacobites that made this book possible.

OUTLANDER AND THE REAL JACOBITES

Scotland's Fight for Freedom

Shona Kinsella

PEN & SWORD HISTORY

AN IMPRINT OF PEN & SWORD BOOKS LTD.
YORKSHIRE – PHILADELPHIA

First published in Great Britain in 2022 by
PEN AND SWORD HISTORY
An imprint of
Pen & Sword Books Ltd
Yorkshire – Philadelphia

ISBN 978 1 39900 471 8

A CIP catalogue record for this book is available from the British Library.

Typeset in Times New Roman 11.5/14 by
SJmagic DESIGN SERVICES, India.
Printed and bound in the UK by CPI Group (UK) Ltd, Croydon, CR0 4YY.

Pen & Sword Books Limited incorporates the imprints of Atlas, Archaeology,
Aviation, Discovery, Family History, Fiction, History, Maritime, Military, Military
Classics, Politics, Select, Transport, True Crime, Air World, Frontline Publishing,
Leo Cooper, Remember When, Seaforth Publishing, The Praetorian Press,
Wharncliffe Local History, Wharncliffe Transport, Wharncliffe True Crime and
White Owl.

For a complete list of Pen & Sword titles please contact
PEN & SWORD BOOKS LIMITED
47 Church Street, Barnsley, South Yorkshire, S70 2AS, England
E-mail: enquiries@pen-and-sword.co.uk
Website: www.pen-and-sword.co.uk

Or
PEN AND SWORD BOOKS
1950 Lawrence Rd, Havertown, PA 19083, USA
E-mail: Uspen-and-sword@casematepublishers.com
Website: www.penandswordbooks.com

Contents

Contents

PART 6: THE AFTERMATH

Concerning Dates

During the time period in which these events took place, Britain was still using the Julian calendar (Old Style or O.S.), while the rest of Europe had already adopted the Gregorian calendar (New Style or N.S.). This means that the date in Britain was 11 days behind the rest of Europe. In general, the dates given here will correspond to the country in which the events are taking place. Where there is any doubt, I have added (O.S.) or (N.S.) for clarity. To further complicate matters, the Julian year traditionally began on 25 March, a custom that was kept in England, but not Scotland, where the year was considered to start on 1 January. Therefore, any dates between 1 January and 25 March would be written as (for example) 17 January 1745/6, while after 25 March the date would simply be 1746.

Introduction

Like many people, I first came to *Outlander* through the television series. I had been hearing about it for a while but dismissed it as a historical romance at first, which wasn't the type of show I was looking for. Eventually though, the buzz won me over and I decided to give it a try. I have to say that I am very glad that I did. Within two episodes I was utterly captivated by Claire's adventures in the past, aided by the delightful highlander, Jamie Fraser. The show led me to the books, which are just beautifully written, and ultimately to a deep interest in the struggle of the Jacobites.

You see, as well as a thrilling backdrop for a dangerous romance, the 1745 Jacobite uprising was something of a turning point in Scottish history, the results of which can arguably still be seen today. The Bonnie Prince lives on in our memories and in our folk music, with songs such as *Charlie He's My Darling*[1], *Johnny Cope*[2] and, of course, *The Skye Boat Song*[3], which will be familiar to viewers of the *Outlander* television series as the theme song for the show. These songs all contribute to our cultural memory of the young man who sparked a rebellion with little more than his strength of character.

It's clear that Diana Gabaldon did a huge amount of research during the writing of the *Outlander* series, as so many of the details in the narrative clearly show. According to Dr Gabaldon[4], she had decided that she wanted to try her hand at writing a book and had settled on a historical novel, but had no particular knowledge of any time period and so knew that she was facing a lot of research, whatever time period she chose. She was watching an old episode of Doctor Who one night, which featured a young Scottish Jacobite who sparked her imagination. Interestingly, the character was named Jamie McCrimmon and was played by actor Frazer Hines[5]. It seems likely that this is the origin of the name of *Outlander's* leading man, James Alexander Malcom MacKenzie Fraser, however, there was a historical Jacobite named James Fraser, whose actions finally forced the 'Old Fox' Lord Lovat to openly side with Prince Charles[6]. Perhaps this James was part of the inspiration – or perhaps it's just a coincidence. James would have been a common name at the time, especially amongst those loyal to the Stuarts.

Outlander tells the story of Claire Randall, an English woman who served as a combat nurse during the Second World War. The book begins in 1945, when Claire and her husband Frank visit Inverness for a second honeymoon of sorts, an effort to reacquaint themselves with each other after the long separation of the war. One day, while exploring a nearby stone circle, Claire inadvertently passes through some sort of portal to the past, arriving disoriented and confused in 1743. She is soon set upon by an English soldier (commonly referred to as the Redcoats, due to their distinctive uniform) and 'rescued' by a group of highlanders who then take her hostage. Claire is caught between the English army, suspicious highlanders, and a group of Jacobites working to support a Stuart restoration. The following text will contain spoilers for the first three books in the series: *Outlander, Dragonfly in Amber, and Voyager* and the first three seasons of the television series. So, if you haven't read/watched those, you might want to do that first and then come back to this.

The word Jacobite comes from the Latin, Jacobus, meaning James[7]. The Jacobites were, simply put, supporters of the exiled King James II and VII. In order to understand the events of the 1745 uprising, it would be useful to take a brief look at the circumstances which led to it.

In 1676, James Stuart, brother of King Charles II, and heir to the throne, converted to Catholicism. This caused a great deal of panic in the Protestant circles of power, but was tolerable until 1685, when James assumed the throne upon the death of Charles. At this time, James' eldest child, Mary – a Protestant – became heir, a situation which somewhat reassured those that were unhappy with a Catholic monarch. In June 1688, James's wife, Queen Mary, gave birth to a son, James Francis Edward Stuart, who immediately displaced Princess Mary as heir. James Francis Edward, the Prince of Wales, was going to be raised Catholic, like his parents and for some of the most powerful Protestants in England, this could not be tolerated. They reached out to William of Orange, husband of Princess Mary, and asked him to invade, removing James from the throne. William was only too happy to help.[8]

By December 1688, James fled to France and on 13 February 1689, William and Mary were crowned King and Queen of England. Scotland's Jacobites first rose only a month later, led by Major-General Viscount Dundee. They faced a number of battles with the Redcoats before agreeing to peace in December 1691, with many of their officers travelling to France. William of Orange had offered amnesty to any Jacobites who took an oath of fealty to him before 31 December 1691. MacIain, chief of the Glencoe MacDonalds, was late in taking the oath and as a punishment, Sir John Dalrymple, Secretary of State for Scotland, ordered the massacre of the Glencoe MacDonalds[9] in order to set an example to any remaining Jacobite sympathisers.

In 1707, the Act of Union united the kingdoms of England and Scotland, a development with which many Scottish Jacobites were unhappy. In 1714, the throne passed to George, Elector of Hanover, in line with the Act of Settlement 1701. In 1715, the Scottish Jacobites rose again, led by the Earl of Mar, John Erskine. They were joined in December by James Francis Edward Stuart, James the VIII of Scotland and III of England. James remained with them until February 1716, when he fled to France and the Jacobite army disbanded. The Jacobites were punished harshly – especially those from England – with the punishment of being hung, drawn and quartered, with those who were spared often losing their lands and titles. In Scotland, the penalties were lighter, such that George demanded some Scottish Jacobites be marched across the border and tried in English courts[10].

There was a small, local uprising in 1719, which ended after one decisive battle, after the Spanish failed to send support that had been promised. After that, things settled down in Scotland for a number of years, however Jacobite activity did not truly cease; they were waiting for a better time to act.

In 1720, Prince Charles Edward Stuart – Bonnie Prince Charlie – was born in Rome. Jacobites everywhere celebrated this extension of the Stuart line. Perhaps from that moment on, the events of 1745 and 1746 were inevitable.

PART ONE

Highland Life in the 1700s

Chapter One

The MacKenzies and the Frasers –
What Was Clan Life Really Like?

When Claire arrives in 1743, she is rescued/captured by a group of men belonging to Clan MacKenzie. They take her to their home, Castle Leoch, where Callum/Colum (this character is called Callum in the books but Colum in the TV series. For consistency, I'll be using Callum throughout) MacKenzie invites her to stay as a guest – although it is soon made clear to her that she is not at liberty to leave. Claire subsequently spends several months living alongside the MacKenzies.[1] But what was clan life really like?

The word 'clan' comes from the Gaelic '*clann*' meaning children, or more broadly, descendants. It was believed that clans were large, extended family groups, bound by descent from a common ancestor. The reality seems to have been a little different. Clans in Scotland formed during the early Middle Ages, when people did not trust the crown to protect them. Instead, they gathered around men of charisma and influence, forming communities that were tied by strong bonds of kinship, loyalty and responsibility.[2] Indeed, according to the contemporary letters of English engineer Edmund Burt, many clansmen viewed their duty to their chief above even their duty to the crown.[3]

The clan chiefs were feudal landowners[4], who then rented land to tenants, who often took on subtenants of their own in order to work the land. The clan chief provided protection of the land and livestock (cattle raiding was a common pastime in the highlands; that was what Dougal and his band were up to when they stumbled across Claire at the mercy of Captain Randall) as well as supporting his people through times of scarcity and need. In exchange, the tenants paid rent to the chief (as often in goods as in money) and pledged their military service to him, should it be needed. This was far more effective than trying to maintain a standing army in the difficult lands of the highlands, but it also meant that the loyalty of any army from the highlands and islands would be to their chiefs – and there was no guarantee that the clan chiefs' loyalties lay with the crown[5].

The highlands and islands of Scotland during that time period operated on what is called subsistence culture, meaning that the produce and livestock that were farmed were largely required for the survival of the people who lived and worked on the land. Cash was relatively rare, especially in comparison with today's society – the most common form of exchange was the barter system, where one farmer would exchange cheese or milk for grain or meal from another[6]. Goods and services were often traded in this way meaning that the entire community depended upon each other for survival and most likely had strong bonds as a result. This ties in with the life that Claire experiences at Castle Leoch, as well as the smaller towns and villages that she visits later with Dougal and Ned, while collecting the rents owed to the MacKenzies.

In Leoch, we see that everyone has a job, be it working in the kitchen or stables, hunting or farming, and in exchange, everyone has room and board, clothing that they need, and medical care provided. Soon after her arrival, Claire is put to work as the clan's healer, taking over from the recently deceased Davie Beaton, who we are told was from a family of renowned healers. In exchange for her room and board and clothing, Claire uses her skills to treat the mostly minor ills of those from the castle and the local village. After proving her mettle as a healer during a hunt, where one man is severely injured and another killed, Dougal decides to take her with him and his men as they travel around the MacKenzie lands, collecting rent. This gives Claire the opportunity to observe everyday life in the highlands during the eighteenth century.

Coming from the grand stone structure of Leoch, the small cottages and blackhouses – often built with stones without cement, with thatched roofs, windows without glass and often with a dirt floor[7] – must have been something of a surprise to her. The majority of these homes had only one room in which the entire family lived and slept, sometimes alongside their livestock. Despite having little space, travellers would be made welcome and given somewhere dry to sleep, even if it was only on the floor by the hearth, and families would share what food they had. Some of the larger towns had inns, such as the one where Jamie and Claire spend their wedding night, but many of the smaller settlements visited by the MacKenzie party were too far from the main roads through the highlands to see many visitors.

During this trip, in one village, Claire is invited to take part in 'waulking the wool' – an invitation that would have been considered quite an honour[8]. Waulking was an important part of tweed production, almost always carried out by the women of the community. When a tweed was ready, the weave was still quite loose; in order to tighten and soften the cloth and set the dye, the fabric was soaked in *maistir* – stale urine. The cloth was then rhythmically pounded on the table until it shrank and softened. The work was accompanied by traditional songs that have been passed down for hundreds of years. This was a very social time for the women carrying out the work and this is caught beautifully in Claire's experience, sharing whisky and gossip while singing and laughing and working together.

The MacKenzies

The first clan that Claire has experience with are the MacKenzies of Leoch, led by Callum MacKenzie. As mentioned earlier, the clans formed around men of power and influence and although leadership often passed to the son of the previous chief, it was not always automatic. An important role of the chief was to lead the clan in battle, and if there was a reason to believe that the obvious heir was incapable of this, leadership could pass to another. This is an area in which we see the real strength of character shown by Callum MacKenzie. As the eldest son, Callum was heir but, after a bad fall from a horse when he was eighteen, it became apparent that he had a degenerative medical condition which would prevent him from leading the clan into battle. This could have resulted in the mantle of chief passing to his brother, Dougal, a great warrior, respected for his fighting prowess. However, Dougal is hot-headed and impulsive, not qualities that one would usually look for in a chief.

The two brothers make things work by each contributing their own strength for the good of the clan; Callum became Laird and clan chief while Dougal took on the role of war chieftain. There are many differences and conflicts between the brothers, but the greatest is over support for James, the 'king over the water'. Dougal is a staunch Jacobite, using his tour of the MacKenzie lands to raise money for the cause, while Callum is more cautious – while he may support the Stuarts in principle, he is

4

unwilling to risk the lives and future of the clansmen by committing them all to an uprising.

But what about the historic MacKenzies? Where did they stand?

The MacKenzie clan came to prominence in Scotland during the fifteenth century, receiving a crown charter in 1476 for lands in central Ross-shire[9], an area that lies close to Inverness – or close enough that it makes sense for Claire to be found by a band of MacKenzie men when she first comes through the stones at Craigh na Dun, outside of Inverness. After this, they ruthlessly expanded until their lands stretched from Lewis on the west coast, to Ross on the east. A story is told[10] that in the early 1600s, King James VI sent the MacKenzies to subdue the Macleods of Lewis. Eventually, the Macleods retreated to the island of Bearnaray, where they holed up in a fortress which had withstood many sieges over the years. However, some of the clan's women and children did not make it to safety; the chief of the MacKenzies had them gathered up and abandoned them on an island that disappeared during high tide, leaving them to drown unless the Macleods surrendered. Obviously, the Macleods were forced to surrender, and the MacKenzies claimed their land. However, not all expansion was at the detriment of other clans – the MacKenzies also secured land and power through strategic marriages and enfolding smaller clans who relied on their more powerful neighbours for support and defence[11].

By the eighteenth century, the MacKenzie seat and home of the clan chief, was Castle Leod, located in Easter Ross, which is still the home of the current chief of Clan MacKenzie, the Earl of Cromartie. Interestingly, the family actually lost the castle and lands after taking part in the uprising in 1745 but they were bought back by Lord Cromartie's son, John, and have remained in the family since[12].

It's clear from this that the MacKenzies took part in the uprising, although it seems that they did not join immediately, despite Lord Cromartie being known to Charles as an ardent supporter[13]. It seems that George was initially reluctant to call his clan to arms in support of Charles, despite his Jacobite sympathies, perhaps because of the lack of French support. Regardless of his concerns, George and his son, Lord John Macleod, eventually came out in support of Charles and joined the second Jacobite army that was forming around Perth. John was captured after the Battle of Meikle Ferry, while George was arrested after capturing

Dunrobin Castle (although this was made somewhat easier by the fact that the Countess of Sutherland had Jacobite sympathies herself).

Both men were taken to London for trial. George, the Earl of Cromartie was sentenced to death but his wife, Isabella, six months pregnant at the time, petitioned King George II for mercy, and was supported by Prince Frederick. Cromartie was released and lived the rest of his days in banishment in Devon[14]. Upon his release from prison, John served in the Swedish army and received high honours there, becoming an Earl Marichal and being given the created title of Count Cromartie of Sweden. When he returned to Scotland, he and his brother George raised an army unit that would become known as the Highland Light Infantry and went to fight in India on behalf of the government. Ultimately, John was able to return to Scotland and pay substantial back taxes on the Cromartie estate, making Castle Leod his family home once more[15].

The Frasers

Clan Fraser play both a larger and a smaller role in *Outlander* than Clan MacKenzie. During her enforced stay with the MacKenzies of Leoch, Claire becomes very attached to a handsome young highlander, who is introduced to her as Jamie McTavish. Later, she discovers that his name is James Fraser, and that he is an outlaw, with a price upon his head. The MacKenzies are protecting him because he is nephew to Callum and Dougal. Through family schisms and clan offshoots, Jamie is a laird in his own right, Lord Broch Tuarach, a Fraser chief, and heir to the estate of Lallybroch.

Claire spends some time at Lallybroch and gets to know some of Jamie's people in *Outlander* before they are forced to flee to France. Jamie is a Jacobite at heart, but Claire's knowledge of the future convinces him that he must try to prevent the uprising, which we will discuss further in later chapters. Jamie is eventually forced to call his men to arms and join Prince Charles Edward Stuart in his attempt to take the throne.

The larger part of the Fraser clan answers to Jamie's grandfather, Simon Fraser, the eleventh Lord Lovat. This character would appear to be based heavily on the real historical figure, even down to carrying the nickname, the 'Old Fox'. What do we know of the historical Lord Lovat?

Many of the details given in *Dragonfly in Amber,* when Jamie is telling Claire about his grandfather, are based on stories of the real Lord Lovat. Simon Fraser allegedly secured the title of Lord Lovat for himself by a forced marriage to Lady Amelia Lovat, the widow of the tenth Lord Lovat. He lost the title when his marriage was annulled, and he was forced to flee the country to escape retribution from Lady Amelia's family. He then spent several decades claiming to be a Jacobite, while reporting to the Hanoverian Crown, attempting to appear loyal and curry favour with both sides. He regained the title and estates of Lord Lovat in 1733 through the legal system[16].

In 1742, Simon Fraser, Lord Lovat, signed a letter in support of the Stuart claim to the throne which advised that there would be at least 20,000 clansmen ready to rise and dedicate themselves to the cause[17]. Despite this, we know that Lord Lovat did not openly rebel until the actions of one of his men – a James Fraser – caused him to be arrested. He then escaped and raised his clan to join the Prince's army[18], although it seems that he may have been working behind the scenes on the Prince's behalf the whole time. It is unclear to what extent this is true, as he also wrote to the government in London, claiming that his son was the Jacobite and that he, himself, had no hand in raising the clan. The government were not impressed with this excuse. Lord Lovat was captured following the Jacobite defeat at Culloden and was executed for treason.

Like the MacKenzie estates, the Lovat title and estates were also seized by the crown in punishment for the Frasers' part in the uprising. Also, like the MacKenzies, the title and lands were won back by the Old Fox's son, also named Simon. Young Simon raised a large regiment of foot soldiers and fought with them on behalf of the British government, in North America, winning distinction for his military skills and earning a seat in Parliament. The traditional Fraser lands and title were restored in 1774[19].

Chapter Two

Claire the Hostage – How Were Women Treated in the Highlands?

When Claire first comes to in 1743, she is disoriented from her trip through the stones and stumbles around, trying to find her way back to the road and to her car. She comes across a group of highlanders being closely pursued by a company of dragoons and initially assumes that she has wandered into some sort of re-enactment. That is, until she finds a man in a Redcoat uniform who bears a striking resemblance to her husband, Frank. This man introduces himself as Jonathan Wolverton Randall, Captain of Dragoons, the very ancestor that Frank had been researching on their trip to Inverness. As soon as he hears Claire's educated English accent, he becomes suspicious and attempts to arrest her, after taking a little pleasure for himself…so Claire is immediately faced with an attempted rape at the hands of a man who looks like her husband and is in a position of authority.

One of the highlanders doubles back and rescues Claire from Captain Randall. He takes her to meet with the other highlanders, who are also suspicious of a clearly well-educated English lady wandering around the remote Scottish countryside, unaccompanied, and wearing a 1940s summer dress which, to them, appears to be her shift. Claire is taken to Castle Leoch, where her story of having been attacked by bandits on the road and losing her escort and belongings is not really believed. The MacKenzies think that she might be an English spy, there to look for Jacobite sympathisers; or perhaps a French spy, reporting back to the Stuarts or Louis XV. Callum decides to keep her close until they can establish who she really is and where her loyalties lie. All the while, Claire wants nothing more than to find her way back to Craigh na Dun and attempt to get back through the stones to Frank.

Claire is restricted by the fact that she has no money and no means of travel but those are not the only things keeping her at the mercy of the MacKenzies. She is a woman travelling alone in a time when that was very uncommon. She is English, in a place where high-born English women do not often travel. Her background as a nurse makes her valuable as a healer, but also may have brought suspicion down upon her with regards to witchcraft, as will be discussed later. Claire as a woman, is forthright, outspoken, she swears in a way that is completely at odds with a highborn lady of the time (and was fairly unusual in a polite, married lady in her own time as well), fiercely independent and not at all inclined to play the role of the 'little woman'.

On the surface, this does not seem consistent with the roles and expectations placed on women in Scotland during that time. We know that women were largely expected to be subordinate to their husbands, an expectation which was included in the marriage ceremony itself[1]. Prior to marriage, it was expected that a woman was obedient to her father (or another male relative) in all things and following marriage, her husband was her master[2]. Women were not allowed to enter into any legal obligations such as contracts or buying and selling property, without the permission of her husband or father[3]. A woman would not be recognised as a witness in court and could not testify on their own behalf, with the notable exception of the witch trials[4].

At the time of her arrival in 1743, Claire assumes the role of a widow, as her husband is not alive in this time period. This would have placed her into one of the most economically vulnerable groups of the time[5]. There were a few notable widows who inherited their husband's business interests, or can be found in records running schools, or brewing ale and were able to establish themselves, but it was by far more common for widows to be forced to rely on charity[6]. In Claire's case, it also puts her in the unfortunate position that, with no one to come looking for her, no husband or father to negotiate with Callum on her behalf, she is entirely at his mercy, indeed, at the mercy of any man who decides he can claim some authority over her, as Captain Randall attempts to do, later.

Although women were generally unable to hold property or access money in their own rights, they were a valuable part of the economy, undertaking a great deal of the work that was done, especially in rural communities. There were jobs which required a man and wife team, such as coal mining and agricultural servants in the Lothians[7] but even a man working for himself in farming would often require the assistance of a wife, who may have caried out much of the harvesting work as well as various other tasks. Many women from rural communities also undertook paid work around the obligations of farm life and the family. In the later 1700s, four out of five women in Scotland were in some way employed in the manufacture of wool and linen, using spinning wheels and drop spindles in their homes[8]. Despite the fact that women were undertaking a great deal of work both inside and outside the home, for employment, they could expect to be paid no more than half of what men were paid for the same work, except perhaps at harvest time, when there was so much work that needed to be done in a short time that labourers held a little more bargaining power[9].

Much of the work of the time was allocated to gender roles, but perhaps not in the same way we would expect today. For example, while we largely associate beer with men now, traditionally brewing was a woman's job. History tells us that women were brewing beer at least as far back as 4,000 years ago[10]. It was after all, originally a domestic task. In the eighteenth century, beer was drunk at least as often as water and for poor people was a necessary addition to their diet for the nutrients contained in the brew. Most housewives would have included brewing as one of their regular tasks[11]. Some widows and unmarried women sold beer in the local markets as a way of earning some money, while skilled married brewers would establish businesses with their husbands. This association of women and brewing only changed as the economic model changed – brewing moved out of the domestic realm and became more about business and men swooped in to take over[12]. They even went so far as to accuse women brewers of witchcraft, giving us a legacy which endures today. Many brewers who sold their beer at market wore tall, pointy hats, so they would be easily spotted in a busy marketplace. They brewed their ale in cauldrons and often kept cats, not as familiars, but to keep the mice away from the grain. These are all items linked with witches to this day.

It was not at all unusual, then, for Claire to be put to work around Castle Leoch to earn her keep. When she is not running her surgery, she often works in the castle garden, tending to the plants which keep everyone fed, under the supervision of the formidable Mrs Fitzgibbons. Affectionately known as Mrs Fitz, this woman runs the household staff at Castle Leoch, making sure that all necessary jobs are taken care of as well as looking after the staff and essentially mothering them. She is a wonderful example of how women could be the master of their domain. No one would dream of mistreating Mrs Fitz or even talking back to her. Anyone – male or female – lounging around without a job to do will quickly be put to work, but anyone who is poorly or dealing with a difficult situation will be taken care of with kindness and generosity. Although, as a woman, she is technically lower in the social hierarchy than the men of the castle, in reality, she answers only to Callum and his wife, Letitia. Even Dougal would face a swift telling off for intruding on her domain.

When we meet Jamie's older sister, Jenny Murray, we see another woman who is very much the head of her household, having become the woman of the house upon the death of their mother when she was just ten years old. After Jamie had left Lallybroch and their father died, Jenny took over the running of the estate and the care of the tenants until she married Ian Murray, at which point they carried out the work together, very much as equal partners.

In Jenny's story we do also see some of the chauvinism of the time. When Jenny was still a young, unmarried woman, some Redcoats visited Lallybroch and were harassing her. Jamie stepped in to protect her and was beaten, although he did a fair amount of damage to the soldiers himself. This was the moment when Jamie and Jack Randall became enemies, a situation which would haunt them both for years to come. Randall threatened to rape Jenny if Jamie did not submit. Jamie stopped fighting and allowed himself to be beaten and arrested in an attempt to protect his sister, but Randall took her into the house with the intention of raping her anyway. Jenny escaped this by laughing at Randall, leaving him unable to perform and so furious that he beat her senseless. The chauvinism in the story isn't just the way that Randall treated Jenny, though. It's in the way that Jamie stayed away for years to come because he believed that his sister lost her virtue over him. It's in the fact that Dougal told Jamie that Jenny had birthed Randall's illegitimate child as a result of the attack and that Jamie considered this something shameful and a reason to stay away from home. It's in the fact that these men thought that they had some right to a woman's body – to use it or to police it – an attitude that pervaded society at the time and is still far too common in our own.

We see from history that not all women were meek and mild and though they were generally expected to obey their husbands or fathers, there were plenty who had their own minds and made their own decisions. Three such women played a particular role in the 1745 uprising.

Lady Anne Mackintosh was born Anne Farquharson in 1723, the daughter of John Farquharson of Invercauld[13]. At the age of nineteen, she married Angus Mackintiosh, chief of Clan Mackintosh, and a captain in the Black Watch, an infantry regiment in the British army, made up of clans who were loyal to the Hanoverians[14]. Despite this, Anne maintained her own loyalty to the Jacobite cause and, when Charles raised his standard, she raised a regiment from both the Mackintosh and the Farquharson clans which joined Charles at Bannockburn just before the battle at Falkirk. Her husband reportedly called her 'Colonel' after he was released from Jacobite custody and the nickname stuck, although she never led men in battle. Lady Anne went on to host Prince Charles at her home, Moy Hall, which we shall discuss further later.

Lady Fortrose, wife of Kenneth Mackenzie, Lord Fortrose, also raised a regiment, despite the fact that her husband was a loyal Hanoverian[15].

Flora MacDonald was the stepdaughter of Hugh MacDonald, a captain in the militia which had been raised to help defend against the Jacobites, and to locate Charles when he fled after the battle of Culloden. We will discuss Flora's story in more detail later but she risked both her freedom and her life to help Charles escape.

These brave women all went against the official positions of the men in their lives to follow their own principles, at no small personal danger.

Chapter Three

A Twentieth Century Nurse Practicing Eighteenth Century Medicine

In 1945, Claire Randall has spent the last several years serving as a combat nurse on the front lines during the Second World War[1]. She is a medic used to dealing with traumatic injuries in a difficult setting, patching up wounded soldiers in the tents and chaos of an active war zone rather than treating patients in the quiet, surgical environment of a hospital. This experience will serve her well when she finds herself in the wilds of rural Scotland in 1743. The first time she meets Jamie, he has a dislocated shoulder and she immediately saves him from the further damage his friends were about to inflict in trying to help him. Later the same night she treats him for a stab wound that caused him to faint and collapse from his horse.

Having revealed her experience as a healer, Claire is soon put to work as the castle healer in exchange for her room and board in Castle Leoch. But what would she treat, and how would she do so without the benefits of modern medicine?

For the most part, around the castle, Claire treats minor complaints, cleaning, stitching and dressing small wounds and burns, removing warts and cysts, helping with headaches and minor stomach complaints. Her more regular task is assisting Callum MacKenzie with the pain in his legs, brought about by a degenerative illness which Claire identifies as Toulouse-Lautrec Syndrome, a condition not yet recognised in the eighteenth century. Caused by a genetic defect, the syndrome causes bones to be unnaturally dense and brittle as well as affecting the formation of muscles and connective tissues. Callum's condition was discovered after he fell off his horse and broke his legs. The fractures did not heal well and were followed by another fracture when he tried to do too much after the original injury. It became apparent that Callum's legs would never be as they were and by the time he meets Claire, his legs are bowed and wasted and he has difficulty walking. Despite the constant pain that he is in, Callum never allows his condition to prevent him from leading his clan.

Claire, with her future knowledge, knows what Callum is suffering from, and although she cannot cure him, she can offer him some relief from the pain by massaging a bundle of nerves at the base of his spine. She is also able to use her knowledge of herbs and medicine to mix concoctions that provide some pain relief.

During a hunt that takes place at a gathering of the MacKenzie clan, Claire saves the life of one man who is injured but is unable to save another. Instead, she helps him to die easily and stays with him, holding his hand and talking to him about his home until the end. Dougal MacKenzie is present and sees in Claire someone who is clearly familiar with traumatic injuries and is a capable medic, but also has a deep well of compassion.

In addition to her surgical experience, Claire has an interest in, and extensive knowledge of, herbalism and this is knowledge she is able to use throughout the books to replace more modern medicines, whether it's using garlic as an antiseptic or stewing ginger to help with seasickness. She also picks up some uses of various local plants from both Mrs Fitzgibbons and Geillis Duncan.

After Jamie's incarceration in Wentworth prison, Claire uses her medical knowledge to save both her husband's life and his hand. Jamie has had his hand crushed, and Claire performs a very delicate surgery, resetting the bones in every finger, while in hiding in a nearby house. Jamie is offered some laudanum – a solution made from alcohol and opium – for the pain but refuses it. Claire is successful in saving Jamie's hand, although he never regains full function of it. An amazing achievement considering that the surgery would have been extremely challenging even under 1940s hospital conditions. Later, when infection sets in and Jamie's life hangs in the balance, she uses a variety of plants in salves and concoctions, to bring down his fever and act as an antiseptic. From thistle to St John's wort, vinegar and yarrow, she tries everything at her disposal to fight the infection without the benefit of antibiotics.

In France, Claire makes use of her medical skills by volunteering at L'Hôpital des Anges, a charity hospital for the poor run by a convent[2]. On her visit, Claire impresses Mother Hildegarde, the nun who runs the hospital, by diagnosing a woman with diabetes (called the sugar sickness) after tasting her urine to check the sugar levels. Unfortunately for the patient, the diagnosis does not help her much, since insulin was not available for the treatment of diabetes until the 1920s. In 1744, the diagnosis is pretty much a death sentence.

Claire treats a variety of ailments at the hospital and learns a lot from Mother Hildegarde and from Monsieur Raymond, a local apothecary whom she befriends. He sells her herbs to be used as a contraceptive, for her maid, as well as herbs to help Jamie sleep. Monsieur Raymond also sells a potion of bitter cascara to customers looking to buy poison. The cascara makes those who consume it violently sick for a day but does no lasting damage. Claire considers using this to mimic the effects of smallpox. When she first arrives in Paris, Claire actually prevents an outbreak of smallpox by identifying it in a sailor who is brought ashore. Her diagnosis causes the rest of the sailors to be quarantined and the cargo and ship to be destroyed, earning her the enmity of the powerful Comte de St Germain.

In eighteenth century Europe, smallpox was responsible for over 400,000 deaths a year[3]. An incredibly infectious disease, it killed around a third of people infected and left others blind and/or permanently scarred. It began with a fever, vomiting and mouth sores, followed by a distinctive rash that left extensive scarring, if the patient survived. It could be passed on by contact with an infected person – or with items that they had touched, which was why it was necessary to burn the ship and cargo which the infected sailor had been in contact with. Claire, having been born in 1918, has been inoculated against smallpox and therefore can't catch it but the people of Paris in 1744 were not so lucky. The first successful vaccination for smallpox would not be developed until 1796.

The times when Claire's skills as a healer are put most dramatically to the test are when she is forced to perform what often amounts to surgery. After the campaign is underway, Claire serves as a medic for the Jacobite army, setting up a field hospital for the battle of Prestonpans[4] (which will be discussed in more detail later). She knows that the biggest challenge will be keeping the wounds clean and preventing infection, particularly vital in a time without access to antibiotics. She commandeers a house and puts together a team of women to keep fires stoked, and scrub down all of the furniture. She makes bandages from any fabric she can find and has them boiled constantly so that they are sterile and ready whenever required. She has her instruments boiled and has large quantities of alcohol on hand, both for external use as an antiseptic, and for internal use to numb the pain[5], as she has no anaesthetic available for her patients. Without antibiotics, Claire is inventive with her use of plants that have antimicrobial properties, such as garlic and witch hazel, as well as honey.

We see another kind of inventiveness from her in her treatment of Alex Randall in *Dragonfly in Amber*. The young man is very unwell and his older brother, Jack Randall, persuades Claire to treat him in exchange for passing on information on the movements of the British troops. Claire visits Alex in the small apartment that Jack has acquired for him. The cold and damp conditions have worsened his already poor health and Claire diagnoses him with tuberculosis (TB) and congestive heart failure. In Claire's own time, the TB could be treated with a course of antibiotics but in the eighteenth century it would likely have been fatal. Today, congestive heart failure would be treatable with medications such as beta blockers and ACE inhibitors[6], although neither of these medications were available in Claire's time.

A cure is beyond Claire's skills – and would have been even in the 1940s – but she does have a few tricks to ease his suffering a little. Mary Hawkins, Alex's fiancée, has been treating him with laudanum but Claire tells her to stop as too much will make him worse. Instead, Claire makes him a mixture with lavender, mint and just a touch of poppy syrup (laudanum) to help him sleep. She also manages to create a digitalis extract using dried foxglove leaves, which she has Alex smoke from a pipe. This helps to ease both his cough and his heart palpitations. These things make him a little more comfortable but cannot extend his life and unfortunately, Alex will not survive to see the aftermath of Culloden.

Chapter Four

Witches or Time Travellers?

Not long after arriving at Castle Leoch, Claire befriends the mysterious Geillis Duncan, the local procurator fiscal's wife. The two women share an interest in herbalism and healing and exchange knowledge about the uses of various local plants. Claire slowly discovers that there is more to Geillis than meets the eye. The two of them are out foraging for medicinal plants one day when they hear a baby crying. Geillis explains that the baby is a changeling – a baby that was born healthy but has become poorly and failed to thrive. The parents believe that the baby has been stolen by the local fae, with a fae child left in its place. They have left the baby on a fairy hill overnight, in the hope that the fae will swap the babies back.

Claire is distressed at the idea and wants to go to the baby, knowing that the child will be unlikely to survive, left exposed to the elements. Geillis discourages her from interfering, saying that it doesn't matter what Claire believes, they are living amongst a superstitious people who will not appreciate her involvement. The two women argue and eventually Geillis leaves while Claire goes looking for the baby, which is dead by the time she reaches it. Claire is devastated and remains there, holding the baby, until Jamie arrives and takes her home, having been told by Geillis where to find her.

One night, Claire witnesses Geillis dancing a ritual in the woods, which clearly has pagan origins. It is at this time she learns of Geillis's pregnancy. The procurator fiscal's wife is carrying the child of another man but says that she has petitioned the gods to help her. Just a short time later, Geillis's husband falls dead at a banquet, seemingly having choked on a piece of meat. Claire attempts to resuscitate him and feels an odd tingling on her lips but doesn't think too much of it at the time.

Soon after this, Jamie departs on a hunt with Lord Sandringham and Claire receives a message that Geillis has taken ill. She goes straight to the other woman's home in the nearby village of Cranesmuir, where

Geillis is confused – she is not ill and sent no message to Claire. Moments later, a mob descend upon the house and both women are arrested as witches[1]. They are both thrown in the thieves' hole, where they await trial and Claire learns a lot more about Geillis.

The trial which follows is harrowing to read and also difficult to watch in the Starz screen adaptation[2]. Despite this, the treatment that Claire and Geillis received was actually much kinder than that faced by many of the accused witches in Scotland's history.

Witchcraft was a capital crime in Scotland from 1563–1736. Diana Gabaldon took a little liberty with the timeline here, as Claire and Geillis were tried in 1743, seven years after the statute was removed from the books, but otherwise, the details are fairly true to life, although the ladies did avoid some of the more gruesome practices from the past.

Witchcraft trials were unlike our ideas of what a trial should look like now. They were often initiated when someone made a complaint to the local kirk session that they had been the victim of some malicious magic. The kirk session would then investigate the accusations, and this is where some of the really awful practices came in. The accused witch would be interrogated by the kirk session, often over several days, during which time they were deprived of sleep in an attempt to wear them down and extract a confession[3]. It was not unheard of for other forms of torture to be used against the accused witch, but sleep deprivation appears to have been the most common one.

One of the really interesting things about the Scottish witch trials was the disconnect between what the church and state were looking for in witches and what the original accusations actually involved. The church and state were very interested in witchcraft as being something that came about as a result of the witch having made a pact with the devil, which was often sealed with sex[4]. The main crime here was the rejection of God and all that is holy, rather than any specific action taken against another. It was not required that the witch actually cause harm to anyone as having made the pact was crime enough. This interest in the demonic though was definitely a feature of church and state rather than a concern of the peasants who made up most of the accusers. The initial accusation of witchcraft usually came from a neighbour of the accused, often following a quarrel and some misfortune suffered by the accuser assumed to be magical harm, such as in the 1597 case of Janet Wishart who was accused of using witchcraft to kill the daughter of a man she had quarrelled with when he refused to sell her some wool[5].

We see this same pattern time and again in the original accusations. One witch was accused of killing a neighbour's dairy cow after a quarrel, while another was thought to have cursed a mill after arguing with the miller about prices. Life in the early modern period was hard and the loss of a cow or the malfunction of a mill could have a huge impact on not only the perceived victim of the witchcraft, but also on the wider community as they were tightly knit and often relied upon one another for survival. So, we see that the accusers were concerned with harm done, while the church and state were more concerned with ungodliness and the essential wickedness of the witch entering into a pact with the devil. By the time the kirk sessions had investigated the accusations and were making applications to the Court of Justiciary or Privy Council for permission to conduct a trial, the devil was more often mentioned. If permission for a trial was granted, then the outcome was almost a foregone conclusion.

We see more evidence of this focus of church and state on a demonic pact, with the search for the devil's mark – something described by King James VI himself in his book *Daemonologie*[6]. As part of the kirk session's investigations, it was common for the accused witch to be stripped naked and examined for this 'devil's mark', which could be any small blemish on their body. This examination was often conducted in full view of their accusers, friends and neighbours, in a society where modesty was an important virtue. The devil's mark could be anything from a spot to a mole to a freckle – the sort of small mark that the vast majority of people will have on their body somewhere. Imagine, for a moment, the sense of violation, the excruciating embarrassment for the accused, the knowledge that the examiner is bound to find some little blemish that they can use to suggest that a pact has been made. All of this added to days without sleep, the mistrust and anger of the people around them, a sense of hopelessness, that no matter what the accused said in their own defence, there was no way for them to prove that they had never consorted with the devil or used magic to cause harm to their accuser.

One thing that set a devil's mark apart from any other ordinary blemish, was that it was said that the witch would feel no pain if this mark was pricked with something sharp. This gave rise to the profession of the Witch Pricker – a person who travelled around the country testing accused witches. This person would stick a needle into the suspected devil's mark – or indeed any part of the accused's body, should such a mark not be found – and it was claimed that the witch would not feel the prick of the needle and that the mark would not bleed. This was seen as incontrovertible proof of the accused entering into a pact with the devil. However, the Witch Pricker was paid for finding witches – they had a vested interest in making sure that they found a mark. One of the most well-known Witch Prickers, John Kincaid, was eventually arrested for fraud and confessed to using fraudulent means to find witches. Many innocent women would have been sent to their deaths based on testimony from this man. It is thought that some Witch Prickers may have used a retractable needle, which would appear to onlookers to enter the skin without causing pain or bleeding. They would also carefully select calloused areas of the body, such as the heel of the foot, where the skin was thicker and therefore less likely to cause pain or bleeding. In other cases, the accused witch was pricked so many times that they confessed just to stop the pain[7].

The devil's mark plays an important role in Claire and Geillis' trial. When it becomes apparent that the only way the trial will end is with a conviction and execution, Geillis confesses and claims that Claire was an unwitting pawn in her machinations. She rips away the sleeve of her tunic and reveals a mark that Claire recognises as a smallpox vaccination scar but the audience to the trial accept as the devil's mark. This confirms to Claire that Geillis is also a time traveller, that she too must have come through the stones at Craigh na Dun, as the vaccine was not available in 1743. Ultimately, Geillis saves Claire's life with a false confession, as we would assume that the confessions of the real women who were executed for witchcraft were false.

Chapter Five

Who Were the Redcoats?

The term Redcoat began to be used in the sixteenth century in Tudor Ireland, to refer to the British army because the soldiers there wore red coats as part of their uniform. Over time, it became the standard uniform for the British army, most likely because red was the cheapest and easiest colour to use at the time[1]. By the 1740s, when Outlander is set, it was standard for British soldiers to wear a red coat with different coloured facings (lapels and collars) denoting different regiments.

Following the 1715 rebellion, the government began recruiting soldiers from the clans which were loyal to the Hanoverians, eventually being able to form a full regiment of highlanders in 1739, the 42nd Regiment of Foot. The majority of the British soldiers in the area though, would have been English, or from the lowlands which, as far as some highlanders were concerned, was just as bad. There is a common perception that the 1745 uprising involved an army full of Scots on the Jacobite side, with the British army consisting of only English soldiers, and that wasn't the case. Both sides fielded soldiers from Scotland, England and Ireland.

After the 1715 uprising, barracks and forts were built throughout the highlands in an attempt to suppress any thoughts of future rebellions. Garrisons of Redcoats were stationed at each of these, and the garrisons were often supplied by levies upon the local area, a situation bound to stir a little resentment in the population around the barracks. As previously noted, the highlands were a subsistence culture, where there wouldn't have been a lot going spare. Having to support a garrison of soldiers, many of whom came from far away and didn't understand local customs, and treated highlanders generally with suspicion, must have felt like an onerous burden to people who barely had enough resources to support their own families.

As a group, the Redcoats were probably much like any other large group of people, made up of mostly decent hardworking people, with a few bad apples thrown into the mix. It is to Jamie and Claire's misfortune that they cross paths with one of the bad apples.

Jonathan Wolverton Randall

When Claire first arrives in 1743, she stumbles across a Redcoat who looks exactly like her husband, Frank. He introduces himself as Captain Jonathan Wolverton Randall, of His Majesty's 8th Dragoons. She knows this man to be an ancestor of Frank's and is shaken and confused to meet him. She knows from Frank that Captain Randall was more commonly known as 'Black Jack' Randall, and she will soon have occasion to discover why. Claire's accent marks her as a well-educated, and therefore high-born, English lady. She is wandering around the Scottish Highlands, unescorted, and wearing a 1940s summer dress, which looks to Randall much like her shift. He reacts aggressively and when he doesn't get the answers he wants, he attempts to rape Claire. She is rescued by a highlander who then takes her hostage, being suspicious of her for the same reasons that Randall was.

The next that Claire hears about Randall is the story of how he lashed Jamie half to death when he was a prisoner at Fort William. Jamie's back is a mess of scars caused by 200 lashes, a stark and constant reminder of Black Jack's brutality. Throughout both *Outlander* and *Dragonfly in Amber*, Claire and Jamie repeatedly encounter Jack and each time they are left with more damage. Jack is a sadist who becomes obsessed with the pair, desperate to break them somehow. Despite coming close once or twice, he never succeeds, and both of the Frasers outlive him.

Fans often ask whether Black Jack is based on a real historical figure, as so many of the characters are. Unlike Bonnie Prince Charlie, Simon Fraser of Lovat and the Duke of Sandringham, to name just a few, there is no direct historical figure that the character is based upon, however, there were a few notoriously badly behaved Redcoats who could have contributed to the inspiration for this truly despicable villain.

Captain Caroline Frederick Scott was born in 1711, son of James Scott, Lord Advocate for Scotland. He joined the dragoons in 1737, serving in the West Indies, Gibraltar and Flanders before returning to Scotland during the rebellion[2]. In March 1746, Scott was sent to command Fort William and managed to hold the fort against a siege by the Jacobite army. After the battle of Culloden, Scott was sent out at the head of one of the groups which were hunting prince Charles. There are reports that Scott encouraged his men to rape women and young girls to get information, burn down houses, steal livestock[3], hang a man without trial or judge, and flay livestock, leaving them alive to run around mad[4]. When staying with Isabel Haldane, the wife of the Clan Stewart chief, Charles Stewart who led the clan at Culloden, Scott had the orchard cut down and all of the doors, windows, slates and wood paneling removed from the house, before ordering that the house be burnt to the ground. The heavily pregnant Isabel and her children were turned out with nothing but the clothes on their backs[5]. In 2011, Captain Scott was named along with others as an officer who would have been guilty of war crimes, had his actions been carried out today[6].

One of Scott's compatriots, a Captain John Ferguson, was known as the Black Captain because of his notorious abuses of prisoners after Culloden. Perhaps this is where Black Jack got his nickname from. The captain of the ship *HMS Furnace,* Ferguson had managed to get hold of a torture device created by MacDonald of Barisdale, a rack-style device that a person was strapped into. A commonly reported story tells of Felix O'Neill, a Jacobite officer, who had been captured and taken aboard the *Furnace.* He was brought before Ferguson to be questioned about the whereabouts of Prince Charles and when he would not reveal the prince's location, Ferguson ordered that O'Neill be stripped of his clothing, strapped to the rack, and whipped until he confessed all he knew[7]. Apparently, a Lieutenant McGaghan, serving in the Scots Fusiliers under Ferguson, objected to an officer being treated in such a manner and threatened to leave

Other prisoners were, however, tortured and the information that they provided led to the arrest of Flora MacDonald for her part in helping Prince Charles escape. Like Scott, Ferguson and the soldiers under his command have been linked with the rape of women and girls all across the highlands, as they searched for the prince and any other surviving Jacobites[8].

Major James Lockhart, a soldier in Lord Cholmondeley's regiment, was known for raping and pillaging his way across the highlands. He was apparently known for hanging men and gang-raping women whether there was any proof of Jacobite involvement or not, exactly the sort of tactic that would have appealed to Jack Randall. There is a story about Angus Grant, who did not fight in the rebellion but nonetheless saw his house burnt to the ground by Lockhart before being forced to watch the hanging of three dead highlanders who had been shot the day before while working in their fields[9]. It hardly seems likely that these were Jacobite soldiers, recently fled from Culloden, if they were out working in the fields in plain view, although according to the story, Lockhart didn't bother to take the time to find out.

Colonel Edward Cornwallis was born in England in 1713, to a wealthy family, and became part of King George II's court from a young age. He joined the army in 1730 and did not distinguish himself as skilled in any way. After the battle of Culloden, Cornwallis was sent with 320 men, apparently with orders to do as much damage as he could all through Lochaber[10]. Michael Hughes, who fought alongside Cornwallis, writes of how men, women and children were shot or burned to death in their homes[11]. Property was looted, cattle were driven away and there were accounts of men being shot in the back, presumably as they tried to flee.

In 1749 Cornwallis was sent to the colonies to found Halifax, where the British settlers clashed with the native Mi'kmaq people. Cornwallis decided to pacify the area much as he had in the highlands and offered to pay a bounty to any soldiers or settlers who killed a Mi'kmaq adult or child. The subsequent war bankrupted the settlement[12].

It's clear that any one of these men could have served as inspiration for Jack Randall and there were no doubt others who acted in similar ways.

Chapter Six

Outlander Locations

Fort William

The first time Jamie is arrested, he is taken to Fort William, where he is initially whipped for resisting when the Redcoats were at Lallybroch. Before his back has fully healed from that punishment, Jack offers Jamie a choice; submit to Randall sexually or face another hundred lashes. Jamie refuses and Jack orders the lashes. When he sees that Jamie will not break and scream out in pain and fear, Randall takes over the whip and beats Jamie until he hangs from the whipping post, unconscious, but still, our hero does not break. When he has begun to recover from this second whipping, some of Jamie's friends sneak him out of the fort and a soldier is killed. Jack Randall blames Jamie for the death and puts a price on his head, forcing him to live as an outlaw[1].

Later, Claire is taken to Fort William as a prisoner, having been caught by a Redcoat patrol while trying to reach the stones at Craigh na Dun. There, Randall interviews her, giving her wine and faking courtesy, before describing in great detail the way he felt while whipping Jamie. He attacks Claire and is about to rape her when Jamie appears in the window. Randall holds a knife to Claire's throat and forces Jamie to hand over his gun. He then attempts to shoot Jamie, only to discover that the gun is empty. Jamie takes advantage of Randall's momentary confusion to knock him out and the Frasers escape through the window, jumping into the river[2].

Like many of the locations mentioned in the series, Fort William is a real place. In 1654, a new fort was built on the banks of River Nevis as part of Oliver Cromwell's attempts to settle the area after the English Civil War. An earth and timber structure designed to house a garrison of 250 men and known as the Garrison of Inverlochy, it was abandoned in 1660, following the restoration.

Thirty years later, following the 'Glorious Revolution', a much larger fort was built on the same site by General Mackay and was named Fort William after the king of the time, William of Orange. The new fort was built of stone and designed for 1,000 men. Its north east wall abutted the River Ness (allowing Claire and Jamie to jump into the river and escape).

During the 1745 uprising, the Jacobite army took the other two forts along the Great Glen (Fort George and Fort Augustus) but could not take Fort William, despite a five-week siege. After the Jacobites were defeated, Fort William served as a base for the hunt for Prince Charles and any Jacobite soldiers who had fled after Culloden. The fort remained in use as a garrison until 1864. Eventually it was sold to the West Highland Railway Company, who demolished most of the buildings. The remainder was demolished after the Second World War[3]. Now, the fort is gone but Fort William remains a thriving town and a popular tourist destination in Scotland. There you will find the West Highland Museum, which has an extensive Jacobite collection.

Because the fort is no longer standing, filming for the *Outlander* television series had to take place at an alternative location. The Fort William scenes were all shot at Blackness Castle, which sits on a piece of land that protrudes into the Firth of Forth, near the village of Blackness. The castle was built in the fifteenth century but was altered in the sixteenth century to become a major stronghold and state prison, which it remained throughout the sixteenth, seventeenth and eighteenth centuries. From 1870 until shortly after the First World War, it was used as the main ammunition depot for Scotland[4].

Over the years, the castle housed some high value prisoners, including Cardinal Beaton, the Archbishop of St Andrews, imprisoned in 1543 for opposing greater links with Protestant England; Andrew Melville, Provost of New College, St Andrews, imprisoned in 1583 for slandering James VI from the pulpit; and Lord Maxwell of Caerlaverock, imprisoned in 1584 for displaying pro-Catholic tendencies[5]. In 1691, the castle was filled with prisoners who had resisted the 'Glorious Revolution' and the ascension of William of Orange and Mary Stuart to the throne.

In 1919, the War Office handed over the castle to the Office of Works, who undertook a major program of repair and restoration. During this process, a rusted iron manacle was found in the 'pit prison' which was still clamped around the wrist bones of a long-departed prisoner.

Blackness Castle is currently looked after by Historic Environment Scotland and is open to the public. During filming for *Outlander*, the castle closed for two months to allow for acting, as well as time to replace the modern fixtures and fittings with replicas of eighteenth century ones[6].

Wentworth Prison

After rescuing Claire from the witch trial, the two flee Leoch and Cranesmuir and Jamie takes his new wife home to Lallybroch, where they live in relative peace and contentment for a short time. Before long though, trouble arises, and Jamie is arrested by Redcoats. He manages to escape and goes into hiding, while Claire and Murtagh travel all across the highlands, trying to find him. In trying to reach them, Jamie is once more arrested and this time he is transported to Wentworth prison, where he is to be hanged for murder.

His execution is delayed by the arrival of Jack Randall, who moves Jamie to a dungeon in the prison, there to torture him for days. Claire manages to rescue him with the help of Murtagh, some MacKenzies and a herd of cattle[7]. Jamie's time in Wentworth and his treatment at the hands of Jack Randall while in there are key to his character development so this is a really key location in the series.

Wentworth itself is a fictional location. There was no prison in Scotland by that name, although there were others like it, as we saw with our discussion of Blackness Castle. For the television series, filming of the Wentworth scenes took place at two different locations: Linlithgow Palace and Bamburgh Castle.

Linlithgow Palace is just a short distance from Blackness Castle, where the Fort William scenes were shot. Originally built in 1424, the palace was popular with the Stuarts as a rest point between Edinburgh and Stirling. It also saw the births of James V in 1512, Mary, Queen of Scots, in 1542 and Princess Elizabeth in 1596. In 1603, James VI moved his court to London and Linlithgow Palace fell into disrepair[8]. It was occupied by both the Jacobite and the Hanoverian forces during the 1745 uprising, and following the Hanoverian occupation in January

1746, a devastating fire broke out and the palace was never again used as a residence[9]. In 1787, the ruin was visited by Scottish poet Robert Burns and in 1874 ownership was transferred to Her Majesty's Office of Works, which went on to become Historic Scotland. It is now open to the public and you can even take an *Outlander* tour there.

The internal scenes with Claire wandering through stone corridors and past cells full of prisoners, all while dodging Redcoats, were all shot in the passages and rooms of Linlithgow Palace[10]. Outside, the palace is surrounded by the Peel, a royal park, which is of historical interest on its own account. It is believed that there has been a settlement of some sort there since the first century AD[11].

Bamburgh Castle in the north east of England was used for the outdoor shots of Wentworth Prison, although this was visually altered with CGI. You can still see the distinctive outline of the castle in the scenes showing the approach to and departure from Wentworth. Bamburgh Castle has a history going back to 547 AD and the Anglo-Saxon kings. As the largest and wealthiest of the seven kingdoms, Northumbria was a power in the Anglo-Saxon world and its kings made Bamburgh their capital[12]. There followed centuries of wars between the Anglo-Saxon kings, followed by Viking raids and bloody feuds with the Danes. In 1095, the Normans arrived in the north and wrested power from the Northumbrian kings. Bamburgh became an important garrison for the newly-united kingdom of England to use as a border defence against the Scots and as a base for sending war parties into Scotland. A strong keep was built, which remains the heart of the castle as it stands today[13].

During the Wars of the Roses – a series of English civil wars in the fifteenth century between two branches of the Plantagenet family tree, over the throne of England – Henry VI made Bamburgh Castle his home. It came under an incredible amount of cannon fire and became the first castle in England to be destroyed in this manner[14]. In 1610, the castle passed into private hands and over the years, it has served as a hospital, a school and a base for the earliest version of the Coastguard. The very first lifeboat in England was launched in 1786 from Bamburgh. After a great feat of money and time, Bamburgh Castle was fully restored and now serves as the private residence of the Armstrong family, who are committed to maintaining this historic building. It is open to the public and hosts weddings as well as holiday accommodation[15].

Castle Leoch

Castle Leoch is the fictional seat of Clan MacKenzie in *Outlander* and is the first place Claire stays when she arrives in the past. It is situated near the fictional town of Cranesmuir, where Claire visits Geillis Duncan and is eventually tried for witchcraft. Jacob MacKenzie seized the castle from Donald MacKenzie who died under mysterious circumstances. Jacob married Donald's widow and they had six children together: Callum, Dougal, Ellen, Janet, Flora and Jocasta. Ellen went on to marry Brian Fraser and have three children with him, one of whom was Jamie[16].

Upon Jacob's death the castle passed to Callum, as eldest son. Had it not been for the 1745 uprising, Leoch would have passed to Hamish, Callum's son, upon his death, however, as punishment for fighting with the Jacobites, the MacKenzies were stripped of their titles and their lands. By 1945, when Claire visits the castle with Frank, prior to her trip through the stones, Leoch is in ruins[17].

The real seat of Clan MacKenzie is Castle Leod, a fact that Diana Gabaldon did not know until after she had created the fictional Leoch[18]. The first stone built keep at Leod was built in the eleventh century by Norse Earls. By the fifteenth century, the building looked much like it does today[19]. It has always been a stronghold of the MacKenzies and is the current home of the clan chief, the Earl of Cromartie[20]. Castle Leod was briefly lost to the MacKenzie family after having the titles and lands stripped from George MacKenzie, the third earl of Cromartie for his involvement in the 1745 uprising. It was however restored by his son, after providing service to the crown. The titles were restored to the family in 1861, when Queen Victoria granted the title of Countess of Cromartie to Anne Hay MacKenzie[21].

Filming of Castle Leoch for the television series took place at Doune Castle in Perthshire, a building with a long and detailed history. All of the exterior scenes at Castle Leoch were filmed here and the production sets which were used for the interior scenes were built using moulds and measurements from the castle. The majority of the existing structure of the castle can be attributed to Robert Stewart, Duke of Albany, who was one of the most powerful men in Scotland during his lifetime. Albany was second in line for the throne and therefore this castle was built as an intended royal residence and was very luxurious for its time[22]. During the fifteenth and sixteenth centuries, Doune Castle served as a royal retreat and was the dower house for several queens, but it fell into disuse after James I and VI moved his court to London. By this time, the castle was in poor repair and James VI appointed a keeper and had the building repaired.

During the 1745 uprising, Doune Castle was briefly occupied by Jacobite forces and used as a prison for British soldiers who had been captured, including those from the Battle of Falkirk. Notably, John Home, who went on to write an account of the rebellion, was imprisoned there and escaped by using knotted sheets as a rope to climb down the side of the building[23].

Renovations were made to the castle in the 1880s, with part of the roof being replaced, as well as new fittings being created for the castle, in a style appropriate for its age and history. It passed into the care of Historic Environment Scotland in 1984 and can be visited by the public[24].

Lallybroch

Lallybroch, also known as Broch Tuarach, is Jamie's family home. On the border between the MacKenzie and Fraser lands, it was gifted to Brian and Ellen after their marriage. When his father died, the estate passed to Jamie although he did not return for several years. In his absence, Lallybroch was taken care of by Jenny, first by herself and then along with her husband, Ian Murray[25].

Broch Tuarach means 'north facing tower' and the colloquial name, Lallybroch, means 'lazy tower'. Claire is confused about how a round tower could be either north facing or lazy and Jamie explains that the door faces north and that the tower leans over a little from falling down and being rebuilt, hence being lazy[26]. The estate supports around sixty crofts, as well as the local village, Broch Mordha[27].

During her time at Lallybroch, Claire makes regular visits to the village and crofts to offer healing where necessary and also advice on preventive medicine, for example, encouraging the highlanders to eat more vegetables in order to avoid scurvy[28]. In *Dragonfly in Amber*, between leaving France and discovering that Charles had turned Jamie into a traitor, the Frasers lived happily at Lallybroch for several months, working with Jenny and Ian in running the estate. During the uprising, when it became clear that the Jacobites would not win the day, Jamie signed a deed of sasine, signing the estate over to Young Jamie, Ian and Jenny's eldest child. This prevented Lallybroch from being stripped from the family after Culloden.

The real-life filming location for the fictional Lallybroch, is Midhope Castle, which is near Linlithgow and Blackness. Midhope Castle was first mentioned in a 1458 document concerning a boundary dispute between John Martyne and Henry Livingstone. Ownership of the castle passed to Henry Livingstone in 1478 and to Alexander Drummond in 1582. Following this, Drummond carried out renovations, rebuilding the tower and turrets. Further renovation work was carried out in 1678 by John Hope, who removed an entrance tower and increased the size of the extension. In 1988 restoration work began, including replacing the roof and windows in places. The inside of the building is sadly dilapidated now, but visitors can access the exterior[29].

Cranesmuir

Cranesmuir is the fictional village closest to Castle Leoch, where several important plot points take place. Claire gets to know Geillis Duncan in her home at Cranesmuir and is drugged by her there. Mrs. Fitzgibbon's ill nephew lives in Cranesmuir and Claire visits, saving his life, and making an enemy of the local minister at the same time. And it is in Cranesmuir that Claire is arrested and tried for witchcraft.

The village's real-life counterpart is an historic town in Fife, called Culross. The town has been conserved by the National Trust for Scotland and retains many of the features it would have had in the eighteenth century. During the sixteenth and seventeenth centuries, Culross produced vast amounts of both coal and salt, making it a very wealthy town. It was declared a Royal Burgh, giving it equal footing to cities such as Edinburgh and Aberdeen and it was involved in international trade. It is said that at times there could be as many as 170 ships anchored off the coast at once[30].

A dreadful storm in 1625 destroyed the mine and by the 1700s the wealth was gone, but the town was maintained and now serves as a historic backdrop in filmmaking.

A local legend claims that in the sixth century a young woman named Thenaw was cast off a cliff by her father because she was pregnant to a partner that her father did not approve of. Thenaw survived the fall and arrived in Culross, where she was rescued by local monks. She gave birth to a son whom the monks named Kentigern. The boy grew up to be St Mungo, patron saint of Glasgow, much beloved in Scotland[31].

PART TWO

Bonnie Prince Charlie and the King Across the Water

Chapter Seven

Charlie's Early Life and Claim to the Throne

Prince Charles Edward Louis John Casimir Sylvester Severino Maria Stuart was known by several names during the uprising. The usurper, the chevalier, the young pretender...but perhaps the name that he is most well-known by is Bonnie Prince Charlie, or just the Bonnie Prince. He is said to have been a very handsome young man, earning his moniker of bonnie, a Scots word meaning handsome or attractive.

Charles was born in Rome on 31 December 1720, to James Francis Edward Stuart and Maria Clementina Sobieska. Charles was grandson to the deposed King James VII and II and therefore, heir to the throne after his father. To understand his mentality and all that came later, it's useful to take a look at his early life.

King James III and VIII

Charles's father, James Francis Edward Stuart left England at only six months old, during the 'Glorious Revolution', smuggled out of the country for his own safety and that of his parents. He was raised in France, surrounded by his father's supporters, people who believed in the divine right of kings – the idea that kings were appointed by God, not man. James was raised believing that he was chosen by God to sit on the throne of Scotland, England and Ireland, a belief that was passed to his son.

James spent his life working towards a Stuart restoration, travelling to Scotland at the head of a French army in 1708, only to be repelled from the coast by a squadron of English warships. James requested to be put ashore alone if necessary, confident that he would find support from the people of his homeland, but the Admiral in charge of the French ships refused and James was taken back to France[1].

In 1711, James was offered the throne as the heir of his sister, the reigning monarch, Queen Anne, but only if he agreed to convert to Protestantism. This offer was made by Robert Harley and Henry St John, leaders of the Tory party and James took their approach at face value. He wrote to his sister and spoke of his affection for her and his plans to protect the Anglican church but received no reply.

In 1713 Great Britain signed the Treaty of Utrecht, which required that James and his court be removed from France. James initially settled in the Duchy of Lorraine, where he established a court at Bar-de-Lac, receiving visitors and trying to maintain relationships with his supporters.

Back in Britain, support for the Jacobite cause and a Stuart succession was growing while Queen Anne's health was failing. Both Harley and St John wrote to James and advised him that, if he wanted to succeed his sister to the throne, he must convert to Anglicanism, as the government would in no way accept a Catholic monarch. James responded in an open letter, in which he promised his support to the Anglican church but made it clear that he would never convert. This effectively prevented James from being named heir and ended the possibility of a peaceful restoration, but for James it was an important matter of principle. He could convert to claim the throne, but he would always be Catholic at heart and refused to lie to his people for his own gain[2].

On 1 August 1714, Queen Anne died, and the throne passed to Georg Ludwig, the Elector of Hanover. Georg was technically a blood relative of the queen but he was fifty-eighth in the line of succession – so there were fifty-seven other people with a better claim to the throne in terms of their blood ties, but these were all barred for being Catholic. King George had never before been in Britain and spoke English poorly – indeed, he communicated with government ministers in French or Latin. He was considered rude by many and his very presence actually strengthened support for the Jacobite cause.

This strengthened support led to the 1715 Jacobite uprising, led by John Erskine, the Earl of Mar, who managed to raise a substantial army, however he failed to coordinate with James or with other Jacobites who may have been inclined to work with him. Mar turned out to be a poor commander and, after taking control of Perth, wasted time waiting for James to arrive and lead them. This could have been avoided, had he made plans with James in advance of raising the banner. In November of 1715, Mar's army began the march south, planning to meet with another group of Jacobites who were rising in the north of England, but just south of Stirling, they were forced to face the British army, led by John Campbell, Duke of Argyll.

The Jacobite army significantly outnumbered the British force that they faced. During the battle, both sides took heavy losses, but instead of pressing his advantage for a decisive victory, Mar withdrew his troops when the Duke of Argyll was almost overwhelmed. Perhaps he judged that he had done enough to win the day, but in the end both armies claimed it as a victory and the Jacobite army was thoroughly disheartened. They retreated to Perth and by the time James was able to join them, their force had dwindled from around 20,000 to only around 5,000, the path to England was no longer open and they faced a far more prepared Duke of Argyll.

In January 1716, with the Duke of Argyll approaching and risk of the king being captured, the Jacobites withdrew from Perth and eventually James was convinced by his advisors that he would best serve his supporters by leaving the country, to live and fight another day. He returned to France, where he visited Queen Mary in secret before moving his court to Avignon[3], where he stayed for only a short while. By 1717, George was insisting that James be expelled from Avignon. James made his way to Rome, where he was welcomed by Pope Clement XI, and given both a home and a pension.

With the death of King Louis XIV, James lost the much-needed support of the French court, but all was not lost. He remained an important person on the European stage with allies in Spain, Russia, Sweden and the Papal States.

In 1719, Spain offered their support for another uprising, but nothing quite went to plan, and James did not make it to Scotland this time, although it was his intention to do so. Upon his return to Rome, James married Princess Maria Clementina Sobieska. King George did everything in his power to prevent the marriage taking place but was unsuccessful and the couple settled in Rome, where in 1720, Prince Charles Edward Stuart was born.

Charlie's Early Life

Charles was raised in Rome, but by all accounts, not in a happy home. His father's court was plagued by treachery and his parents' relationship was rocky, at best. They lived in lavish apartments in Rome, were visited by dignitaries and supporters from around the world, and were sure to maintain the stature and appearance of royalty at all times, although money was a regular concern.

Charles had tutors who provided him with only a mediocre education[4] causing contemporary visitors to observe that neither Charles nor his brother Henry were educated to the level that would be expected of princes of their age[5]. Charles was known to be a keen hunter and a skilled horseman. He often spent days away in the Campagna where he slept outdoors and often went barefoot, activities which must have gone some way to preparing him for the deprivations that would come during his campaign. He was a sensitive young man, weeping so much over the death of his mother in 1735 that the court feared for his life. He is reported to have taken after his mother in temperament, being both willful and moody, prone to see betrayal and treachery all around, perhaps hardly surprising in light of the fact that James's court was, in fact, plagued by betrayal, with trusted advisors such as Mar found to be spies for the Hanoverians.

It was common for British travelers to visit Rome and pay their respects to the Stuart court while there, or at least to attend balls, parties and the opera where the Stuarts were often to be found. It was important for the Stuarts to be seen as royalty, but also for them to be seen as British. James Francis Edward was only six months old when he was taken from England and his sons had never set foot on British soil. A large part of the dissatisfaction with the Hanoverian king stemmed from his perceived foreignness, his lack of English, his lack of British manners, his strangeness to the ways and traditions of the British court. It was imperative then, for the Stuarts to maintain the appearance of Britishness, to appeal as a natural alternative to the Hanoverians. In pursuit of this goal, they were often heard conversing in English, spoken with an English accent, despite the fact that neither James nor his sons were raised in Britain.

Letters written by Samuel Crisp describe observing the Stuarts at a masked ball in 1739, where the two young princes led the party in dancing some traditional English country dances. Two years later, John Russell describes seeing the Stuarts at another ball, which was opened by Charles. The prince was dressed all in Highland clothing, complete with a broadsword[6]. Another pressing reason for the Stuarts to be seen out and about in Rome was that it would be considered treason for any visiting British national to visit James's court at Palazzo del Re, however a chance encounter at a ball or coffee house or the opera could be easily explained away.

So, Charles grew up being paraded around Rome, shown off so that visiting supporters and spies alike could be impressed by the charming young Prince of Wales, but simultaneously living in an atmosphere of secrecy and danger. He lived with constant reminders that his father's throne had been stolen from him, against the will of God. He was no doubt regaled with tales of the 1715 rising and the mass of support that was initially shown for the cause. The stream of visitors that snuck up the secret staircase, past the household staff and straight to James's private rooms to bring information and pay their respects must have created a sense of great support at home for the deposed royal line. By all accounts his father was loving, but somewhat melancholy – and the letters that we have which were sent between Charles and James certainly suggest a close and loving relationship.

We begin to see a picture of a young man, who not only believed that the throne of England, Scotland and Ireland was his own destiny, but had been stolen from his father, against the will of their subjects, the majority of whom, he had been led to believe, wanted the Stuarts to come home. A young man who had been taught that God chose his family to be kings, who watched his father always working towards a restoration, often sad, but always making time to receive and entertain and Jacobites who travelled to Rome. It's easy to imagine that such a young man would begin to see it as his duty to reclaim the throne for his father, would perhaps even believe that this was the reason God had put him here.

The Prince Charles that we come to know in *Outlander* is headstrong and inexperienced and perhaps lacking in wisdom. Given that the real Charles was not included in his father's briefings and planning sessions until he was around nineteen years old, long past the time he would have been considered no longer a child, it seems likely that he was, in fact, rather inexperienced and perhaps lacking in wisdom. He was, however, a devoted son.

Both in the fictional portrayal of *Outlander* and in life, Bonnie Prince Charlie only ever claimed the throne on his father's behalf. Yes, had he been successful, he would have ultimately become king upon his father's death, but there is nothing in the surviving accounts to suggest that this was his driving force, or even a significant part of his motivation. He acts in his father's name, speaking only of his father's throne, his father's subjects and the wrongs that had been done to his father. There is a sense that Charles is desperate to return the throne to his father, thereby making James happy.

Chapter Eight

Charles in France: Jamie and Claire Come to Visit

After Jamie's escape from Wentworth, he and Claire flee to France, where Jamie has family who will help them and give him space to recover from both the physical and mental injuries inflicted upon him by Jack Randall. During this time, Claire befriends a priest and tells him her story, seeking some sort of guidance as to her purpose here in the past.

Claire knows what is coming for the Jacobites – she knows that they will be defeated at Culloden and that this defeat with signal the end of the highland way of life. The more time that she spends with the highlanders, the more she comes to know and love them, and the more this knowledge weighs upon her. She begins to wonder if it is possible to change the future and protect these people who have become her family and friends. The priest suggests that God has allowed her to travel through time for a reason and points out that she has already changed the future for every person whose life she has saved with her medical knowledge since first arriving through the stones. Claire tells Jamie everything she knows and together they decide to try and stop the uprising.

They travel to Paris, where Jamie's cousin, Jared, gives them a place to stay, an income and an introduction to Prince Charles Edward Stuart. Jamie presents himself as a loyal Jacobite supporter and becomes one of Charles's inner circle. It's not hard to see how the young prince, inexperienced, alone, at the mercy of his cousin Louis XV who refuses to acknowledge that he is there, would become enamoured with Jamie, a strong, educated man, only a few years older chronologically, but with so much more life experience that it would have seemed that he knew everything. Jamie is connected by blood to two powerful clans, both the Frasers and the MacKenzies, he has experience as a soldier and speaks multiple languages. Although back home at Lallybroch, Jamie is as likely to be found mending a fence or digging a ditch as anything else, he was raised to be Laird, and has the manners and sophistication to move with ease amongst the French nobility, a skill which would have been very useful indeed to Charles, who was not officially present in Paris and therefore could not approach the French court himself without putting his cousin, Louis XV, in an embarrassing situation[1].

So, why was Charles in Paris at all, and what did he hope to achieve? For that, we turn to history.

Louis XV

It became increasingly apparent over the 1720s and 1730s that the only hope of a Stuart restoration would be with the assistance of another European power, most likely Scotland's old allies, France. However, the situation was far from straightforward. Louis XIV had always been a supporter of the Stuarts, believing absolutely in the Divine Right of Monarchs, as well as being a devout Catholic. He allowed James VII and then James VIII to reside in France until the Treaty of Utrecht forced him to expel the Stuarts from his country. He even went so far as to provide ships and men to James VIII in 1708 for an attempted uprising, one which ended before it began when the French fleet encountered the British Navy waiting for them and were unable to land. Upon his death in 1715, the French throne passed to his five-year-old grandson, who became known as Louis XV and the Stuarts found themselves without strong support in his court.

Between 1715 and 1723, France was ruled by a regent on behalf of the child king, his great uncle, Phillipe Charles, Duc d'Orléans. He died shortly after Louis reached his majority at thirteen and after a brief time, Louis appointed his tutor Cardinal André-Hercule de Fleury to the role of his chief minister[2]. Fleury had no particular love for the Stuarts and no interest in supporting their cause. As time went on, it became increasingly apparent that Louis was content to leave the running of the country to Fleury and that there would not be any support forthcoming for another restoration attempt.

In 1740, English Jacobite James Barry, the Earl of Barrymore, paid a visit to the Cardinal, hoping to convince him that the time was right for another rising, with French support. It would seem that his attempt was unsuccessful as no support from France was forthcoming.

In 1742, a truly extraordinary letter was sent to the Cardinal. In it, multiple Scottish peers begged French support for an uprising, with a promised 20,000 men, who would secure the Scottish throne for the Stuarts. The writers believed that with this position of strength, the English Jacobites would then rise and allow for a full restoration. The letter was signed by some of the most powerful Scottish Lairds of the time: James Drummond, Duke of Perth; Lord John Drummond; Simon Fraser, Lord Lovat; Lord Linton, Donald Cameron of Locheil; Sir James Campbell of Auchinbreck, and William MacGregor of Ballhaldy[3], together calling themselves 'the Association'. If they were accurate in the number of men they could field, then this may have been the best opportunity the Stuarts ever had to reclaim their throne, but again, Cardinal Fleury did nothing.

The elderly cardinal's health began to decline, and it was expected that he would be succeeded by Cardinal Guérin de Tencin, French Ambassador in Rome and advisor to James Francis Edward Stuart. Not only was Tencin one of James's advisors, but he actually owed his position in the College of Cardinals to James. His elevation to Louis' chief minister would have been a significant development for the Stuarts, placing someone concerned with their interests into Louis' inner circle. Unfortunately for James, Louis had other ideas, and, upon Cardinal Fleury's death he announced that he would be running the country by himself from now on, with no chief minister.

At this time, on the wider European stage, several countries were fighting in the war of Austrian Succession. On one side were France, Prussia and Bavaria, while on the other were Britain, the Dutch Republic and Hanover (although other countries were drawn in over the course of the war, which lasted for eight years). In June 1743, France's army was defeated by British, Hessian and Hanoverian troops, and forced to withdraw. It was, then, in France's interests to create a distraction for the British; another rising at home may force George II to withdraw his troops from the continent[4]. However, Louis remained cautious and was unwilling to commit resources without a clearer picture of how things stood in Britain.

In August 1743, with the cardinal dead, John Murray of Broughton approached the French Secretary of State for Foreign Affairs, to follow up on the letter from the Association, sent to Cardinal Fleury. He was given only lukewarm assurances that Louis cared about the plight of his cousin

James and would help when he was able to. This seemed discouraging, but when Murray returned to England, he was accompanied by Lord Ballhaldy, the secretary of the associated Scottish lords, and Louis' master of horse, James Butler, to talk to the English Jacobites and gauge support for another rising.

James Butler, Louis' master of horse, was given two lists: one naming prominent Jacobites from each county of England, and the other listing members of the Corporation of London (the governing body of the city) and indicating their loyalties, mostly either Jacobite or Whig. These lists showed that there was widespread support for a Stuart restoration among the gentry and other powerful persons throughout England. Butler was also given a note of the support that they would request from France in order to bring about a restoration. They wanted 10,000 men and arms to march on London as a priority. They requested that the French force be led by the Protestant general, Maurice de Saxe and that a separate force of 3,000 troops, led by the exiled George Keith take the Scottish highlands[5].

The information that Butler took back to France was enough to convince Louis to act, and he began making plans for a French invasion to support a Jacobite uprising and put his Stuart cousins back on the throne.

Charles in Paris

There is some confusion around Charles's arrival in Paris. We know that the plan was for Charles to head the invasion with documentation from James naming him Regent, which would make it clear that this was in fact an attempted restoration and not a land grab from France. The problem was that the Stuarts were watched very closely, so if Charles left Rome, the Hanoverians would have warning that there was something going on, allowing them to prepare a defence. It therefore would have made sense for Charles to remain in Rome until the last possible moment, but that does not seem to be what happened.

Charles left Rome on 9 January 1744, under cover of a hunting trip with his brother. It seems that this ruse delayed suspicion about his departure for about two weeks. Charles arrived in Paris on 8 February 1744, a month after leaving his father's household, where he took up residence, initially, with Lord Sempill. There he was visited by the Earl Marischal and Lord Elcho. Charles gave them both places in command of men and required them to report to Dunkirk at the end of February[6].

Charles himself travelled to Gravelines on the northern coast of France, just fifteen miles from Dunkirk, where 10,000 men were waiting to board ships for England. However, before they could depart, two severe storms hit the French coast, scattering the fleet that were to distract the British Navy from the transports and destroying twelve ships.

The British had been warned of the plan to invade and, as well as preparing the navy to prevent any ships that attempted to make the crossing, they were using emergency legislation to arrest and detain leading Jacobites in England without trial, causing many others to go into hiding. King George also now had the opportunity to strengthen his army with the addition of Dutch troops, which could be requested as well as returning British troops from Flanders. The Stuarts had lost the element of surprise and the Earl Marischal warned Charles that they would likely have to put their plans aside for some time[7].

There followed days of uncertainty as Charles waited for Louis to give the order to proceed and the Earl Marischal gave every warning not to trust Louis or any advisor who claimed to speak for him, convinced that to act now would be a mistake and would serve France's interests but not the Stuarts'. Charles was left sitting around in Gravelines, waiting to find out what other people would decide about the expedition and his hopes to reclaim the throne of his father. A young man of twenty-three, so far having led a sheltered life in Rome, while also being aware of the danger of treachery from friends and advisors, something which had plagued his father's court throughout his life, Charles must have been frustrated beyond all measure – to have been so close to embarking only to be prevented at the last moment and stuck in this limbo.

On 30 March the state of limbo ended. Louis officially abandoned the invasion and France declared war on Great Britain.

Charles was furious and exchanged letters with his father voicing his frustration. James empathised but advised Charles to remain calm and do whatever Louis said, knowing that France was still their best chance for military support. The French court instructed Charles to leave Gravelines and go into hiding until they were ready to proceed. He was supposed to disappear into rural France and stay out of the way; instead, he secretly travelled to Paris. Charles was amused by the fact that no one seemed to know where he was and wrote to his father telling him of how people would say to his face that they wondered where the prince was. While the average person may have been unsure of the prince's location, it is highly unlikely that Louis did not know exactly where his younger cousin was and what he was doing with himself.

By May of 1744, there was talk of Charles joining Louis on military campaign in Flanders, something the prince was very keen to do, no doubt in part just to alleviate the boredom of waiting for something to happen. Perhaps he also hoped to impress his royal cousin and encourage him to move forward with the plans to invade Britain. Charles wrote to his father, speaking of Louis' kindness towards him and hinting at a frustration with the Earl Marischal who was very much against the idea. The Earl had pointed out that for Charles to fight alongside an army who were on the opposite side of the battlefield to the British would likely disgust some people who would otherwise support him. The fact that Charles hadn't considered this by himself is probably as a result of his sheltered upbringing, but it does show a great lack of forethought and political understanding.

This impression ties in with the fictional version of Charles whom we meet in *Outlander*. The young prince befriended by Jamie in 1744 is impetuous and naive, frustrated with the lack of attention from Louis XV and the need to hide, he drinks too much and spends a great deal of time in brothels, where he meets with prominent Jacobites, bankers, and members of the French court. He is also often seen to be short of funds, a situation we know to be true, with finances being a constant concern for James and his court. In the novel, during this time, Charles begins an affair with Marie Louise de La Tour d'Auvergne, a noblewoman who has befriended Claire. Louise confides in Claire that she is pregnant but that she cannot keep the baby because then her husband will know that she has taken a lover. Claire convinces her that she should resume marital relations with her husband and keep the baby. The problem is that Charles is very jealous, a fact which Claire and Jamie think to use to their advantage.

Jamie congratulates Louise and her husband on their pregnancy at a dinner party attended by Charles, in the hope of causing Charles to embarrass himself and reduce the likelihood of the other attendees being willing to lend him money or to support his cause in the French court.

Unfortunately for Jamie, Charles remains polite and his dinner party is ruined by other events.

The historical Charles Edward Stuart did in fact have a relationship with Marie Louise de La Tour d'Auvergne, but not until 1747. The couple were actually first cousins; Marie Louise's mother was Maria Karolina Sobieska, the older sister of Charles's mother, Maria Clementina Sobieska. In 1743, the young Marie Louise was married to Jules Hercule Mériadec de Rohan and the couple settled in Paris, where they were part of the French court. In November 1746, Marie Louise contracted smallpox, a disease that was often fatal. She was, however, fortunate enough to recover and in summer 1743, she met her cousin Charles Edward Stuart for the first time. The couple fell in love and began a passionate love affair, which they attempted to hide from Marie Louise's mother-in-law, who had the young woman closely watched.

Louise became pregnant and was forced to end the affair with Charles though it broke her heart to do so. Charles, it seems, was rather less broken hearted; he moved on quickly to a love affair with Clementina Walkinshaw.

In *Dragonfly in Amber,* Charles attempts to secure financing for his venture by taking out a bank loan and investing it in some wine with the Comte St Germain, a business rival of Jamie's cousin, Jared, and an enemy of Claire. If the wine deal were to go ahead, Charles would be in a much better position to travel to Scotland and begin the uprising which Jamie and Claire were desperately trying to prevent. They take inspiration from the incident which caused the enmity between Claire and the Comte St Germain; upon their arrival in Paris, they had witnessed a ship arriving in port and an ill sailor being carried into a warehouse. Claire followed in an attempt to help, but it was too late, the sailor was dead. Claire recognised his symptoms as being smallpox. In order to prevent an outbreak in the city, the sailors were all quarantined and the ship and its cargo – both belonging to the Comte St Germain – were destroyed.

While Jamie and Claire cannot engineer an outbreak of smallpox, Claire can use her knowledge of plants and medicines to simulate the symptoms of one. Jamie and Murtagh join the cargo ship as passengers and fake a case of smallpox, forcing the ship to abandon its journey to Paris and securing the wine for themselves. Charles is left once more in financial difficulties. By this time Louis XV has arranged a pardon for Jamie back in Britain and tells them to leave France. They return to Scotland, having done everything in their power to prevent Charles from embarking on his venture. This is where the narrative leaves Charles until his arrival in Scotland, so we must once more turn to history to find out how he came to travel to Scotland with so few resources.

By August of 1744, Charles was struggling. He had no money to speak of and had been technically in hiding for months, caught in the agony of waiting for a seemingly indifferent cousin to decide if and when he would be given the resources to complete his mission. From his letters to his father, it would appear that the French court were stringing him along somewhat, telling him that the undertaking was still possible, that Louis XV was still keen to support the Stuarts in their cause, but that it would all be decided upon 'soon'. It's hardly surprising then that Charles was becoming impatient. Even James, ever the voice of reason and patience, was growing frustrated, revealing in a letter to Lord Sempill in August that he felt that his son had been sacrificed for the interests of France[8].

At this time, John Murray of Broughton, an influential Jacobite from Scotland, came to visit Charles in Paris. In his memoirs, Murray stated that he visited the prince and made it clear to him that the position of the Scottish Jacobites was not as strong as Charles had been led to believe by Lords Sempill and Balhaldy. It was Murray's belief that far fewer men would join an uprising than the 20,000 that had previously been suggested. Despite Murray's warnings, Charles stated that he would be in Scotland the following year, whatever may happen. Murray claims that he tried to discourage Charles from coming to Scotland without French support, for he did not believe that any uprising could be successful without it and that some of the Lords who claimed to support the Stuarts would fail to act if the prince came alone. However, it seems that Charles had made up his mind and would not be persuaded otherwise[9].

Charles wrote to his father, expressing his loneliness and frustration and hinting at an intention to land in Scotland without French support, believing that if he did so, the English Jacobites would rise and it would force Louis into finally acting[10]. In his response, James advises caution but admits that he has limited perspective since he is not in France and present at the various meetings. He does state that he is not keen on an attempt to take only Scotland – this is quite possibly a key reason for some of Charles's later decisions.

Over the winter, Charles was persuaded to retire to a country estate, where he was comfortable but lonely. The French Court seems to have wanted to keep him handy for their own purposes, but out of the capital and out of the way. The prince amused himself by making secret trips into Paris to visit friends and relatives, as well as attending the occasional masked ball at Versailles, right under Louis XV's nose[11].

For over a year, Charles was confined to this life of waiting, reliant upon Louis for all things and unable to make any firm plans or move forward. Thinking about this and comparing it to 2020/21, years that were times of waiting and restricted movement for so many, perhaps we have a greater understanding of Charles's frustration than we would have liked.

Chapter Nine

Charles Arrives in Scotland

After their abrupt departure from France, Jamie and Claire return to Lallybroch, where they live in peace for several months, hoping that they have done enough to prevent the uprising. Unfortunately, their peace is shattered upon receipt of a declaration from Charles of his intention to retake the throne on his father's behalf and signed by some prominent supporters – including Jamie. Charles has signed Jamie's name to the declaration, thus marking him a traitor to the Hanoverians and leaving him with no choice but to join the rebellion and do his best to help Charles win.

Jamie and Claire gather a force of thirty men from Lallybroch and leave to join the Jacobite army, meeting up with Dougal and a few of the McKenzies on the way. While en route, their camp is infiltrated by a young English soldier, John Grey, who attacks Jamie, who is impressed by the young man's bravery. Jamie pretends that Claire is his hostage and threatens to harm her if Grey does not give them information about the English forces, which John does. Jamie then leaves Grey tied to a tree near the English army camp and sabotages their wagons and cannons, before going on to meet the Jacobite army at Prestonpans[1].

In history, Charles did not force anyone's hand, at least not by signing their name to any declarations. By June 1745, Charles had decided that he would wait no longer for Louis XV to make up his mind. He wrote to John Murray, stating his intention to come to Scotland that summer, even without troops or many resources[2]. Charles does reveal that over the previous months he had been surreptitiously gathering money and arms, which he intended to bring with him. He had also managed to arrange transport and an escort ship, seemingly all without Louis' knowledge. Knowing, however, that Louis had an extensive network of spies, it seems likely that he was aware of his cousin's actions, at least to some extent, and either tacitly supported them or chose to ignore them for his own reasons. After all, France and Britain were still at war, it may be that Louis considered Charles's plans a useful distraction for the British.

Whatever the reasons, Louis did not interfere, and Charles made his plans, believing that they were unknown. It was only when he was ready to depart from Paris that Charles wrote to both his father and Louis, informing them of his plans. It is from these letters that we gain some insight into the prince's thought process. He suggests that the Scots were planning to rise with or without support, and that he saw it as his duty to lead them and aid in their attempts to reclaim the throne for James. This is not at all the impression given by other writings of the time, such as James Murray's memoir, but it is possible that this is entirely believed by the prince. He goes on to point out that James did a similar thing himself in 1715 but that the circumstances now were more favourable, with a significant portion of the British army tied up in Flanders, facing the French forces. He expresses again to his father how he has been poorly treated by the French and suggests that by beginning an undertaking without them, it would force Louis' hand into providing proper support[3].

Charles gathered to himself men who were loyal to the cause, and especially those who could be of use in inspiring others to join the uprising upon his arrival in Scotland. These men were instructed to travel, individually, to Nantes, where they were to stay away from each other, in order to avoid raising any suspicions as to the prince's plans, while preparing to leave for Scotland. Charles remained at the Château de Navarre, under the pretense of spending the summer there in sport, while preparations were made, travelling to Nantes only when he had received word that all was ready. The prince travelled to Nantes and met with his men in early July and from there travelled to Saint-Nazaire and set sail for Belle Île, where his ship, the *Dutillet,* would await its escort, the *Elizabeth,* a French man o' war. In the early morning hours of 15 July 1745, both boats set sail for the Western Isles of Scotland, carrying Prince Charles to his ancestral homeland for the first time in his life[4].

The crossing from France was not to be uneventful. As they passed the Lizard Peninsula off the southwest coast of England, they encountered the British navy warship, the *HMS Lion*, commanded by Captain Percy Brett. The two warships engaged while the *Dutillet* stayed safely out of range. They fought a battle which lasted for hours, leading to multiple deaths and heavy damage on both sides. Eventually, the *Lion* withdrew, which technically gave the victory to the *Elizabeth,* but it didn't matter because she was so badly damaged, it was clear that she could not complete the journey.

This was devastating for Charles because the troops and arms that he had secured were all on board the *Elizabeth*. The ship was too badly damaged to attempt a transfer at sea. Charles now faced a difficult decision; should the *Dutillet* return to France with the *Elizabeth* and await refitting or the chance to source a new boat, or should they continue to Scotland without the arms and men that the *Elizabeth* carried? The logical thing may have been to turn back to France and wait for a better opportunity, but some decisions cannot be made on logic alone. Consider the circumstances of the prince when making this decision; a young man of twenty-four who has been raised to believe that the sole purpose of his life was reclaim the throne that had been so cruelly stolen from his grandfather, for no reason other than his religion. By this time, Charles had spent over a year in France, waiting for Louis XV to launch the attempt he had promised, becoming increasingly convinced that Louis would not act unless his hand was forced. He had also been convinced that the majority of British subjects wished to see the Stuarts restored to the throne, and that they suffered under the Hanoverian reign. Add to that the knowledge that turning back now would likely be seen by friends and enemies alike as yet another failed attempt and there was really no way that Charles could decide to do anything other than continue on to Scotland.

So it was, that the *Elizabeth* turned back with the troops and arms while the *Dutillet* continued the crossing, alone, carrying the young Jacobite prince[5].

At around 3.00pm 23 July 1745, Prince Charles Edward Stuart first stepped onto Scottish soil on the remote island of Eriskay, in the Outer Hebrides[6]. The island was part of the lands controlled by Clan MacDonald of Clanranald, staunch Jacobites, who could be counted on to protect the prince. Charles spent the night in the home of an islander who had no idea whom he hosted. The next day, messengers were sent out to some of the local clan chiefs and Charles was visited aboard the *Dutillet* by Alexander MacDonald of Boisdale, who bore bad news. He refused to join any uprising that was not supported by troops and arms from France and advised Charles to return there and wait for more favourable circumstances. He also stated that he had spoken with Norman MacLeod, Chief of Clan MacLeod and Sir Alexander MacDonald of Sleat who both shared his position[7]. This must have been devastating news for Charles, who had practically convinced himself that all he had to do was set foot in Scotland and every highlander would rise in his support.

Nonetheless, Charles was undeterred, and he travelled from Eriskay to Arisaig, where he stayed for the next two weeks. While there, the prince sent messengers out to many of the clan chiefs that he believed would support him, advising them of his arrival and requesting their help and loyalty. He had more refusals, all based on the same arguments as those made by Boisdale; that to rise without proper support from France would be likely to end in disaster and that Charles should return there to safely await better circumstances. To be fair, this was also the advice given by Lochiel, who nevertheless ended up raising his clan and being one of the first to do so. In his memoirs of the time, he states that he made multiple attempts to persuade the prince to return to France but when he was unsuccessful, his loyalty to the Stuarts meant that he could do nothing else but support his prince.

To make it clear that there would be no turning back, Charles sent the *Dutillet* back to France and settled in Borrodale, from where he sent out more letters and messengers, asking the clan chiefs to rise. On 18 August, Charles was joined in Borrodale by John Murray of Broughton, who became his personal secretary. Later the same day, Charles and his party left, travelling to Glenfinnan, where he had requested that the clan chiefs meet him with their men. He arrived on the afternoon of 19 August, accompanied by three hundred of Clanranald's men, and could do nothing but wait and pray that he would be joined by others. Before the afternoon was out, Lochiel arrived with several hundred Camerons, as well as 350 MacDonalds, led by Alexander MacDonald of Keppoch.

One can only imagine the relief that the prince must have felt upon seeing all of these highlanders streaming into the valley; after the less than enthusiastic reception upon his arrival, it must surely have crossed his mind that the clans may not rise at all.

With around one thousand men gathered, Charles ordered the standard raised and read out his manifesto and declarations, including a proclamation that his father, James Stuart, was the king and that he, Charles, was acting as his father's regent[8]. After the appropriate ceremony, the fledgling Jacobite army remained at Glenfinnan for a short time, to await further expected support, and for them to begin training in preparation for the coming battles. John O'Sullivan was made Adjutant-General and given command to start forming the men into something resembling an army[9].

PART THREE

The Campaign

Chapter Ten

Edinburgh

Perth

From Glenfinnan, Charles made his way south, heading for Edinburgh, Scotland's capital city and seat of her kings. By this time, the Hanoverians knew that Charles had arrived and a price of £30,000 had been placed on his head, a value roughly equivalent to £7,100,000 today[1]. A substantial amount, yet no one ever turned him in. This is another indicator of how much loyalty the young prince inspired in those around him. To the tenant highlanders, who often paid rent in grain or chickens rather than cash, this amount of money would have been truly life changing. As the campaign wore on, and the conditions became increasingly difficult, it becomes even more impressive that none of the Jacobite army – especially those pressed into service by their clan chief, rather than because of their own support of the cause – ever tried to claim the reward money.

On the way to Edinburgh, the Jacobite army came to the town of Perth, Cameron of Lochiel arriving first, on 3 September, with a small force of men and taking possession of the town for the prince. He immediately took the town piper and drummer to the town square, where he declared James III King and Charles his Prince Regent[2]. Some of the town officials panicked and fled south, to Edinburgh. Lochiel did not attempt to stop them from leaving.

The next evening, Charles and the rest of the Jacobite forces arrived in the town, to be greeted warmly on the whole, the people cheering and ringing the church bells. Observers commented on his appearance and the fact that he wore highland dress. It was important for Charles to make a good impression; his army still needed recruits. As well as recruits, Charles's army desperately needed money and while in Perth, they levied taxes upon the town and surrounding county in the king's name, raising around £500[3]. This money would be used to buy the supplies needed to keep the army fed and provisioned while marching south.

While in Perth, the prince attended a ball thrown in his honour by the ladies of the town, but he did not stay long, withdrawing after only one dance. From the modern perspective, this is not particularly surprising; after all, we know that the young prince had spent most of his life attending balls and similar social events, while all the time he was waiting for an opportunity to head an army and take back the throne that had been stolen from his family. Now that the venture was underway, it makes perfect sense that he would be far too preoccupied with the army to be able to enjoy a ball.

While in Perth, Charles was joined by one of the most significant actors in the uprising, Lord George Murray, younger brother of the Duke of Atholl. A lifelong Jacobite, Lord George had taken part in both the 1715 and 1719 uprisings, living on the continent until receiving a pardon from the crown in 1720, when he returned to Scotland and married. When he was approached prior to the prince's arrival in Scotland, he refused to take part[4]. However, when the rising was underway and Charles, accompanied by Lord George's older brother, William Murray, the Marquis of Tullibardine, arrived at George's home, Blair Castle, he reluctantly joined them.

We know from a letter sent to Lord John Murray, the Duke of Atholl, that George really struggled with this decision and did not hold out much hope for success. He regretted the trouble this would cause for his wife and children as well as for his brother, but in the end, felt that honour demanded that he fight for the cause which he believed so strongly in[5].

Lord George was one of the few men with prior military experience, having fought in Flanders, as well as the two previous uprisings, and therefore he was given a position of command as a Lieutenant-General, a position shared by Lord John Drummond, the Duke of Perth. As the three commanders of the army, then, the relationship between these two men and the prince would be very important to the army and its eventual defeat, as would Lord George's relationship with O'Sullivan, the Adjutant-General and now quartermaster, as well as one of Charles's closest confidantes. According to the writings of James Johnstone, one of Lord George's aide-de-camps, Lord George was a strong leader, able to easily win the hearts and minds of those he commanded, while being able to put men to the best use their experience and disposition allowed for. Johnstone does admit that Lord George had his flaws, being haughty and often unwilling to listen to advice, while wishing to control everything himself. If that were the case, then sharing command with Lord John Drummond must have proven a challenge for Murray[6].

It could be this perception of Lord George as haughty that caused the first cracks beginning to show in the command team before the army even left Perth. According to the account of Sir John MacDonald, a few days after Lord George's arrival in Perth, a MacDonald woman came to him to warn him that Lord George was an enemy to the prince and that she had overheard him telling some Atholl men that they were to fight for John Cope, the commander of the Hanoverian forces in the area, something the men had refused to do. Sir John decided that it was his duty to give this information to the prince. There is no record of the prince's response, and since no changes were made to the command structure, we must assume that he didn't take it too seriously, at that time. However, in Lord George's own account of events, he recalls that as the army were leaving Perth, Sir John made an offensive comment to him, which he was advised by Keppoch to ignore.

With the benefit of history, it seems ridiculous that anyone could seriously suggest that Lord George was anything other than devoted to the Stuarts. He had already fought in two previous uprisings, risking his life not only on the battlefield but in the knowledge that capture would mean execution. We have his letter to his brother, where he clearly expresses his loyalty to the cause and his willingness to risk everything he has once again, in support of his king. The man may have had faults, perhaps even many, but disloyalty to the Stuarts was not one of them.

Edinburgh

Charles and his army marched south, skirting around Stirling, where the castle was held by government soldiers. As they passed, the garrison fired cannons at the royal standard in the centre of the Jacobite forces, but they did not cause any harm. On Sunday, 15 September, the Jacobite army reached the outskirts of Edinburgh and camped at Slateford, around two miles away from Edinburgh castle, which was held by government forces. Charles settled in to a two-storey house next to a flour mill, while his men made camp in the surrounding fields. From here, he wrote to the civic leaders of Edinburgh and demanded that the city receive the Jacobite army peacefully and make sure that no Hanoverian troops were welcome in the city. In addition, he warned that any action taken against them would have dire consequences[7].

The town council decided that, with no armed support from government forces, and the most senior legal men and government representatives having all fled, there was nothing to be done but to surrender the town. However, they decided to delay the inevitable for as long as possible, perhaps in the hope that Hanoverian forces would arrive and protect the city.

A delegation was sent to negotiate with the prince. They arrived at the mill and were greeted by Secretary Murray and advised again of the prince's wishes. They requested additional time to talk it over and Charles grudgingly agreed to give them until 2.00am to open the gates of the city. The young prince saw their play for time for the delaying tactic that it was and sent a small force, led by Lochiel and Secretary Murray, to follow them to the city and be ready to take it by force if necessary.

A second delegation from the city was sent to the mill but the prince did not meet with this group – they were sent on their way with a note reiterating the previous instructions. By this time, the 2.00am deadline had passed, and Lochiel's group were preparing to attempt entry to the city. As they gathered near the city gate, the coach which had carried the second delegation to the Jacobite camp approached, returning to the city. Lochiel and his men quietly followed the coach through the city gates and the guards fled. So, the delegation which was sent to waste time and delay the Jacobites, inadvertently was the means by which they took the city without violence, just as Charles had wished.

Once inside the city, O'Sullivan took charge and posted men at all entrances to the city as well as at Parliament House. He found the town leaders gathered at a tavern, awaiting news from the group sent to the prince. O'Sullivan held the town leaders there and informed them that any resistance in the city would be met with violence but that anyone who conducted themselves as a loyal subject of King James would be treated as such. He ordered beer and bread to be taken to the men guarding the city and required that bakers and butchers continue their work in preparation for feeding the main army as they arrived over the course of the day[8].

Prince Charles led his army to the city, carefully keeping a mile distance between them and the castle, which was still occupied by Hanoverian forces. The garrison at the castle fired three cannon shots at the Jacobites but were unable to harm them or halt their advance, since they were well out of range. As they made their way through the city, crowds formed to see the prince. Some waved and cheered while others just looked on, but even those who supported the Hanoverians could not help but be curious about the young pretender, the Stuart heir who claimed the throne for his father. Although Charles had not set foot in his ancestral homeland until very recently, dressed in highland garb, he must have seemed more like a Scottish king than the Hanoverians, who seemed to largely treat Scotland as an afterthought.

People who witnessed the events of the day wrote that Charles dismounted from his horse and walked alongside while crossing the steepest part of Kings Park. The crowd pushed in, reaching to touch him or kiss his hand, measure themselves against him or perhaps just satisfy themselves of his royal bearing. The crowd pressed in so close that at St Anne's Yard, Charles had to remount his horse. It was agreed that the troops would set up camp here in the park, while Charles proceeded to take possession of the Palace of Holyroodhouse.

Setting Up Court

Holyroodhouse was originally founded as an Augustinian monastery by David I in 1128. In 1501, James IV had land cleared around the Abbey and built the palace where he subsequently lived with his wife, Margaret Tudor, sister of Henry VIII, a marriage which bound a peace treaty between Scotland and England, and ultimately led to the union of the crowns in 1603. Their son, James V, added a tower to the palace and a new west front. Mary, Queen of Scots grew up in Holyroodhouse and married two of her husbands there.

After the restoration, Charles II had extensive renovations made to the palace, although he never lived there, and indeed, never returned to Scotland[9]. The palace was subsequently the home of James VII and II, Bonnie Prince Charlie's grandfather.

It was, no doubt, with a feeling of homecoming that Charles approached the palace along the Duke's Walk, so called because of his grandfather's fondness of it[10]. He paused here and dismounted to take in the view, while the crowd cheered and pressed close to him. Put yourself in his shoes for a moment. He is a young man, sheltered and protected on the one hand, while never knowing who to trust on the other. He has been waiting for this moment all of his life – he has been raised believing that this is the purpose of his life, that God made him to be king of this land, as his ancestors have been for centuries. He has grown up watching his father mourn his lost throne, always hopeful of a restoration, but melancholy, nonetheless. He has set off on this venture, alone, with few resources and little support, with no reason to believe he will be successful other than his firm faith that this is God's will.

And now, here he stands, looking at the palace where so many of his ancestors lived but his father has never seen. So far, everything has been easy; he has met no real resistance since arriving in Scotland and has taken possession of the capital without a single shot fired. He must have felt as though all of his dreams were coming true, that God really was guiding him to restore the Stuart line to the throne.

Charles remounted his horse and rode the rest of the way to the palace. It seems that his intention had been to just walk into the palace without any pomp or ceremony although at least one of his followers disagreed with such an approach. James Hepburn of Keith stepped in front of the prince, knelt to him, and then drew his sword and held it aloft, guiding the prince into the palace, lending an air of gravity to the moment[11].

Charles took up residence in the Duke of Hamilton's apartments and was said to sleep in the four-poster Darnley bed, which was usually reserved for the Duchess of Hamilton. Each day, he held an audience in the grand gallery, surrounded by portraits of his ancestors, stretching back to King Fergus of Scotland, from around 330 BC[12]. The women of Edinburgh flocked to the palace to kiss the young prince's hand and shower him with gifts. He was, after all, handsome and unwed, as well as being heir to the throne.

During his time there, Charles is said to have risen early, held a council of war every day with his chief advisors, dined publicly at lunchtime, and then spent the afternoon training with his troops, before returning to the palace for evening entertainments, most likely including at least one ball, where he would mingle with the local gentry and try to secure further support for his cause. He was hardworking and determined, as well as charismatic[13].

The same day that he took possession of the palace, Charles had his father declared King James VIII and III at the Mercat Cross, as well as having his people read out his father's declaration of regency and his own manifesto. Various writers describe this scene differently; Jacobite supporters write that all of Edinburgh came out and cheered the prince, the ladies all waving hankies in celebration, while the Hanoverian writers suggest that there were no men of any note in the crowds and that many stayed silent at the announcement, showing their disapproval. The reality is most likely somewhere in between, with many people drawn by curiosity and the pageantry of it all, regardless of their feelings towards the crown. It's also important to note that many of the residents of Edinburgh quite possibly didn't care who was on the throne, any more than the average person cares today.

Chapter Eleven

Prestonpans

Charles barely had time to catch his breath in Edinburgh before he had news that General Cope and his dragoons had arrived at Dunbar. On 20 September, the Jacobite army began marching east, to meet with Cope and have their first military encounter. It was important for Charles that his army perform well here – not just for the outcome of the battle itself, but because he still hoped to draw more support. An early victory against the Hanoverian forces would improve the chances of persuading more clan chiefs to join the uprising.

When the Jacobites reached Musselburgh, a town six miles to the east of Edinburgh, they received news of the government forces' position, close to Tranent. They assumed that the British army would attempt to engage them on the moors west of Tranent, in a position that would be likely to favour the regular soldiers over the highlanders. To Cope's surprise, the Jacobites' response was to increase their speed and make haste for the battle ground. It became clear that the British force would not reach their preferred ground before the Jacobites, so instead they selected a large open field near Prestonpans to make their stand. This ground still favoured their tactics, being two miles long and a mile wide, and open with lots of space for the cavalry to act[1].

As the Jacobite army arrived, they came to the same conclusion as Cope, noting that there was no way for them to approach the British force without being exposed to heavy fire from their guns and mortars[2]. They set up camp for the night on the other side of a marsh, an obstacle which neither side would choose to be the first to cross, as it would slow down any attack, making the attackers more vulnerable to gunfire from the opposing side.

In *Dragonfly in Amber* this is where Jamie and Claire rejoin the prince. Jamie's small force of men from Lallybroch are welcomed and Claire immediately gets to work setting up a field hospital to treat the wounded after the inevitable battle. Jamie joins the prince and his advisors as they try to figure out the best plan of attack. Fergus (a young boy that Jamie and Claire brought home with them from France, who is utterly devoted to Jamie) brings news that a local man can offer them a path through the marsh. Claire arranges for the man to speak to Jamie, who immediately takes him to the prince. Charles and his advisors decide to have the man lead the army through the marsh before first light for a surprise attack.

Jamie and the Frasers from Lallybroch are one of the first groups through and attack the British soldiers through the mist, in the early hours of the morning. They catch the British camp almost completely unawares – with some of the soldiers still asleep – and quicky win the day, although not without casualties.

All morning, Claire is kept busy with wounded soldiers from both sides being brought to her temporary hospital. Charles has insisted that the British forces must be treated too, as they are also his father's subjects. This causes some grumbling from the Jacobites, but Claire will treat anyone who needs her, earning grudging admiration from the men on both sides of the conflict.

In real life, there is some confusion about who really informed the prince of the path through the marsh. Some accounts suggest that Lord George Murray was responsible, knowing the area himself and having a few men with him who were familiar with the path. Other accounts suggest that the knowledge came by way of the landowner, Robert Anderson of Whitburgh, who approached the prince and informed him of the path. Either way, at some point on the evening of 20 September, the Jacobite command became aware of a path that would lead them safely through the marsh; a path which was not guarded by the British force, despite the fact that one of General Cope's officers was local to the area and would likely have known of the path[3].

The Jacobites rose before dawn and quietly, carefully, made their way over the marsh and formed battle lines on the left flank of the British forces. They were spotted before they could finish forming their lines but as soon as the alarm was raised, Lord George ordered the charge, before Cope's men could get into position to face the new angle of attack. He gave instructions to attack the cavalry first, aiming for the horses' heads, with the intention of causing confusion in the opposing ranks. The highlanders did as he ordered, and the plan worked perfectly. The dragoons could not control their horses, which caused chaos and confusion throughout the

British ranks. This led to the dragoons fleeing the field of battle. Suddenly, the British infantry found themselves surrounded by Jacobite forces on three sides, unsupported by the cavalry, which they had expected to make short work of the highlanders. The loss of the dragoons sent panic flying through the infantry and only moments after the battle started, the main part of the British forces broke and fled. The Jacobites won a decisive victory in a battle that lasted only around fifteen minutes[4].

Despite so many of the British troops fleeing, only a small number of them actually escaped, those being mostly dragoons, some of whom did not stop running until reaching the town of Berwick-upon-Tweed, some fifty miles south, just across the English border[5]. Of the rest of the British forces, around 300 were killed and around 1,500 taken prisoner, 400–500 of whom were wounded[6]. In comparison, the Jacobite army was relatively untouched, with 30 dead and 70 wounded[7].

At the beginning of the battle, the two forces were of similar size, with the British fielding somewhere between 2,200 and 2,800 men (500 of which were dragoons on horseback), while the Jacobites numbered between 2,000 and 2,500. On the face of it, then, they seem somewhat evenly matched. That's not really the case though – while many of the British troops were, reportedly, somewhat inexperienced as recent recruits, they had the benefit of training as part of a regular army, whereas the Jacobite army was made up of clans in varying numbers and positions, some of whom were vying for position with other clans. Some of the clan chiefs had forced tenants and members to join the rebellion under threat of violence, so that there were men in the ranks, in unknown numbers, who had not chosen to be there and perhaps did not even believe in the cause they were fighting for. Some of the men had no previous military or battle experience and many of them were poorly armed, with some carrying only clubs or scythes on poles[8]. Those Jacobite soldiers who carried muskets were untrained and had no idea of volley fire. In contrast, the government forces were all well-armed, had signed up as volunteers, had trained as part of a regular army and were supported by heavy artillery, of which the Jacobites had none. The field of battle also favoured the government forces, as they had arrived first and chosen a large, open space, suited to cavalry and far less so to the famous highland charge.

So, with all of that taken into account, it really was an incredible victory for the Jacobites. Some of it can be ascribed to the element of surprise they gained by popping up on the left flank unexpectedly, but it wasn't as dramatic as the version portrayed in *Dragonfly in Amber*. The Jacobites did not attack out of the mist, while the British army still slept. The government forces had time to begin forming the battle line, repositioning from their original positions to face the threat from a new direction. It has been suggested that, as they travelled towards the battle, the government troops were exposed to stories of the fierce highlanders they would soon face and that in general, the populace supported the Stuarts and therefore offered little support or encouragement to the soldiers[9]. While this may well have been disheartening, it hardly seems sufficient for the mass panic that overtook the battle.

There is some discrepancy in the descriptions of Charles's behaviour following the battle. Perhaps unsurprisingly, the British commentators reported him as having dined on the battlefield, amongst the dead and injured, while delighting at his success. The writer, Andrew Henderson, takes care to note that Charles spoke to one of his advisors in French – clearly painting the prince as foreign, which is somewhat ironic as the Hanoverians who held the throne were Dutch, and indeed, George I did not speak English at all. Henderson clearly views Charles as callous and 'other', a view that is perhaps to be expected from those he fought against.

The Jacobite writers however report that Charles was calm and caring, making sure that medical care was provided to the enemy wounded, even at the expense of his own men (the attitude we see portrayed in *Dragonfly in Amber*). Jacqueline Riding suggests that both reactions are likely, pointing out that Charles was young and inexperienced and that this was his first taste of battle close up and personal and therefore, he probably was jubilant over his victory, especially as it was achieved so quickly and with so little loss of life amongst his own men. As someone who repeatedly spoke of God's will, this must have seemed like a sign of divine favour for his venture. This win put all of Scotland into his hands, with only small pockets of Hanoverian forces holding Edinburgh and Stirling castles and four garrisons at Fort William, Fort George, Fort Augustus and Ruthven. Riding then suggests that when the first flush of victory passed, Charles made sure that provision was made for medical care and reminded himself that these men too were his father's subjects. Any lapse in his earlier conduct was most likely caused by immaturity and inexperience, rather than him taking any real joy in the slaughter, as had been suggested[10]. This is supported by the fact that he ensured the prisoners were treated well, regarding them as prisoners of war rather than rebels – an important distinction as rebels can be executed without trial in such circumstances. Instead, Charles made sure that the wounded received medical treatment and then took the prisoners with him back to Edinburgh, where the officers were paroled[11].

As well as prisoners, the Jacobites retrieved the British soldier's weapons, including cannons which the Jacobites had none of, meaning that they would be much better equipped when next they faced government forces. They also captured General Cope's baggage train, which included a war chest of around £2,000, funds which Charles sorely needed if he was to pay his soldiers and provide food and equipment. Charles returned to Edinburgh on 22 September, triumphant, and in a far better position than he had been when he left the palace at Holyroodhouse only days before.

Chapter Twelve

Building an Army

In *Dragonfly in Amber,* Jamie and Claire travel to Edinburgh with Charles and are given a room in the palace itself, as Jamie is one of the prince's closest advisors. While in residence there, Jamie does all that he can to guide the prince to actions that will change history, however Charles tends to hear only what he wants to hear. Claire is approached one day by Jack Randall, who begs for her help in caring for his brother, Alex, who is deathly ill. Jack is stationed at Edinburgh castle, where a small garrison is still holding out. In exchange for Claire's help, he offers to pass her information on the movements of the British forces. Despite her hatred of Jack, Claire agrees to help Alex, as much because her conscience as a nurse insists that she must, as to gain any information that Jack may be able to provide.

This is a time of planning, and of reaching out to the lords and clan chiefs who were still on the fence, hoping that the success at Prestonpans would draw them into the cause. In both the book and the TV show, this time is something of a pause, while the characters catch their breaths and prepare for the next big push.

The real Charles Edward Stuart returned to the palace at Holryroodhouse on the evening of Sunday, 22 September, accompanied by a piper who played his return. He took up residence in the Hamilton apartments, an extensive suite of an appropriate level of luxury for the heir apparent and regent. It was important that Charles be seen as suitably royal if he were to convince people to support the Stuart claim to the crown, and therefore the trappings of royalty were more than mere decoration.

On 23 September, Charles issued a proclamation concerning the battle. He expressed affection for all of his father's subjects and appreciated their desire to celebrate his victory at Prestonpans. However, he reminded the populace that the victory had cost the lives of many of his father's subjects and so he believed that public rejoicing would be wrong and forbid any such celebrations. It is a commonly held belief that a ball was held at Holyroodhouse, celebrating the victory at Prestonpans, with commemorative fans made specially for the occasion and handed out to the ladies who attended. Although there are examples of such fans, it seems unlikely that the story is true, given the prince's proclamation. It would have been highly hypocritical of him to ban public celebrations and then hold one of his own and would no doubt have been written about by his detractors in Edinburgh, from whom we have many writings, but none that mention a victory ball. If there had been such a ball, it would have had to have been held on the Sunday night, when Charles had just arrived back at the palace. This seems unlikely both because it was the Sabbath, and because it wouldn't have given adequate time for the making of the fans that were allegedly given out as gifts.

On 24 September, Charles issued another proclamation, this one offering pardons to anyone who had acted against him on the condition that they presented themselves before him at Holyroodhouse, within twenty days, and pledged to live peaceably under Stuart rule from now on[1]. This tells us two things about Charles at this time – that he wanted to settle things as peaceably as possible and win as many people to his side with charm as he could, and that he intended to stay in Edinburgh for at least the following three weeks. At this point Charles had a choice to make. He could stay in Edinburgh, ruling Scotland as Prince Regent, and await reinforcements from France/the arrival of his father, while building support from the Scottish people and making preparations to defend themselves from any attack from the British army. Or they could march into England, attempt to take London, reclaiming the entirety of his grandfather's kingdom, while hoping for word from France as he travelled. The fact that he intended to be in Edinburgh may indicate that he had not yet decided on which course of action to take.

During his time at Holyroodhouse, and indeed throughout his campaign, Charles held a council of war each morning with all of his advisors. In *Dragonfly in Amber,* Jamie attends these council meetings and is, in the beginning, one of the voices Charles is most likely to listen to. These meetings are often portrayed as fraught and full of bickering, which seems to be a fair representation of the real thing. According to the writings of Lord Elcho[2], these council sessions were often fractious. He states that Charles would begin by announcing his plans for moving forward and then go around each person in turn, asking for his opinion.

Elcho then suggests that Charles did not like hearing any opinion that was contrary to his own and wanted to be surrounded by sycophants who would say yes to everything he mentioned. This doesn't seem as if it can be entirely accurate though. The fact that Charles held these council sessions every day and gave each person the opportunity to voice his opinion, rather than just passing down commands from on high, as he likely would have considered within his rights as Regent, does rather suggest that he sought genuine opinions and advice. Of course, just because one asks for advice does not mean one will necessarily like what one hears.

Lord Elcho goes on to complain that Charles's 'favourites' were the Irish contingent, mostly Thomas Sherridan, the prince's tutor, and John O'Sullivan, his companion since Paris. Lord Elcho argues that, being Irish, these men had nothing but their lives on the line, unlike the Scottish clan chiefs, whose families would lose their titles and lands should the uprising fail. Reading Lord Elcho's words today, it's hard not to wonder if he was a little jealous of the Irish and the favour he believed that they received from the prince, if perhaps he wasn't being entirely fair.

James Maxwell of Kirkconnell, one of the prince's aides-de-camp, wrote in his memoirs[3] that Charles always gave the main council the opportunity to speak their minds and that he never took any significant action without their agreement. This is a rather different picture than that painted by Lord Elcho. It is important to note that Maxwell was not a member of the council, but as the prince's aide, he was an observer to the meetings. In his opinion, the true problem with the council was the lack of unity. He writes of factions creeping in and this leading to ideas being discounted because of who proposed them rather than being considered on their merits.

Charles had already observed such infighting in the movement while he was in France. Indeed, he wrote to his father about it at the time, frustrated that the Jacobites spent so much time fighting amongst themselves, instead of directing that energy at achieving their goals. Managing such a fractious group would take a strong, wise and personable leader. While we see many of these qualities in Charles, he was a young, inexperienced man who had never been in the position of leading such a disparate group before. Although he was a prince, many of the men he was leading were older than him, some having fought in the 1715 uprising, before Charles was even born. These men were also nobility themselves – they were Dukes and Lairds and Clan Chiefs, used to being considered important. It's easy to see how they might have bridled at the young prince, essentially a stranger to Scotland, telling them what to do and expecting them to work together when he had no real understanding of the politics and feuds and alliances between the various families and clans.

It's also possible that there was a bit of a mismatch in aims between Charles and the rest of the council. Whatever Charles personally thought, his father had made it clear that he would not settle for Scotland alone. James VII had been King of Scotland, England and Ireland and James VIII would accept nothing less. The prince almost certainly saw it as his duty to present his father with the throne to all three nations. The council, however, were largely Scottish lords, who were quite content to see the Stuarts restored to the Scottish throne and the ties with England severed.

Most days in Edinburgh, following the council meeting, Charles would dine in public – the curious were allowed to enter the palace and observe the prince at his meal[4]. This more closely resembled the style of the European courts than was usual in Scotland, but was probably a wise move at this time, as he still sought to win over the people. This was important not just to fill his army but, ultimately because without people accepting the Stuarts as the rightful kings, the future would be a constant fight to keep the throne.

After his meal, Charles would ride out to Duddingston, where the army was encamped, and spend the rest of the day training with his men. He also frequently stayed there overnight, sleeping in a tent alongside his army. This was, at least in part, to encourage the troops, but knowing that Charles enjoyed camping out even when he lived in Rome, it may also have been his own preference. There is no doubt that Charles was taking all of this very seriously. This was not some grand game to him as some have suggested, but an undertaking which he had every intention of seeing through the end, however he could. Even on the days when he returned to the palace after his visit to the camp, Charles still set a gruelling pace for himself. He received visitors from the ladies of the town, dined in public and then there would be music in the evening before he retired for the night, ready to do it all again the next day.

We know that a ball was arranged by the ladies of Edinburgh and that Charles looked in upon it, but did not stay long, famously saying 'I have now another Air to dance, until that be finished, I'll dance no other.'[5] This seems at odds with Lord Elcho's assertion that there was often a ball after supper[6], although it is possible that there were balls which the prince did not attend, although there are not many contemporary accounts which mention them if they took place.

About a week after the battle at Prestonpans, the Jacobites faced another problem. The castle was still occupied by a garrison of British soldiers, who were currently cut off from supplies and reinforcements. On 29 September, they sent a letter to the city's Lord Provost, stating that if they were not reconnected with their supply line, they would begin firing on the Highland Guard, and if that didn't work, they would turn their cannons on the city. A six-day truce was negotiated but lasted only two days before the Highland Guard fired upon a group carrying provisions to the castle. The castle responded by firing at the houses on Castle Hill, which they believed to be occupied by Jacobites.

The following day, Charles declared that the castle should be cut off and that anyone attempting to supply provisions or communications to the garrison would be executed[7]. The garrison commanders kept to their word and began firing on the city itself. While they did appear to be aiming for the Highland Guard, innocent bystanders were killed, and homes damaged by the cannon fire. After three days, Charles declared that communications with the castle could resume because the deaths in the city pained him. It seems important to underline the fact that the deaths here were caused by the British – government – soldiers firing cannons into the city, at their own citizens, fairly indiscriminately. The Jacobites took possession of the city with no loss of life but the government forces fired on civilians to force the reinstatement of their supply lines, despite the fact that the castle was actually very well provisioned and could have held out for months, had Charles not relented[8].

Good news for the Jacobites arrived in Edinburgh on 14 October, in the form of Alexandre de Boyer, Marquis d'Éguilles of Aix-en-Provence, an envoy from Louis XV and the French court. He had brought with him some men, weapons and much-needed money – although not as great an amount as Charles would have wished. He also brought the news that more ships were attempting to reach Scotland, carrying men and arms. This was an important moment for Charles – if he could persuade d'Éguilles that he had a reasonable chance of success, this would increase the likelihood of Louis sending more help, preferably (for Charles) in the form of an invasion of England, timed to coincide with his own arrival there.

D'Éguilles brought with him 2,500 French army muskets, six Swedish cannons and £5,000 in gold coins as well as Major Baggot of the Irish Brigade Cavalry and Colonel Grante, a gunnery expert[9]. Both men would be of great assistance to the army, commanded largely by men who had very little military experience.

During this time in Edinburgh, more clan chiefs came to join the uprising, including Lord Forbes of Pitsligo, Lord Balmerino, Lord Ogilvy and Lord Kilmarnock, bringing with them men to join the army. Although these would be a welcome addition, they were more men to arm and pay, putting more pressure on Charles to find funds. Even with the £5,000 from Louis XV and the captured £2,000 from General Cope, Charles's war chest was running low. They were surreptitiously aided by John Campbell, a cashier at the Royal Bank of Scotland. All of the bank's coins had been removed to the castle, where it was under guard by the British troops. Campbell approached the governor at the castle and explained that the bank needed the coins to carry out its day-to-day business and could not function without them. The governor allowed him to remove over £7,000, which he gave to the Jacobites to help finance the next stage of their campaign[10].

Chapter Thirteen

Heading South

Given what we know of James's letters to his son and the king's position towards an endeavour in Scotland only, it was perhaps inevitable that Charles would, sooner or later, march into England and attempt to take the throne there too. James would not be content with the throne of Scotland alone and therefore neither would Charles. It's easy to imagine how this could have felt like a snub to the Scottish clan chiefs who were risking everything for the Stuarts – who had been the royal family of Scotland for centuries before the union of crowns, after all.

With hindsight, one has to wonder if the outcome of the uprising would have been different had Charles dug in and strengthened his position in Edinburgh rather than crossing the border. If he had reformed the Scottish Parliament, which had been disbanded with the Act of Union in 1707 when he declared the union dissolved, he could have waited for his father to arrive, all the while gathering taxes and showing the people what kind of sovereign they could expect from him. He could have used the time to charm more of the clan chiefs into supporting him, bringing his considerable charisma to bear. It's possible that King George II would have waited and watched without taking decisive action, since he had shown very little interest in Scotland until this time and his troops were already stretched thin. Of course, it's easy to speculate on what might have been, but much more difficult to make decisions in the moment.

From the writings of people who were privy to the council discussions, Charles faced a great deal of opposition from his men over the plan to invade England, although the reasons for such opposition are different depending on whose memoirs one is reading. According to Lord Elcho[1], Charles wanted to cross into England at Berwick-upon-Tweed, and march to Newcastle upon Tyne to face the government force led by Field Marshall George Wade. Secretary Murray writes that Charles argued that the troops there would be tired from their long journey back from Flanders, that morale in the government forces would be low after the decisive Jacobite victory at Prestonpans, which was still fresh in everyone's memories, and that winning a victory in the affluent north of England would be massively beneficial to the cause, both in potentially securing income and in encouraging English Jacobites to rise[2]. These all seem like sound arguments. By this time, Charles and his army had been in Edinburgh and the surrounding area for around six weeks. There was a real risk of losing his army as men grew bored with the inaction and decided to head for home, where there would doubtless be work that needed to be done.

Money must have been a factor in Charles's plans as well. He had limited funds and no guarantee of where the next injection of money would come from. He was currently paying an army to camp outside of Edinburgh which no doubt seemed to be doing little to advance his cause. Sooner or later, he would face the prospect of running out of money and then his campaign would be over. That must have lent a sense of urgency, a need to move and take as much ground as possible before the chance passed.

Lord Elcho had a different view of the prince's reasons for wanting to cross into Northumberland and meet Marshall Wade's army. He believed that Charles had been misled by the courtiers and visitors to his father in Rome, who had given the impression that the vast majority of people in both Scotland and England hated the Hanovers and only awaited the presence of the Stuarts to rise up and overthrow the usurpers. Lord Elcho suggested that the reception in Edinburgh had only strengthened this idea in Charles's mind and even led him to believe that the British forces would not fight against him as they would recognise him as their true prince.

Such naive ideas would of course meet opposition from the clan chiefs, who would be all too aware that, even if support for the Stuarts was indeed widespread, only a small number of those supporters would be likely to come out and risk their lives fighting in the Jacobite army and soldiers in the British army would do as they were ordered or be shot for treason. If Charles did indeed base his plans upon such assumptions, it is not surprising that his council were not in support of them. In his *Memoirs of the Rebellion*, Captain Johnstone states that some of the clan chiefs told the prince in no uncertain terms that their support extended to putting the Stuarts back on the throne of Scotland and no farther; they had no interest in England and would not risk everything to invade it[3].

Despite their reluctance, Charles somehow persuaded them to march for England. Johnstone accuses the prince of having lied about receiving letters from prominent English Jacobites who were planning to meet them at the border with a large force to join their numbers[4]. Whether this is true or not, we know that at this time, Charles was still hopeful of a French invasion, led by his brother, arriving in the south of England any day, a notion that seems to have been encouraged by the Marquis d'Éguilles, who is said to have supported Charles's plans in public, but privately told the clan chiefs that France did not care who sat on the throne of England, only that a Stuart ruled Scotland[5].

Whatever the arguments he made, his success at winning the council over is further evidence of the charisma and force of personality that Charles must have had. To some extent, he could lean on the ancestral support of his family, but that likely would not have been sufficient on its own to persuade the clan chiefs to follow him, when they expected failure and knew what it would cost them. And so, on 1 November, Charles and his army set out from Edinburgh, some 5,000 men, by this point made up of both highlanders and lowlanders, leaving behind a city that did not know if they would ever see him again[6].

Chapter Fourteen

Carlisle

Although Charles did persuade the clan chiefs to march, he compromised on the plan for entering England, agreeing that instead of crossing the border at Berwick-upon-Tweed, they would instead enter England in Cumbria, a more mountainous region that was thought to be more suited to the usual tactics used by the highlanders in battle. When the army marched out of Dalkeith, near Edinburgh, Captain Johnstone tells us that they split into three columns, which each took one of the three main routes from Scotland into England, thereby to confuse the enemy as to what their intentions were[1]. On 9 November, all three columns met about a quarter of a mile from the town of Carlisle.

On 10 November, the Jacobite army approached the town walls and began to prepare for a siege, raising a battery for their weapons – a move considered foolhardy by Colonel O'Sullivan, since they did not have sufficient weapons to do any significant damage to the walls of either the town or the castle. The garrison fired upon the Jacobites, who withdrew. As he had with Edinburgh, Charles sent word to the Deputy Mayor of the town that he had come as regent for his father, the rightful king, and that if the town was opened to him and the residents behaved peaceably, then all would be treated as loyal subjects of the crown. If, however, they failed to comply, then he would not be responsible for any regrettable consequences of the town being taken by force. There was no response from the town.

That night, Charles received news that Wade was marching from Newcastle upon Tyne towards Carlisle to meet them. The prince immediately told his men to prepare to march for Brampton, a town to the east of Carlisle. On 11 November the Jacobites marched there and settled in to wait for Wade. The country there favoured the Jacobite army, being hilly and unsuitable for cavalry. Charles was delighted, sure that a victory here would allow him to take occupation of Newcastle upon Tyne. They waited at Brampton for two days, hearing conflicting reports of Marshall Wade's movements, before a heavy snowfall made it unlikely that the British troops would now march out to meet the Jacobites. Rather than fully retreat back to Carlisle, Charles split his forces, sending a contingent back to Carlisle under the leadership of Lord George and the Duke of Perth, while the rest of the army would wait at Brampton, should the British forces under Wade act unexpectedly and come out to fight after all.

Outside Carlisle, Lord George and the Duke of Perth conspicuously dug trenches, rolled out their cannon and cut down trees to fashion scaling ladders, all while under fire from the town. They did not, however, fire at the walls, knowing that their cannons were too small to have much effect, and not wanting the residents of Carlisle to discover this fact. In terms of laying siege, the townsfolk and veterans in the castle were in a far better position than the Jacobites. It was mid-November by this point and freezing, with snow coming down on the Jacobite forces as they dug the trenches. They did not have sufficient weapons or men to storm the town and with every day that they were encamped outside the walls, the possibility of British forces arriving to relieve the town drew closer.

The one thing the Jacobite army did have on their side was a fearsome reputation. By now, everyone knew that this was the army that defeated General Cope in fifteen minutes at Prestonpans. Agents of the British government had been spreading anti-Jacobite propaganda, convincing people that the highlanders were savages, men who would destroy anything in their path, Godless creatures who would eat human flesh if the opportunity presented itself. On 10 November, Charles had lodged in the home of a Quaker in Moorhouse, near Carlisle, and discovered that the lady of the house had hidden her child under the bed, convinced that the Jacobites would eat him because there wasn't much food in the house[2]. Charles had already subtly played on those fears with his letter citing unspecified 'dreadful consequences' if the town did not capitulate[3].

In the end, it was likely the fear that the British government had spread which led to the fall of Carlisle. The militia holding the town walls were tired and frustrated at the lack of relief from the army. They went to the commander of the castle garrison, Lieutenant Colonel James Durand, and explained that they could hold out no longer without relief from the army and intended to surrender to the Jacobite army. Colonel Durand tried to persuade them to hold fast a little longer, pointing out that he didn't believe the Jacobites had the artillery to breach the town walls – in which he was correct – and that he was convinced the trenches and earthworks were built only to intimidate the town. The militia were not satisfied and went to the mayor, asking him to join them in surrender. Ultimately, a town meeting was held, at which a majority of the townspeople agreed to assist in defending the town but even then, the militia were not satisfied. Fear had taken hold and they were determined to capitulate, whatever the townspeople and garrison said. Eventually, the townspeople agreed to join them, and the militia sent word to the army camped outside the walls, while the garrison and any who would join them retired to the castle.

The next morning, Colonel Durand received word that the surrender had been refused. The Duke of Perth had insisted that both town and castle must capitulate together or there would be no peace. He said that if the castle attempted to hold out, the town would be destroyed and all within put to the sword, but if the castle and town surrendered together, the garrison would be allowed to leave freely. We know that this was a bluff as the Jacobites were not in a position to take the town by force, but the castle garrison could not be entirely certain of that, though they suspected it, and the Jacobites had all of the fearmongering carried out by agents of the British government working in their favour.

Colonel Durand called a war council at the garrison. The soldiers there were all infirm, older men, veterans of previous wars, none of whom were in a position to fight. The militia would not assist in the defence of the town and there was no sign that relief was imminent. With all of this in mind, they decided that the only reasonable way they could fulfil their duty was to capitulate with the town and preserve as many lives as possible[4].

Both town and castle surrendered and the Jacobites took possession of yet another town without a shot fired from their side and only one casualty. This can only have fed into Charles's belief that God was on his side and that the people of Britain were desperate for the Stuarts to return.

On 16 November, The Duke of Perth proclaimed for King James III accompanied by the town's civic leaders, who are then said to have travelled to Brampton to present Charles with the keys to the town – on their knees[5]. The Jacobites now had a firm foothold in the north of England and took possession of all of the arms in the castle, adding muskets and gunpowder to their supplies.

Despite their continued success, all was not well in the Jacobite command. Lord George seems to have gotten a bee in his bonnet over the prince delaying the rotation of troops in the blockade, a situation which lasted only days before the town capitulated at any rate. As a result, Lord George resigned his commission, stating in his letter that he felt the prince did not listen to him or take his advice. He went on to state that his loyalty to the king would not allow him to leave so he would continue as a volunteer but no longer lead. It seems that initially the prince accepted his resignation and in some places is reported as being rather cold towards Lord George[6], possibly as a result of other people who were close to the prince having taken against him. We already know that people were accusing him of being a spy or having Hanoverian sympathies before the Jacobite army even took Edinburgh; it's possible that such thoughts were preying on Charles, a young man who was no stranger to betrayal.

After hearing of what had happened, the Duke of Perth also resigned his commission, in favour of serving only as commander of his own regiment[7]. This suggests that the reason for Lord George's resignation was to do with the relationship between him and the Duke of Perth as joint commanders, and indeed some texts hint at this[8] however, Lord George never mentions the Duke of Perth or the shared command in his letter of resignation. Conflicting accounts make it impossible to know exactly what passed between the prince and Lord George, but ultimately, he was reinstated as sole commander of the army beneath the prince.

Before leaving Carlisle, the prince held another council of war to discuss what to do next. Charles was resolved to push on, further into England, sure that more supporters would flock to his banner and that Louis XV was preparing a French invasion, headed by Charles's younger brother, Henry. Some of the clan chiefs argued for a return to Scotland, while others wanted to wait at Carlisle for some sign of English support or an imminent landing from the French. As with previous councils, Charles was able to persuade them to follow him whether through pretence, as suggested by Johnstone[9], or through sheer force of personality. On 20 November, the Jacobite army was on the march again, leaving behind Colonel John Hamilton, with around 100 men to hold Carlisle.

Marshall Wade

Throughout this time, Field Marshall Wade and his reported 11,000 troops had remained in Newcastle upon Tyne, kept from leaving by the harsh weather conditions. He finally was able to march for Carlisle on 16 November, despite the still-challenging weather conditions, but while en route he was notified of Carlisle's surrender. With no artillery to retake the town, and leading exhausted and poorly provisioned troops, he had no choice but to turn around and return to Newcastle upon Tyne. The freezing temperatures, lack of forage and difficulty of travelling during inclement weather are all reasons that military campaigns at that time were usually avoided in the winter months. While in this instance that worked in Charles's favour, that would not always be the case during the coming months.

Chapter Fifteen

Traveling South Again

What we know about this time, comes mostly from the reports of observers, people sending letters to loved ones or the British army, warning them of numbers and direction of travel of the Jacobites.

On 20 November, a Mr Cowper stood on the main street of Penrith, watching the Jacobite army arrive in town, twenty miles south of Carlisle. In a note to a postmaster in a nearby town, he described the army swarming into town like bees, and passes on numbers and the names of commanders. Another gentleman from Penrith wrote that all of the shoemakers in the area had been commanded to provide all of the men's shoes they had, for which they would receive the usual price. Failure to comply would result in military execution[1].

On 21 November, some of the Jacobite army had reached Kendal, twenty-seven miles south of Penrith. What this tells us, is that at this point, the Jacobite army was spread all the way from Carlisle to Kendal, roughly forty-seven miles. This was in part because of the need to billet the soldiers – the harsh winter conditions meant that they couldn't just sleep outside as they had in Edinburgh. This also made it easier to find food for the soldiers. It was the wrong time of year to find much that they could hunt or forage and no town in winter could feed 6,000 extra mouths at short notice. So being spread out like this was a sensible choice, but it did leave the army vulnerable. If the British forces, or even a local militia had gotten organised they could have attacked the vanguard, who would have been unable to defend themselves for long enough for the rest of the army to catch up.

On 24 November, a British agent, John Beynon, wrote a detailed description of the Jacobite army arriving in Lancaster. He describes how, at noon, a quartermaster, six highlanders, six gentlemen and two servants entered the town, going straight to the town hall and issuing an order for taxes to be paid to the prince, as would be owed to the king, and a deadline given for payment. This was a practice that caused problems for the towns that paid, as George II did not recognise these payments as valid and demanded his own taxes. Of course, Charles had no option but to collect funds from the towns he passed through in order to pay his men and to pay the residents of the town for the food and supplies that he required. Waging war is an expensive pursuit, especially in winter, and Charles did not have the financial resources that he required. After ordering that taxes be paid, Charles then issued an order for all bakers, butchers, etc. to continue in their work and bring provisions for his army.

John Beynon witnessed all of this and noted the numbers coming through the town before someone spotted him and identified him as a British agent. He fled to nearby Preston, where he penned a report on all that he had seen[2].

On 26 November, Lord Elcho was the first of the Jacobite commanders to arrive in Preston, followed by Lord George, who led the vanguard, while the rear column was only just arriving in Lancaster. The prince arrived later that day to a warm welcome and cheers from onlookers. Here, at last, there was sign of English support for the cause, for the first time since they had crossed the border. Despite this apparent enthusiasm though, volunteers were not flocking to the banner as Charles had believed they would. So, what was the cause of this reluctance? Were the English Jacobites less committed than the Scots?

It's possible that there was an element of this; the Stuarts had been the Scottish royal family since 1371[3], far longer than they had sat on the thrones of England and Ireland. It's possible that there was a certain amount of ancestral loyalty that was not there to the same extent in England. However, that couldn't be the only issue, as English Jacobites rose and fought in the 1715 uprising. And therein, perhaps, lies the answer.

Following the 1715 uprising, the retribution from George I was swift and brutal. Although under the Act of Union, the two countries now shared one parliament, Scotland had retained its own legal system, distinct from the English courts. After the 1715 uprising, many more English prisoners were executed than Scots, to the point that George I attempted to have Scots brought to England for trial so that they would be executed[4], but their Scottish lawyers travelled with them and proved to be very capable at defending them. Those captured in England met with a far worse fate.

Peers who had been taken prisoner at Preston were taken to London to be executed. Several were beheaded while others were given the more common sentence for treason – they were hung, drawn and quartered. This sentence was carried out all over the country, in at least one instance with the convicted prisoner's head being mounted on a pole above the town hall[5]. Those that were not executed were often held prisoner in awful conditions, where many starved or froze to death, or died of typhus, also known as gaol fever. Some prisoners were sent to America or the West Indies, where they were sold as indentured servants.

The Protestant state also used this as an excuse to further persecute recusants – Catholics who refused to convert and attend Anglican services. A large number of Catholic estates in northern England were seized and taxes were increased for recusants, while in Scotland, the legal system itself fought against such seizures. Even when Scottish Lairds lost their estates on paper, many still enjoyed at least part of the income[6].

With all of this in mind, it is easy to see why the English Jacobites may have been more reluctant to rise again, especially in light of how small Charles's force was and the apparent lack of foreign support. Even some of the prince's closest advisors, such as Lord George Murray and Lochiel, believed that the uprising would inevitably fail. Is it any wonder, then, that even staunch Jacobites would think twice about coming out to fight for the Stuarts?

In Preston, the same town that had been the site of the final battle of the 1715 uprising, the majority of people gave all appearances of supporting Bonnie Prince Charlie and his action on behalf of his father, but very few were willing to sign up and risk their lives and lands on an apparently lost cause. Predictably, this worried some of Charles's council, who once again argued that they should turn for home[7]. Charles, supported by the Marquis d'Éguilles argued convincingly that a French force was no doubt on the way and indeed, may even have landed already. Once again, he was able to persuade the clan chiefs to go along with what he wanted, even in the face of waning hope for recruitment of English Jacobites.

Chapter Sixteen

Manchester

Manchester in 1745 was a wealthy, but small, market town but was known to have a relatively high level of support for the Stuarts. Charles likely chose this route because he had been convinced that he would find support there[1]. Recovered writings from Manchester resident Elizabeth Byrom tell us that many of the town's Hanoverians fled at news that the Jacobite army was heading their way, leaving shops shuttered and warehouses empty[2]. Some of those who fled were the town magistrates, eager to avoid being forced to declare James as king, as had been done in all previous towns taken by the Jacobites.

On 28 November, the first members of the Jacobite army entered Manchester at around three in the afternoon. Two men and one woman, wearing highland dress, came into town and began calling for volunteers to join the prince regent's army. Accounts of the response to this differ. Elizabeth Byrom writes that no one interfered with the Jacobites, an impression supported by her father, John Byrom, who reported that these three took possession of Manchester without any opposition. Captain Johnstone, however, tells a different story. According to him, a crowd gathered around the recruiters and threatened them, but were scared off by Sergeant Dickson, one of the three Jacobites, when he showed the crowd his blunderbuss (a short gun with a flared barrel) and threatened to shoot anyone who laid a hand on him or his companions. Thus, he was able to hold the crowd at bay until local supporters arrived and dispersed the crowd[3].

It's important to note that both Elizabeth and John Byrom's accounts agree and those two were actually present for the event. Captain Johnstone was not in Manchester and can only report what was told to him by Dickson and his companions. It's possible that this story was just a bit of propaganda, intended to embarrass the English and highlight the bravery of the highlanders. There is no doubt that the three recruiters who first entered Manchester, without the support of the army that was travelling behind them, were brave indeed. They could not have known that their arrival would be met with so little resistance. Had the Hanoverian supporters not fled the town before their arrival, the three could have found themselves arrested and tried for treason, if not killed outright. Whatever the truth of the matter, the Jacobites took possession of yet another town without being required to fire a shot, an impressive record by this stage. It was understandable in Perth and even Edinburgh, at the beginning of their campaign and before George II had really had time to respond and get his troops in place to counter the rebellion. By the time they reached Manchester, however, they had fought only one battle and continued largely unopposed. It's difficult to understand this lack of real response from the Hanoverians.

Members of Charles's council such as Lord Elcho have suggested that the young prince was naive and convinced that God was on his side and that the British army would not fight against him, as they would recognise him as their true prince. It's possible that this is an exaggeration on the part of Lord Elcho, or evidence of his own bias and apparent dislike of the prince, or at least of the prince's attitude towards him, however, if Charles really did believe these things, his army's largely-unresisted progress into England can only have strengthened these beliefs.

Elizabeth Byrom reports that Lord Pitsligo and his regiment of horse arrived at around eight that night, by which time eighty volunteers had signed up with the recruiters. Not quite the flood of support the prince was no doubt hoping for. Charles himself arrived with the majority of the army the following afternoon, to apparent cheers of support. The town bells were rung, and bonfires lit, and the houses in town were all lit up in what would appear to be celebration, which must have seemed promising to the Jacobites, although some, like Lord Elcho and John Marchant, believed the display to be forced, possibly from fear[4].

The only town officials which remained when the Jacobites arrived were the two town constables, who, despite the risk to themselves, did their best to resist the army, in the small ways that were available to them. They refused to attend when summoned by Lord Pitsligo and then refused to carry out orders given by the Jacobite command, although they had been threatened with military execution. When they were taken to the town square to read the proclamations, both men made various excuses as to why they couldn't read the proclamation, until eventually, constable Fowden was forced to repeat the words of the proclamation,

Right: Portrait of Prince
Charles Edward Stuart
by William Mosman

Below: Midhope
Tower – used as the
filming location for
Lallybroch in STARZ
TV series *Outlander*
M J Richardson/
Midhope Tower/ CC BY-
SA 2.0)

Doune Castle – used as the filming location for Castle Leoch in STARZ TV series *Outlander* (Photograph taken by Steve Collis, used under Creative Commons Attribution 2.0 Generic Licence)

Blackness Castle – used as the filming location for Wentworth Prison in STARZ TV series *Outlander*

Above: Clan Fraser marker at Culloden Battlefield

Right: Scottish Clan Map showing the approximate locations of the major clans during the 17th century

DECLARATION

Lord JOHN DRUMMOND Commander in Chief of his moſt Chriſtian Majeſty's Forces in SCOTLAND.

WE Lord JOHN DRUMMOND, Commander in Chief of his moſt Chriſtian Majeſty's Forces in SCOTLAND. Do hereby Declare, that we are come to this Kingdom, with Written Orders, to make War a-gainſt the King of ENGLAND, Elector of HANOVER, and all his Adherants, and that the poſitive Orders we have from his moſt Chriſtian Majeſty are to attack all his Enemies in this Kingdom, whom he has Declared to be thoſe who will not immediately Join, or aſſiſt as far will ly in their Power, the Prince of WALES, Regent of SCOTLAND &c. His Ally, and whom he is reſolved, with the Concurrence of the King of SPAIN, to Support in the taking Poſeſſion of SCOTLAND, ENG-LEAND, and IRLAND, if Neceſſary at the Expence of all the Men and Money, he is Maſter of, to which three Kingdoms, the Family of STEWART, have ſo Juſt and indiſputeable a Title. And his moſt Chriſtian Majeſt's Poſitive Orders, are, that his Enemies ſhould be uſed in this Kingdom in proportion to the Harm they do or Intend to his Royal Highneſs's Cauſe.

Given at MONTROSE, the ſecond Day of *Decem-ber, One thouſand ſeven hundred and forty five* Years.

236 **J. DRUMMOND.**

Jacobite Declaration of War, Printed Handbill from Lord John Drummond, Scottish Commander, 2 December 1745 (SP 54/26/90B) – held by the National Archives – used under Government Open Licence 3.0

Glenfinnan Monument, a memorial for the Jacobites who rose following Prince Charles raising his standard here on 19th August 1745. The monument was erected in 1815 by Alexander MacDonald of Glenaladale.

Old Leanach Cottage, which stands on Culloden battlefield

The Battle of Culloden April 16 1746 – Coloured Line Drawing by Luke Sullivan – held by the National Army Museum

Memorial Cairn at Culloden, erected by Duncan Forbes in 1881

William Augustus, Duke of Cumberland – Oil on Canvas by David Morier – held by the National Army Museum

as read by one of the Jacobite officers, an act that he was later tried for, as it was considered treason against George II, the Hanoverian King[5]. Both constables were under the threat of military execution, in addition to having their homes burned down and their families killed for defying the Jacobites or later execution for acting against King George. There was no good solution for either of them.

The Jacobite army remained in Manchester for two days, during which time Charles held two evening receptions and was sure to ride through town and make sure that he was visible to the residents, charming and impressing at least some of them as he had everywhere else. Elizabeth Byrom writes of how handsome and noble he was and how excited she was to be taken to kiss his hand. Her father, however, had to be forced into an audience with the prince[6], perhaps because he understood the stakes better. Or perhaps just because he was less won over by the handsome young man than his daughter.

By the time they were ready to move on, there were between two and three hundred new recruits from Lancashire which were formed into the Manchester regiment, headed by Francis Towneley, as Colonel Towneley was held in high regard by the Marquis d'Éguilles and Sir John MacDonald, one of the Irish officers who was close to Charles[7]. A new regiment was not to be slighted, but it was nowhere near the 1,500 troops Charles had hoped to recruit in the area. Lord Elcho suggests that the people in the county were uninterested in the prince and his cause, but this doesn't seem to be the case; many of the writers of the time describe how crowds gathered and cheered for Charles everywhere that he went, how eager people were to see him and to touch him, to bless him and wish him well. It seems more likely that the reluctance was a result of the harsh retribution that was paid in the area following the 1715[8] rising. The majority of the new recruits were young men[8], whom some writers have suggested were just looking for adventure. I think it more likely that the older supporters remembered the hangings and disembowellings of those tried for the treason after the last uprising and were more cautious, especially with no sign of the French forces that were supposed to be on their way to support Charles.

Chapter Seventeen

The British Forces

By this time, the Jacobite army had marched around 130 miles into England, over the course of around three weeks, without meeting any significant resistance or opposition from government forces. So where were the British troops and what were they doing during this time?

Up until the taking of Edinburgh and the defeat of General Cope's force at Prestonpans, it seems that King George and the parliament did not take the rebellion very seriously. This is perhaps understandable, when one considers how small the Jacobite army was and the fact that the British forces were already committed in Flanders, fighting in the War of Austrian Succession, which was not going particularly well for the Pragmatic Allies in 1745. Since France were fighting on the other side from Britain during this war, it is likely that their interest in supporting the Jacobites was more to create a distraction and cause the British to withdraw soldiers from Flanders, rather than out of any genuine interest in restoring the Stuarts to their thrones.

Sir John Ligonier was initially recalled from Flanders in September, along with ten battalions of troops. He arrived in London just before the news of General Cope's defeat at Prestonpans. From there, he wrote to the Duke of Cumberland, Prince William Augustus, the third son of King George II. Cumberland was commanding the Pragmatic Allied troops in Flanders, despite his young age and lack of experience. Born on 15 April 1721 (N.S.), he was a few months younger than Prince Charles although, by the autumn of 1745, he did have more military experience than Charles, having served since 1741. In his letter to Cumberland, Ligonier passed on news of the defeat at Prestonpans and advised that he expected more troops to be recalled soon[1].

Other letters received by Cumberland at around the same time inform him of the sense of panic now being felt in London and express fear for the safety of the king. Letters between Lord Harrington and Robert Trevor and between Ligonier and Sir Everard Fawkner show the sort of misinformation and panic that was happening in London at the time. Ligonier reports that the Jacobite army is said to consist of 16,000 men (we know that there were really around 2,500 at the battle of Prestonpans and no more than double that by the time they left Edinburgh) and both writers share the belief that the Scottish parliament will be recalled, and the union dissolved, with Scotland being placed under the protection of France[2]. How differently things may have turned out if Charles had followed these expectations.

More letters back and forth to Flanders show how eager Cumberland was to come home and face the Jacobites, especially as the campaign in Flanders was winding down for winter. On 21 October, Cumberland wrote to Lord Harrington, stating outright that he was impatient to receive orders to return to England[3]. He was no doubt delighted when those orders finally arrived, a short time later. The Duke of Cumberland arrived home in London on 18 October (O.S.), by which time Field Marshall Wade was already marching north towards Newcastle upon Tyne.

Wade arrived in Newcastle upon Tyne on 30 October, while Charles and his army were still in Edinburgh. Wade's first action was to issue a proclamation advising people that anyone who had joined the rebellion but now returned to their homes before 12 November and wished to live as loyal subjects of King George II once more, would be given clemency for their actions so far[4]. We know that during the coming weeks, Wade led his army towards Carlisle, only to turn back when he received news of the town's capitulation to the Jacobites. The weather was poor in the north of England at this time with heavy snowfall making travel very difficult. Added to that was the exhaustion of his troops and the difficulties in securing supplies[5]. Wade's force had largely just returned from the fighting in Flanders and then marched from London to Newcastle, in winter, when they would usually expect to see some rest. In a letter Wade wrote to Cumberland on 31 October 1745 (O.S.) he explains that some of his soldiers are barefoot, from the rigours of the march.

It was decided that Wade's army was not equipped to pursue the Jacobites as they continued their advance into England, at least until they had been able to rest and secure some provisions. It was now up to Sir John Ligonier and the Duke of Cumberland to defend London and prevent the Jacobites from securing the throne.

On 25 November, with Charles and his army in Lancaster, King George II put the Duke of Cumberland in command of the army and instructed him, amongst other things, to stay in close correspondence with Wade in Newcastle upon Tyne and to offer a pardon to any rebels who surrendered themselves to the British forces[6]. Cumberland immediately travelled to Lichfield, where he took over command from Ligonier on 27 November. At this time, the troops were spread across a distance of roughly thirty-four miles, positioned in such a way as to be able to move towards either Derby or Chester, depending on which way the Jacobites headed.

It seems to have been Cumberland's intention to bring the two forces together, as he writes of Marshal Wade and his force having left Newcastle upon Tyne, although he was not making swift progress. Wade's progress was further slowed by the uncertainty of what the Jacobite army was going to do. Wade, transporting heavy artillery, was limited to using good roads, and still hindered by the weather. His route had to be carefully planned to find roads which could accommodate him. He would not be able to easily change direction should the Jacobites move unexpectedly.

This greater speed and manoeuverability of Charles's smaller force was a distinct advantage throughout their time in England. It allowed them to outpace the British forces at every stage and required fewer resources to maintain. By the time the Jacobites were in Manchester, the British forces were aiming to close in on them and expecting to soon be doing battle. The Duke of Richmond writes to the Duke of Newcastle and details what he believes to be the possibilities facing them in his order of preference.

First of all, the Jacobites could attack the British forces, and this is the option he is hoping for, as long as the two armies are together, for he believes the British will be guaranteed a win. The second option that he mentions is that they could march into Derbyshire. This would give the British more time to bring their two armies together and then cut off the Jacobites from any further advance. The third option was that the Jacobites could march to Chester and besiege the city (we know that they didn't really have the resources to take a walled town by siege, but they had already managed to do so at Carlisle, despite this). Richmond's fourth option was they could bypass Chester and march into Wales. The final option, the one that Richmond hoped for least, was that they could withdraw and go back to Scotland[7]. This is interesting, because we know that this was the last thing that Charles wanted to do, an action that he would consider defeat, and yet it was what this particular British commander feared the most. If the Jacobite army retreated to Scotland – especially if they went into the mountains of the highlands, where the roads were poor and they had the clear advantage in terms of tactics, and the British forces were unlikely to follow – they could sit out the winter and wait for French reinforcements. At the very least, it would cause the rebellion to drag on for months, rather than ending with the swift, decisive victory Richmond believed was possible if they fought soon.

Throughout all of this, the British navy were patrolling the English Channel and watching the north coast of France with some trepidation.

Chapter Eighteen

On the Continent

When James first heard, in July 1745, that Charles had left France for Scotland, he must have been frantic with worry but not entirely surprised. After all, he had been on the receiving end of Charles's letters expressing his frustration and impatience to start the campaign for at least a year by this stage. By August, James was writing to everyone associated with the Jacobite cause in France and entreating with them to support the prince in his endeavours. He could only hope that Charles's actions would shame the French Court into taking the action they had been promising but failing to deliver for so long.

James sent his younger son, Henry, to visit the French Court and make the case for supporting Charles in person. Henry left Rome at the end of August and arrived in Fontainbleu, Louis' palace south of Paris, where he usually spent the hunting the season, on 24 October 1745 (N.S.)[1], despite falling quite ill while travelling. When Henry arrived, the French Court was, as usual, divided. Some members of the court, such as Cardinal Tencin and the Marquis d'Argenson were in support of sending a French invasion force to support Charles immediately. Others, such as the Maréchal de Saxe felt that France did not require to involve itself any further, since the rebellion had already served to distract the British in Flanders and there was no further gain for France in acting at the moment. Louis was holding back from making a decision and had instead sent the Marquis d'Éguilles to Edinburgh for the purpose of reporting back on how things stood in Scotland.

When Louis XV received news of the victory at Prestonpans, he was impressed enough to begin planning an invasion in earnest. He finally committed himself fully by signing the Treaty of Fontainebleau on the very day that Henry arrived.

James received letters from both Henry and Lord Balhaldy telling him that Louis was determined to send troops to support Charles but that divisions in the French Court and indeed amongst the Jacobites at the court, were slowing progress. By now, this must be an old and frustrating tune for James, who was stuck in Rome, unable to act, dependent upon his capricious cousin.

By mid-November, Lord John Drummond and the troops of the Royal Ecossais were ready to embark for Scotland, along with arms and heavy artillery. They were to be joined by men from the Irish Regiments in France. Things continued to progress and, by 26 November (N.S., 11 November O.S.) when Charles was securing Carlisle, Henry was able to write to him and assure him that a French invasion force was preparing to land in the south of England, with Henry at its head. Henry had been reassured by d'Argenson that the invasion would take place by 9 December (O.S.)[2].

On 14 November (N.S.), Lord John Drummond and his men of the Royal Ecossais set sail from Dunkirk and headed for Scotland. Along with men, Drummond brought both arms and ammunition and some large, heavy cannons of the kind that would be useful in a siege as well as a battle, unlike the smaller, light cannons that Charles travelled with. These larger cannons were much more difficult to transport over land than their smaller cousins and slowed an army down considerably – as we have already seen with Marshal Wade's force.

The British navy had ships patrolling the channel and all around the coast, however a storm aided the French fleet, by scattering the navy ships and opening a path to Scotland. On 24 November the first French ship landed at Montrose, a town that was overrun with Jacobites. Some of the French ships were captured but the majority of the soldiers and weapons made it to the shore and the Jacobites were able to secure Montrose harbour – one of the only safe landing points on the east coast of Scotland. The Jacobites also managed to capture one of the British ships, the HMS *Hazard* which they renamed *Le Prince Charles*, a move that no doubt drew the ire of the British forces.

Lord John Drummond wasted no time in issuing a proclamation asserting that he and his troops were here to support the Stuarts in making war against the Hanoverian King and that any who stood against Charles would be treated as an enemy. He also stated that both France and Spain supported the Stuarts in claiming their rightful place on the throne[3].

Whether Charles knew it at this time or not, he now had the French support that he had been trying for so long to secure. But was it too little, too late?

Chapter Nineteen

Derby

On 1 December 1745, the Jacobite army left Manchester and headed towards Derby. While travelling through Cheshire, Charles was greeted by a welcoming party which included a Mrs Skyring, an elderly lady who had grown up devoted to the Stuarts, despite an apparent historic mistreatment of her family by Charles II, the prince's great Uncle. It was said that she had been sending half of her income overseas to support the Stuarts in exile, ever since James II and VII fled to France in 1688. She had now sold everything of any value that she owned and brought the proceeds to Charles to assist in his campaign[1].

Near the town of Macclesfield, Colonel Henry Ker caught the government spy, Captain John Weir or Vere. It was proposed that Weir be hanged immediately but the prince would not allow it and argued that Weir was not technically a spy since he had not been caught in the camp. Instead, Weir was tied to a horse and dragged along behind it, barefoot. Weir gave them information about the size and location of Cumberland's forces, although he exaggerated their numbers. Colonel Ker was able to report on how the army was quartered and as a result, Lord George Murray volunteered to take a column of their forces towards Lichfield, where Cumberland was stationed, in the hope that this would trick the British into believing that the Jacobites were marching to meet them in battle, and pull all of their soldiers together, giving the main body of the Jacobite army time to reach Derby. Lord George and his men would then turn for Derby before coming face to face with the British[2].

This tactic had served them well in the past and it did so again now. The two columns rejoined at Ashbourne for the last stretch of the march to Derby.

At around 11.00am on 4 December 1745, two Jacobite officers arrived in Derby and ordered billets for 9,000. They were quickly followed by thirty Hussars (light cavalry) who took up position in the town square and waited in silence for the main body of the army, which began arriving around three that afternoon, followed by Charles, who arrived on foot around dusk. He made sure that his men were given bread, cheese, beer and straw, before he retired to his own lodgings in Exeter House[3]. There, he spoke about what he should wear when entering London, seemingly unaware of the reluctance of most of his council to go any further. It seems that Charles was not the only one who was unaware of this determination to turn back; the troops who had marched for hundreds of miles in increasingly harsh conditions, were reportedly in high spirits, ready to take on Cumberland's forces or make a dash for London, whichever was required of them. Letters sent home by some of the Jacobite troops indicate that they were excited to have come this far and fully intended to see their prince throned in Westminster[4].

While in Derby, Charles received word from Lord John Drummond that he had landed safely in Scotland and was in command of a force of 3,000 men made up of those he had brought with him and Scots who had been unable to join the prince's army prior to their departure for England. He also advised that there were more Irish and French troops on their way[5].

As was the usual course of affairs, a council meeting was called, where all regimental colonels would be given the opportunity to speak their opinion about the best course of action to follow. Accounts differ as to exactly how that meeting went. Most agree that there was a meeting, that it lasted for a long time (or was possibly two meetings over the course of that day) and that things became heated over the course of the debate. Lord Elcho gives a detailed account of the proceedings, especially of the arguments for retreat put forward by Lord George Murray[6], who opened the meeting.

Lord George argued that the only sensible thing to do was retreat. They had marched around 200 miles into England, almost two thirds of the way to London, through the counties that were known for their Stuart sympathies, all the way expecting to be joined by the English supporters that Charles had assured them would rise. This had not happened. Neither had the French invasion which had been promised. Lord George insisted that this largely Scottish army had done all that could have been expected of them. He then went on to talk of the two English armies that threatened them, the force with Field Marshal Wade and the one under the command of Prince William, the Duke of Cumberland. Lord George argued that, at this moment in time, they had a clear run home, as long as they set off soon, but if they stayed where they were or tried to push further towards London, they would find themselves trapped between these two forces, with another gathering outside of London, at Finchley Common. In truth, the Jacobites had very sparse knowledge of the size or movements of the armies they might face, and that uncertainty could only have fed into the desire to go home. Lord George continued with the argument that, in order to succeed, their small Jacobite army would need to defeat each of these, probably larger and better armed forces, each time losing men to death, injury and desertion, while any British survivors would regroup with one of the other armies, swelling the numbers that the Jacobites must face in the next instance.

Lord George went on to suggest that, should they make it as far as London, the battered and bruised army that would arrive there would be insufficient to hold the capital and hardly likely to inspire support when so little had been encountered so far. He closed by coming back to the assertion that it would be madness to continue without an English uprising or a French invasion in the south-east of England or preferably both.

Johnstone tells us that the prince argued strongly for facing the Duke of Cumberland's army the next morning (6 December) and then marching straight to London[7], a distance of approximately 120 miles, or four day's march. Given that we know now that the French were planning to land an invasion force in the south-east no later than 9 December, then the timing would have been perfect, if all had fallen into place. But either Charles did not know of this date, or the chiefs were not convinced it would happen, because they continued to pressure the prince to turn back.

During the council meeting, a Captain Williams entered the room, claiming to bring them news of a force of 9,0000 troops, commanded by General Ligonier, which was waiting for them on the road to Northampton. Having very little knowledge of the actual constitution of the enemy forces, they believed this, although it was completely untrue. Captain Williams was really a Whig agent called Bradstreet, sent to discover what he could of the Jacobite army and sow doubt and dissension if possible. Charles is reported to have ordered that Williams/Bradstreet be thrown out, but the damage was already done[8].

Lord Elcho speaks of how passionate the prince was, how determined to proceed and how angry and frustrated he became when the chiefs could not be persuaded. Charles even suggested that the chiefs were betraying him. We see this anger in *Outlander* episode 'Vengeance is Mine'[9] which shows this meeting, where Charles was forced by his chiefs to turn back. In *Outlander*, as in *Dragonfly in Amber,* Jamie stands by the prince and argues for advancing to London – not because he expects to succeed, necessarily, but because he is desperately trying to turn aside the course that leads to slaughter on Culloden Moor. In history, Charles did not have even one supporter. Even the Duke of Perth, who generally followed the prince's wishes in all things, did not argue for pushing on to London.

Eventually Charles came to realise that he would not be able to persuade the chiefs to follow him this time and that he had no choice but to agree to the retreat. With the knowledge, or lack thereof, held by the council at that time, it was the sensible thing to do. However, the decision to retreat likely sealed the fate of the Jacobite army and this final uprising.

After much deliberation, the retreat was set for the following morning. In order to both confuse Cumberland's forces and to avoid the inevitable distress in the army at retreating when they were set on battle, flexible orders were given, and the decision was made that the army would begin moving out before first light. Despite the resolution having been taken, it seems that Charles still hoped to overcome the resistance of his council, as he had at every stage until now, and he spent the afternoon in efforts to persuade some of his council to change their minds and support him in an advance[10]. When that failed, he sank into a depression. According to Lord Elcho, he called all of the Scottish officers on the council to see him that night and told them that although he would agree to the retreat, he would hold no more councils and take no more advice[11].

The Jacobite army left Derby early on 6 December, first feinting towards Loughborough before turning back and passing through Derby again on their way north. According to Johnstone, when the light came up and the troops realised that they were retracing their steps, their grief was the same as it would have been had they been defeated[12]. This can only have been added to by Charles himself; instead of marching on foot with the troops, cheering them and keeping their spirits high as he had done throughout the campaign until this point, he rode at the back, his manner betraying the defeat and betrayal that he felt. Had Charles greater age and experience, he may have been able to hold his army together and keep morale high by billing the retreat as a triumphant return to Scotland to meet with the French-supported troops who had landed with Lord John Drummond. Instead, it must have felt to the men that they were running home with their tails between their legs. This little army, which had achieved so much in so little time, now faced forced marches through the winter, desperately trying to outrace the two English armies which would no doubt follow.

At this point in *Dragonfly in Amber,* Jamie and Claire are sent ahead of the main army to secure provisions, Jamie having fallen from Charles's good graces because of his failure to persuade the council to march on London. Their small group are taken off on their own adventure, while the rest of the army march for home.

Although a march on London would have been risky, they still had the advantage of being much faster than the English troops – Cumberland himself thought that if the Jacobites made a dash for the capital, they would arrive there first. The citizens of London were also in a panic, giving the Jacobites a psychological advantage, much like the one that had brought them the swift victory at Prestonpans and had seen so many towns surrender to them without a fight. Help from France was on the way and may have been enough to hold the capital and intimidate George II into fleeing back to Hanover. For some historians, such as Murray Pittock, this was the moment at which the campaign was lost[13].

PART FOUR

The Retreat

Chapter Twenty

The Race North

Most of what we know about the retreat comes from letters which were being sent to and from the Duke of Cumberland, tracing the Jacobites' progress north. After having put his troops through a forced march from Lichfield to Packington, thirteen and a half miles south of Derby, Cumberland was not in a position to pursue the retreating Jacobites in the first instance. In a letter to the Duke of Newcastle, dated 6 December, he explains that his troops have marched long days to get to Packington and cannot go farther without some rest. Had the Jacobite army marched on Cumberland on the morning of 6 December, as both Charles and the troops had wished, they would have found a fatigued force that, in some cases, had worn completely through their shoes[1]. This would have been in contrast to the Jacobites who had just had a day's rest in Derby and were in high spirits, looking for a fight and a chance to prove themselves by defeating another British army. Obviously, a win is never guaranteed, but the Jacobites would have been in a good position. Instead, they were marching back towards Ashbourne.

On hearing of the retreat, Cumberland sent a messenger to Wade, who was at that time in Doncaster in South Yorkshire. The Duke ordered that Wade and his men should immediately march into Lancashire to cut off the retreat before the Jacobites could reach Scotland[2].

On 7 December, Elizabeth Byrom notes in her journal that there is talk of the Jacobite army returning through Manchester and that there have been reports that they are at Leek, a town thirty-three miles south. The following day, she writes of the bellman going around town, reading out a notice that the people of the town are ordered to arm themselves as they can and prevent the Jacobite army from passing, holding them up long enough for the Duke of Cumberland's men to catch up. The first group of Jacobites reached Manchester on the afternoon of 9 December and, according to Miss Byrom, some people threw stones at them. The Jacobites told them to stop or be fired upon, so they stopped. Charles ordered that there would be a curfew in town, and none could gather in the evenings without a Jacobite escort, or they would be treated as rioters. How very different from the festive feeling that Elizabeth described just a week before when the Jacobites had passed through on the way south, and the ladies were all making white cockades for them. On 10 December, Charles ordered that the town pay a contribution of £5,000, although it was eventually reduced by half. The money was to be raised by 1.00pm, and about 1,000 men stayed to collect the money, while the rest of the army left town[3].

A letter from a 'T. Furnivall' to Cumberland, dated 8 December, informed the Duke of the Jacobites' progress towards Manchester, and that a group of five deserters had been seen in a nearby town and had expressed an opinion that there would soon be more[4]. If this was true, then it's hardly surprising. We know that there had been a certain amount of desertion before the march to England and now that the Jacobites were retreating, without the strong leadership from Charles that may have saved morale, some of the soldiers must have felt that their best chance of survival was to flee.

Also on 8 December, Field Marshall Wade held a council of war at Ferrybridge, in West Yorkshire, seventy-four miles from Macclesfield, where the Jacobite army was on 8 December. Having received the orders from the Duke, they resolved to march to Lancashire as quickly as they could, but the quartermaster informed them that they did not have sufficient provisions to march before Tuesday, 10 December. A dispatch was sent to the Duke of Cumberland, advising him of these plans[5]. Facing the pursuit of a smaller, faster, lighter army, it's hard to see how Wade could have justified this sort of delay to Cumberland. Every moment that they spent in Yorkshire allowed Charles and his Jacobites to increase their lead, reducing the likelihood of catching up with them before they crossed the border back into Scotland.

On the same day, in London, much relief was felt at the retreat of the Jacobite army, though there was still concern about the potential invasion from France, expected to land somewhere in the south-east imminently. It was decided that the Duke of Cumberland should go no farther north than Coventry, in case of a French attack on London[6]. It's possible that they were concerned that the Jacobite retreat was a feint, intended to draw troops away from London, opening the capital to attack from France while both the Duke's and Wade's armies were too far north to return quickly, which may have been an effective technique, had the rebels in England and the troops in France been coordinating with each other.

By 11 December, as of yet unaware of his new orders, the Duke of Cumberland and his army were at Macclesfield, having marched fifty miles over difficult terrain to get there. He had hoped to catch up with Charles and his army at Manchester, but the Jacobites had already moved on. On 11 December, Cumberland wrote to the Duke of Newcastle, expressing doubt that Marshal Wade would be able to cut the Jacobites off. He also wrote that there had been some stragglers from Charles's army picked up and that he had encouraged the locals to put to death any rebels they should come across[7].

The next day, the Duke was still in Macclesfield and was excited to hear rumours that panic was spreading through the Jacobite army to the extent that they were discarding their weapons. He believed them to be at Preston, two to three day's march ahead and he was determined to press on and catch up with them[8]. He may have been less excited had he been in possession of the letter sent to him that day by Field Marshal Wade, who advised that he had been forced to stop in Leeds to secure provisions and would not be likely to intercept the Jacobite army before it reached Carlisle. He also stated that his numbers were being reduced due to illness, worsened by the harsh conditions[9].

Cumberland arrived at Preston on 15 December, to receive reports that the main body of the Jacobite army was at Lancaster, around twenty-eight miles away, a distance the duke could hope to cover in one day. What had, at first, seemed impossible, was now within his grasp. However, the new orders from London finally caught up with him in Preston, calling him back south to protect London. His response shows his frustration as he says the orders have saved the rebel army, which otherwise, he would have utterly destroyed with the help of Marshal Wade's force[10].

Despite Cumberland's feelings about it, the command to return south made perfect sense in light of the ongoing activity at Dunkirk, where the French troops were preparing to embark on the invasion led by Charles's younger brother Henry, and the duc de Richelieu, and London was largely unprotected.

The duke may have been called back to London, but it would seem that his army did not head south immediately. Johnstone writes of a confrontation between the rear guard of the Jacobites and some light cavalry of the Duke's army, between Shap and Penrith. He recounts how the rear guard came across the cavalry and then, from beyond a ridge, could hear drums and trumpets making enough noise to convince them that the whole of the English army awaited them on the other side. The Jacobites were cut off from the main part of their army which was already at Penrith; this small force decided that there was nothing for it but to rush the enemy and try to find a way through to Penrith or die trying. According to Johnstone, when they reached the peak of the ridge, they found only three hundred light cavalry, who fled at sight of the highlanders bearing down on them.

A short time later, Sergeant Dickson pointed out a shadow on a hill about a league away and insisted it was Cumberland's army. At first no one else could make out any detail in the shadow and they were unconvinced that Dickson was correct, but soon they could see that he had been right. Johnstone reported that the Duke of Cumberland and about 4,000 men fell on the MacDonalds who were at the rear of the column. Fortunately, the road was narrow with high hedges to either side, preventing the duke's army from surrounding them, allowing the highlanders to repel the cavalry and give the wagons with their artillery some time to move farther along the road. They fought this way for a distance of a mile or so, until they came to Clifton Hall, where the remainder of the Jacobite army was drawn up ready to give battle, the prince having heard what was happening and ordered the men out to assist.

According to Johnstone, the English soldiers drew up into battle lines inside some enclosures on the grounds, behind some hedges. He writes that the highlanders cut down the hedges with their dirks and then immediately attacked the English soldiers, cutting through them until they were eventually forced to retreat. The way Johnstone recounts the story, this was a definite victory for the Jacobites, with Cumberland's army losing perhaps as many as six hundred men, while the highlanders lost only a dozen[11].

Cumberland wrote of this conflict as a 'trifling affair' which increased the panic and fear felt by the Jacobite army as they fled. The duke suggested that his army had won the day, the rebels only being saved by the coming of darkness[12]. In the additional notes of Johnstone's memoirs, there are stories of various accounts put about by the English of this battle going in their favour, with heavy losses to the Jacobites, however the Jacobite accounts all largely agree with Johnstone's[13].

Chapter Twenty-One

Carlisle Again

On 19 December 1745, the Jacobite army marched back into Carlisle, which was still held by John Hamilton. Waiting there were letters from Lord John Drummond and Lord Strathallan, both of whom were writing from Scotland. Lord Strathallan gave details of the army that was now gathered in Scotland and awaiting the prince's return, advising that it was better than the army that the prince had with him. Lord John wrote of the imminent invasion from France and passed on advice from Louis XV that Charles take no decisive action until the French troops arrived to support him and assure his success.

Here, Charles called a council, though this probably was not the same group that he had sworn not to take advice from again at Derby. At the meeting, it was decided that they would march into Scotland and join Lord John Drummond's army there while awaiting further contact from France. It was also decided at this meeting to leave behind a garrison at Carlisle to hold both the castle and the town, made up of the Manchester regiment and over 200 Scots. It's hard to make sense of this decision without any clear account of the thinking behind it. On their march into England, five weeks earlier, the Jacobites had taken Carlisle easily, it's walls and other defences insufficient to stand against even this small army with minimal artillery. It's hard to conceive that Charles or the clan chiefs thought that any small force they left behind would be able to hold the town against the combined might of Cumberland's and Wade's forces and all the artillery they could bring to bear. So why were they left behind?

Johnstone tells us that some thought the prince was choosing to sacrifice these troops in order to delay Cumberland in his pursuit, allowing the rest of the Jacobite army to retreat at a slower pace than that which they had been forced to maintain from Derby to Carlisle. Such reasoning would be rather mercenary on Charles's part and there is no other indication that he considered any of his army to be disposable in this manner. Johnstone also states that others suggested that leaving the garrison behind, especially the Manchester regiment, was intended as vengeance on the English for failing to rise when so many had indicated that they were willing to do so[1]. This motive also does not fit with anything else that we know of Charles. He was young and impetuous, stubborn and misguided, but prior to this, there was no suggestion in his behaviour that he was vindictive or malicious, and it would have made little sense to take his anger out on the men who had signed up and sacrificed everything to fight for him in order to punish those who did not, not to mention the Scots troops that he left behind along with the Manchester regiment. In fact, had he wished to punish people who had let him down, he could have commanded any of the chiefs who argued for the retreat to remain and hold Carlisle.

I find it more likely that the reason Charles wanted a garrison to stay and hold Carlisle is simply that he did not intend to be gone for long. It was always his intention to take both thrones and this retreat had pained him greatly. The news of the force waiting for him in Scotland with Lord John Drummond and the imminent arrival of more French troops likely encouraged him to believe that he would be marching towards London again soon and leaving a garrison here would leave him with a foothold in England. It may also have been symbolic; a clear sign that he was not abandoning his claim to the throne of England.

Regardless of Charles's intentions, the majority of the Jacobite army marched out of Carlisle on 20 December, never to return.

The frontrunners of Cumberland's army started arriving in the area surrounding Carlisle the next day. The Duke of Cumberland wrote to the Duke of Newcastle from nearby Blackhall, where Charles had also lodged. Cumberland told Newcastle that the town and castle were garrisoned and that they had fired upon anyone that had shown themselves. He couldn't pass easily to pursue the fleeing army and so decided to wait there until cannons could be brought, a few days later. He expressed the hope of getting some revenge on the rebels for causing so much trouble – contrast this attitude with Charles, who showed mercy to all of the prisoners that he took after Prestonpans, and even to the British spy that was captured near Ashbourne[2].

A week later, Cumberland had the artillery he required and his battlements in place and he commenced the attack on Carlisle.

On 30 December, the rebel defenders of the castle hung out a white flag and sent a messenger to the duke to ask for terms of surrender. Reportedly, the only terms the duke would offer were that the Jacobites would not be immediately executed but would wait for King George II to decide what to do with them. Colonel Towneley, who had command of the town, was less than impressed with the castle's surrender as it forced him to capitulate at the same time since it would be impossible to defend the town without the assistance of the castle[3]. As previously discussed, the standard penalty for treason was to be hung, drawn and quartered. Facing that punishment, no doubt the thought of dying in battle was far more appealing.

The Jacobite soldiers were kept under guard in the cathedral and treated poorly. According to a James Miller, who had joined them in Preston, they were given no food for three days, and only water from a well broken open in the floor of the cathedral[4].

The Duke of Newcastle sent a letter to Cumberland, dated 28 December, which presumably arrived after the surrender, on the subject of what to do with any prisoners he should take at Carlisle. The letter says that if he should take their surrender, it should be on the condition that they all be sent to the West Indies[5].

Chapter Twenty-Two

Glasgow

The Jacobite army crossed the river Esk into Scotland during the afternoon of 20 December 1745, Charles' twenty-fifth birthday. This normally placid river was swollen from the heavy rains of the season and crossing was treacherous. The cavalry stood their horses in the water to break some of the power of the current, while the infantry crossed downstream, in groups of ten or twelve, with linked arms. Cavalry were also prepared downstream of the infantry to catch anyone who was swept away by the current. Using this method, they managed the crossing without losing a single man. Fires were lit on the far bank to dry out and pipers began to play. According to Johnstone, the highlanders all began to dance, so happy were they to see their country again[1]. This is perhaps unsurprising – many of them no doubt expected to die in battle, somewhere in England. To have returned home must have seemed miraculous, even under the circumstances.

As it had done several times before, the army split into two columns; one, led by Lord George, headed towards Ecclefechan while the other, led by the prince, headed north-west, towards Dumfries. Lord George recalls difficult travelling conditions, with poor roads and driving rain. By the time they reached Ecclefechan, he had caught cold and spent the next day in bed[2].

Charles, travelling with Lord Elcho and the cavalry, pushed on straight to Dumfries, where they arrived on 22 December, having marched through the night in the driving rain. They were unwelcome here, which was only to be expected, since the town had confiscated some of the Jacobite army's ammunition waggons, when they had been marching south. No doubt the residents were concerned about retribution from angry and dispirited soldiers. According to Johnstone, the town was punished by being made to pay a substantial fine[3]. The town failed to pay the full amount of the fine, so two men were taken hostage along with the army, pending payment. It also guaranteed the safety of any

Jacobite stragglers that came through the town after the main body of the army had left[4].

Charles spent Christmas Day at Hamilton Palace, the home of the Duke of Hamilton, widely accepted as one of the grandest stately homes in Scotland[5]. The prince spent the day shooting in the park that surrounded the palace and impressed all onlookers with his skill as a marksman.

By Christmas Day, Lord George and the other column of the army had reached Glasgow, Scotland's second city. A wealthy city, it was predominately a Hanoverian stronghold. The Jacobites would find no warm welcome here. Charles and the rest of the army arrived on 26 December and it was decided to rest the entire army here. They had covered almost 300 miles in just twenty days, during the worst season for such a journey. They were exhausted and in need of new clothes and shoes. While in Glasgow, Charles demanded that his army be supplied with 12,000 shirts, 6,000 coats, pairs of stockings, bonnets, shoes and hose[6].

While in Glasgow, Charles arranged to review his army as a whole on Glasgow Green – after they had received their new clothes and been fed and rested. Marching on the green, with colours flying and bagpipes playing[7] they must have made quite an impressive sight. Contrary to the beliefs of the Duke of Cumberland, they had lost very few men to desertion or panic. On the way into England, Charles had attempted at all times to disguise the true size of his army, a wise course of action, given how few they were. But now, back in Scotland, safe for the moment, due to meet with Lord Drummond and increase their numbers, their small size must have seemed a badge of honour. This was, after all, the army who had defeated Cope at Prestonpans and then penetrated all the way to the midlands, conquering every major town they stopped at, before giving the British army a merry chase north.

It was noted by Lord Elcho that, while in Glasgow, Charles behaved differently to how he had anywhere else. He wore fine French silks rather than his customary highland or lowland garb, and he paid more attention to the people who chose to visit him, taking part in dancing and such-like[8]. It's possible that Charles was taking this opportunity to remind his chiefs that he was, in fact, their prince. He was royalty, born to the crown, and would be recognised as such. It's also possible that he intended for word to get back to Louis XV, whom he needed to align himself with in order to secure additional support from him.

In *Dragonfly in Amber,* unlike in history, the Jacobites returned to Edinburgh at this time, and there, Jamie receives a visit from this uncle, Callum MacKenzie. Callum's debilitating illness has worsened, and he is dying. He comes seeking Jamie's advice regarding whether to commit his clan to the Stuart cause. Jamie knows that the extra men and weight of the MacKenzie clan could, potentially, change the fortunes of the Jacobite army. But he also knows that any clans involved with the rebellion will be almost wiped out following Culloden if the Jacobites lose. This all weighs heavily on Jamie and we see him struggling with the decision. Eventually, he finds that he cannot recommend that the MacKenzies join the fight, even knowing that it might turn the tide in the Jacobites' favour. He warns Callum not to raise the clan.

Unfortunately, Callum dies before he can make his decision known, and Dougal takes over the clan as chief, until Callum's son reaches the age of majority. Dougal, whose loyalty to the Stuart cause has never wavered, immediately raises the clan, bringing the MacKenzies to Charles's banner. Assuming that Jamie persuaded Dougal to raise the clan, Charles sends Jamie to recruit Simon Lovat and the Fraser clan. Although Lord Lovat is Jamie's paternal grandfather, the two have never met and he bears no love for the old man, describing him to Claire as a sly, dishonest person and telling her the stories of how he came to marry each of his three wives.

Jamie, knowing that it's looking more and more like the events at Culloden will come to pass, tells his men from Lallybroch to make their way home and promises to meet them there. In short, he tells them to desert. Claire and Jamie make their way to Simon Fraser's home at Castle Beaufort, where they find a cantankerous old man, determined to turn the situation to his own advantage somehow. During their stay, Claire sees Lord Lovat throw a woman into the hall, a seer who will not tell him of her vision. Claire speaks to the woman and discovers that the vision was of an executioner's axe hanging over the laird's head. Lovat keeps Jamie and Claire there for around two weeks, trying to manipulate Jamie into giving up the title to Lallybroch and joining Lovat's branch of the clan. When that doesn't work, Lovat prevaricates, until Claire diagnoses him with prostatitis, a condition he uses to argue that he is too ill to join the prince. He does, however, send his son, Simon Fraser, Master of Lovat with one hundred and seventy men, although on the muster roll, he claims two hundred men, including Jamie's thirty from Lallybroch. If Jamie hadn't noticed and had it corrected, and the Jacobites won, Lovat could have used this to claim Lallybroch, on the grounds that they answered his call for men.

After seeing young Simon and the troops off, Jamie and Claire make their way to Lallybroch, where they discover that Jamie's men have all been arrested for desertion and are in jail in Edinburgh, so the couple immediately head back to the capital to intercede with Charles and try to negotiate the men's release.

In history, Simon Lovat did finally declare for Charles and raise his clan, but it was not as a result of persuasion by his grandson, but because another James Fraser forced his hand. On the evening of 16 October, James Fraser and a force of around two hundred Frasers, attacked Culloden House, attempting to abduct Duncan Forbes, the highest legal professional in Scotland at the time, and the leader of the Hanoverians in the north-east. Historians disagree over exactly what position Lord Lovat had in all of this. Riding tells us that James Fraser was acting at Lord Lovat's request[9], as does Christopher Duffy[10], while Sarah Fraser argues that Lord Lovat did not order the action, and in fact, wrote to Duncan Forbes to warn him of the impending attack[11]. Even if Lord Lovat did send such a letter to Forbes, this does not prove that he didn't also tell James Fraser to act as he did; Lovat was known for playing both sides and such behaviour could have simply been a way to try and ingratiate himself with the Stuart prince by making the order and the Hanoverians by warning them.

In this case, the Hanoverians were unconvinced by Lovat's protestations of innocence, and on 11 December, John Campbell, 4th Earl of Loudoun had Lovat arrested and brought to Inverness, where he was held until 2 January, when, according to Sarah Fraser, he escaped without difficulty. He was then assisted by Fraser clansmen who took him to Gorthleck House, on the banks of Loch Ness[12], where he waited out the rebellion, never actually fighting himself, although his son, Simon Fraser, Master of Lovat, was present at Culloden.

The Frasers were not the only ones who rose after Charles had left for England. Lady MacIntosh had raised her husband's clan, and Lady Fortrose had managed to gather a regiment of MacKenzies, although both of their husbands were Hanoverian supporters. In addition to this, Lord Cromartie and Lord John Macleod had raised the main MacKenzie clan (so the MacKenzies did rise, just not under Dougal). This army was gathering around Perth in the north-east. Edinburgh had been retaken by British forces only a week after Charles had left; returning there would force a battle with government forces, something the prince wanted to avoid for a little longer. So it was, that he decided to leave Glasgow and consolidate his forces, while awaiting news of a French landing in England.

During this time, Charles received news that Carlisle had fallen. According to witnesses, the prince was very upset by this news and lamented the loss of his men although the blow was softened by news of a Jacobite victory in Aberdeen, involving Lord John Drummond's forces against Lord Loudoun[13].

After a little over a week in Glasgow, the Jacobite army marched out on 3 January, heading north to meet with the other troops.

Chapter Twenty-Three

Falkirk

Stirling Castle was always a strategically important stronghold, as it guarded the gateway between the lowlands and the highlands. Even by 1746, it had an impressive history, having been home to many Stuart kings and queens over the centuries. In January 1746, the castle had not yet been involved in this conflict and was held by a garrison of British soldiers. If the Jacobites were able to take the castle, it would have both practical value as a base of operations – and would be a historically appropriate place for Charles to hold court util the next stage of the campaign – as well as being of great psychological value to the Jacobite troops.

To this end, the Jacobite army marched from Glasgow in two columns to rendezvous just outside Stirling on 4 January. Charles took up residence at Bannockburn House, two miles from Stirling, while Lord George Murray travelled to meet with Lord John Drummond and facilitate the transport of the heavy French artillery, without which they would be unable to meaningfully attack the castle. Lord Elcho settled in Linlithgow with the cavalry, while another part of the army was cantoned in villages just outside of Stirling[1]. This effectively blockaded the town and so began a siege to take the castle. Lord John Drummond finally joined Charles with around four thousand men, roughly doubling the number that had marched to Derby[2]. Johnstone laments that these men had not been with them in Derby. He suggests that if the prince had been a little more patient in allowing more men to gather before marching from Edinburgh, then they surely would have had enough men to crown him in London.

On 6 January, the Jacobite army began opening trenches in front of the town of Stirling, but since the town walls were in a poor state of repair and they had no means of defending themselves, they sought terms for capitulation. Charles agreed that none would be harmed, and the town gates were opened to the Jacobite army on 8 January. The castle did not surrender, having strong walls and being manned by a garrison of several hundred men[3]. The prince took advice from a Monsieur Mirabelle de Gordon, a French engineer who had arrived with Lord John Drummond, with regards to setting up a battery with their artillery in a position which would allow them to breach the castle walls. Johnstone did not think highly of the advice offered by Mirabelle, stating that the engineer lacked discernment, judgement and common sense[4]. There was certainly a difference of opinion about how the battery should be set up.

According to Johnstone, a Mr Grant had proposed a plan of attack to the prince, which involved setting up the Jacobite battery in a cemetery on the outskirts of the town, facing the castle gates. Mr Grant was convinced that this was the only practical place to attack from, as everywhere else, the castle was substantially higher than the surrounding grounds, such that their weapons would be far less effective and even if they did manage to create a breach in the walls, they would be unable to get men through to attack inside the castle. The townspeople were unhappy with this plan and asked the prince to reconsider; they were convinced that if the Jacobites set up in the cemetery then return fire from the castle would destroy the town. Charles asked Mirabelle for advice. The French engineer recommended setting up the battery on a hill to the north of town, where the rock was very close to the surface, making it impossible to dig proper trenches. Johnstone blames this for the substantial loss of men during the siege[5].

During this time, Charles was ill, laid up with what Lord George described as a bad cold, but was quite possibly brought on by exhaustion. He was tended to by Clementina Walkinshaw, who would later become his mistress and mother to the only child that he formally acknowledged.

Upon his recovery, he gathered his army together for review. He had received news that General Hawley – now in charge of the British forces, while Cumberland was in London – was encamped at Falkirk, so Charles marched his army out to meet them, leaving around 1,000 men behind to continue the siege, commanded by the Duke of Perth.

General Hawley did not march out to meet the Jacobite army, so they circled around to take Falkirk Hill, giving them the high ground. Lord John Drummond took some cavalry and foot soldiers, separate from the main army, to serve as a distraction to the British. It seems that this worked – when the British army heard Drummond and his troops coming, they largely dismissed them, without checking to see if the main army followed. According to John Home, Hawley ordered that the men could get ready but that they did not need to be under arms[6] (a state of readiness where the soldiers are in uniform, on duty, and carrying weapons).

At some time between and one and two in the afternoon, British scouts finally saw the main body of the Jacobite army approaching and gave the alarm. The British camp was in disarray, unsure of how to proceed without orders from Hawley, who was still at Callendar House, where he was staying. As soon as he received the news, he rode straight for the field of battle and ordered that the cavalry be brought up first, with the infantry behind them. This was a risky strategy since the Jacobites had so roundly defeated the cavalry at Prestonpans. The horses were not well trained to face a highland charge, and this had not changed between the two battles. It may be that Hawley was displaying a little arrogance here; perhaps he believed that the fault at Prestonpans lay with Cope's leadership rather than the cavalry which had been so thoroughly routed.

There was now something of a race between the two armies to reach the top of Falkirk Hill first, as whichever gained the high ground would have an advantage. In January in Scotland the sun sets early, and it was in this dying light that the battle commenced. What had been a cloudy, damp day, was now turning to wind and heavy rain, giving the Jacobite army another advantage – the rain was blowing at their backs but directly into the faces of the British army, obscuring their view and rendering some of their muskets useless as they were unable to keep them dry[7].

The cavalry slowly advanced upon the Jacobite right flank, led by Lord George Murray, who had ordered the men not to fire until he gave the signal. They held firm until the cavalry were very close, easily within musket range, and then fired. Smoke from their guns joined the wind and rain into the faces of the horses, adding to the confusion and chaos. According to Johnstone, the cavalry crashed into the highlander lines, who then carried out an unexpected manoeuvre; while flat on the ground, they pulled their dirks and began to attack the underside of the horses, stabbing them in the bellies, and pulling some of the riders down by their clothes and stabbing them[8]. After this, all three cavalry regiments turned and fled, one crashing into the Glasgow militia which had been placed behind them. This resulted in the militia firing upon their own cavalry to save themselves from being trampled[9].

Contrary to Lord George's orders, the MacDonalds pursued the fleeing cavalry. Most of the British infantry, who were marching uphill into the battle, wind and rain in their faces, were caught in the confusion and turned and fled. The right flank of the British army held its ground, firing upon the Jacobites, who were prevented from charging by a ravine that separated them from the British. This resulted in some of the Jacobite force retreating; indeed, some left the field of battle altogether and returned to Bannockburn or Stirling. This resulted in the greater part of the British army fleeing to the east, while part of the Jacobite army fled to the west[10].

The remainder of the British army gathered at their camp, where they put fire to their tents to deny them to the Jacobites and then they withdrew to Linlithgow. From that town, Hawley wrote to the Duke of Cumberland with a report of the battle, although he does not give great detail about what happened. Instead, he seems to have been very much overcome by emotion. He describes himself as heartbroken and goes on to say that he is unclear on who won the battle, since both armies had one flank defeated. He reports that he had around two thousand men more than the Jacobites but laments the cowardice of his troops, many of whom quit the field without firing a single shot[11].

As a result of the complete disorder in the British army, a great many officers paid with their lives. Twenty of those killed were officers, from five regiments. Because of the cowardice of the ranks, who fled before they were in any significant danger, the officers were exposed and took a disproportionate amount of fire.

Although the Jacobite army were eventually able to enter Falkirk and could thus declare the battle a victory, Johnstone tells us that it was not as cut and dried as that. They considered it at best a temporary victory and expected to resume battle the next morning[12]. According to this account, immediately following the battle, many of the officers had no idea where Charles was, or even if the prince was safe. With the British having largely fled, night having fallen and the weather worsening, they had no choice but to seek shelter wherever they could and were greatly relieved to learn at last that Charles was safe in Falkirk.

There was much bickering amongst the Jacobite command after the battle as to whose fault it was that their victory was less than decisive. Lord George Murray blamed the MacDonalds for breaking ranks and also Colonel O'Sullivan for apparently not appointing an officer to command the left wing[13]. This does seem like a basic mistake to make, if true.

According to the editors of Johnstone's *Memoirs of the Rebellion,* Home stated that Lord George blamed Lord John Drummond, who should have been in command on the left, while Lord Drummond and other officers blamed Lord George for not giving the MacDonalds free rein in pursuing the fleeing British army[14]. Whatever the individual failings of the officers, it's clear that this lack of cohesion in the command structure cannot have done the Jacobite army any good whatsoever.

Although the battle was not an unqualified victory, it was a victory and, unlike at Prestonpans, this time they had defeated a force full of experienced troops, not new recruits. These seasoned soldiers had still turned and fled from what many of them considered nothing more than an undisciplined rabble. With a clear command structure and less infighting at the top, what might this army have become?

Unfortunately, the infighting was not to stop in the immediate aftermath of the battle and, in fact, only became worse as time went on. It seems that there were rumours concerning Lord George and the idea that he was a traitor to the cause, and always had been. In a letter to an unnamed person, George Colville writes that Lord George has been unfairly maligned and that he is a skilled and dedicated commander, much loved by the clansmen and their chiefs. Colville suggests that the rumours have been started by some envious person and says that Lord George has a sincere devotion for the King (James)[15].

The Jacobite army stayed in Falkirk until 19 January and while there, an incident occurred which would overshadow their success for many of the men. A Clanranald clansman was cleaning his gun and discharged it from the window of the building he was staying in. Unknown to him, the gun was double loaded and discharged while Colonel Angus MacDonnell, son of Glengarry, was walking past[16]. MacDonnell was fatally wounded, much to the distress of the army; it was said that he was well-loved throughout the army[17]. In order to avoid any retribution between the clans, it was immediately ordered that the Clanranald man be executed, which he was. Unfortunately, this did not solve the problem and the execution was followed by a general unrest and several desertions[18].

Despite this, several of the clan chiefs wanted to push on to Edinburgh and force Hawley to quit the capital, but the prince was determined to take Stirling Castle and so ordered the return to the siege[19].

Stirling

Back in Stirling, the trenches around the castle were offered poor protection and General Blakeney, in charge of the castle garrison, constantly fired upon the Jacobites, leading to a considerable loss of life; according to Johnstone as much as twenty-five a day[20]. Charles visited the trenches only once, which can hardly have encouraged the troops risking their lives there. Mirabelle raised a battery by 28 January, on Gowan Hill, firing upon the castle. Unfortunately, Blakeney fired back with very well-aimed fire, and managed to destroy the Jacobite guns within a few hours. It was unclear if Mirabelle was incompetent or had been paid off[21].

On 21 January, Charles wrote to Louis XV, informing him of the victory over Hawley's army at Falkirk and asking for more money and men. He was careful to flatter Louis by complimenting Lord John Drummond and the men he brought with him, men who were ultimately under Louis' command. He also reminds Louis that he is currently risking his life on this campaign and that the French king has the ability to change that by sending the invasion so long promised.[22]

Unknown to Charles, the duc de Richelieu in Dunkirk, called off the plans for the full invasion by the end of January but, following news of the battle at Falkirk, several cavalry regiments were preparing to travel to north-east Scotland to join the Jacobite army.

While the Jacobite battery was being established and then destroyed, the Duke of Cumberland was en route to Scotland to take over command of the British army from Hawley, who was probably lucky not to be facing court martial over the fiasco at Falkirk, as so many of his troops had. Cumberland arrived in Edinburgh on 30 January 1745/6 and took up residence in the Duke of Hamilton's apartments at Holyroodhouse, where Charles had stayed the previous autumn. Cumberland wrote to the Duke of Newcastle with an update on his plans. He advised that he intended to move against the Jacobite army at Stirling and that he believed he had enough troops to destroy the Jacobites completely, if his own men did their duty and stayed on the field of battle. Having learned from the battles at both Prestonpans and Falkirk, Cumberland told Newcastle that he planned to put the cavalry in the third row[23]. Already, he was making better decisions than Hawley, despite the fact that Cumberland was only 24, a few months younger than Charles.

When Charles heard that Cumberland was planning to march to Stirling, he was excited rather than worried, keen to face the British army in a decisive action and drive them from Scotland, once and for all. Charles had Lord George draw up a battle plan, which he approved of. The prince and Lord George were both aware of the problem of desertion from their ranks by this time, but it does not seem to have caused the prince to doubt his ability to defeat the British. He was said to be in good spirits after reviewing the battle plan with Lord George[24].

Unbeknownst to Charles, the clan chiefs met in council with Lord George on 29 January 1745/6 and were far less enthusiastic about the idea of going into battle than the prince was. With so many of their troops deserting every day, from every part of the army, they were unconvinced that they could win against Cumberland, especially since they believed he would be marching with a larger army than the one they had faced at Falkirk. The assembled chiefs also did not believe that the siege would be successful. Given the fact that their battery had been so easily destroyed the previous day, it is perhaps understandable that they had little faith in their ability to take the castle. They believed that it would take weeks or even months to overcome the castle's defences, no doubt by starving the garrison out.

The clan chiefs signed a petition to the prince, advising him to retire to the highlands for the remainder of the winter, driving the British troops from the highland fortresses and resting their soldiers so that, in spring, they would have more men available to them to continue the campaign in any way that Charles would wish. The petition was signed by: Lord George, Keppoch, Lochiel, Clanranald, Lochgarry, Ardsheal, Scothouse and Simon Fraser, Master of Lovat[25].

We know that the prince felt betrayed in Derby when the council voted against him for a retreat from England. How much more so would he feel now, to have the clan chiefs meet in secret, behind his back, and then resolve to retreat again? However reasonable their advice, however necessary retreat may have been at this time, Charles would not have wanted to hear such advice.

The petition from the clan chiefs is said to have arrived at Bannockburn after the prince had retired for the night and Secretary Murray and Colonel O'Sullivan read it and decided not to disturb Charles until the next morning, anticipating his reaction to it. Secretary Murray was heard to have blamed it all on Lord George, suggesting that the commander had turned the rest of the clan chiefs against the prince's wishes.

In the morning, when he was given the petition, the prince apparently hit his head against the wall and complained about Lord George, expressing disbelief that he should have lived to see such actions[26]. The editor who noted this account of the prince's behaviour in Johnstone's memoirs makes it clear that they consider this display of emotion to be immature and selfish and they clearly don't think much of Charles in general. This assessment seems a little unfair. Charles may have reacted strongly in the moment, but he responded to the chiefs in a measured and reasonable way. He did not pull rank and insist that they obey his orders, as their sovereign, instead seeking to persuade them with arguments that held some merit.

In his letter to the chiefs, Charles expressed concern that if they fled north, it would further harm the morale of the Jacobite army, while encouraging the British troops, who should really be still feeling the sting of their defeat at Falkirk. He believed that they would find themselves in a worse position than they had been when he first landed.

After receiving his letter, some of the chiefs visited Charles in Bannockburn to explain their position. Charles again wrote to the whole group, stressing the points he had made previously and begging them to reconsider. He went on to state that if they were set on retreat then he had no choice but to go along with them although he believed the action would be fatal[27].

It's clear from this that Charles believed he had no power over the army, that the clan chiefs would do what they wanted regardless of his opinion. Without a greater number of French troops to offer him support, he was beholden to the chiefs and could not force them to comply with his wishes. This is a curious dynamic for an army led by the sovereign of the country. Charles was in Scotland as his father's regent and therefore should have had the authority of the king, as far as these chiefs were concerned. Would they have treated James the same way they treated his son? Were the Stuarts too long removed from Scotland to command the kind of power and loyalty that a king needs? Or was the problem here that Charles was young and inexperienced? Did they see him as someone to be protected from youthful mistakes?

If we contrast this with the British army, we see soldiers obeying Cumberland without question. Senior commanders in that army wrote of their love and admiration for the duke, their relief when he returned to Britain to lead them. Remember that Prince William Augustus, the Duke of Cumberland, was also young and although more experienced than Charles, he was hardly the kind of veteran that Field Marshal Wade was. What was the difference between these two young men that gave one unquestioning command of the forces beneath him, while the other had his commanders deciding how to proceed without his permission?

Perhaps Charles set too much precedent of leading with consent early in the campaign, leading the clan chiefs to feel that they could tell him what to do. He had always worked with persuasion rather than force and he did so now, although it failed to secure the result that he wished.

The order was given for the retreat to begin on 1 February, though first, the prince wanted to review the troops between Stirling and Bannockburn, hoping that the desertion would not be as serious as previously thought and that he could still, somehow, avoid the retreat. Unfortunately, word of the order to retreat got out early and, rather than wait for the appointed time, many of the troops began marching north immediately so that the number who appeared for review was very poor indeed. There was no option left but to march north.

At this time, there was an odd incident involving a church called St Ninian's, south of Stirling. The Jacobites had been using this church to store gunpowder and during the retreat, it blew up. The local newspaper reported that it had been blown up on purpose by the Jacobites out of malice of some sort. Several townspeople were killed so one can understand why the reporter would believe it had been done on purpose. The problem with this theory though is that some of the highlanders also died, and other important people were put at risk. Charles himself was close enough that he might have been injured in the explosion, and Lochiel was passing at the time with Secretary Murray's wife[28]. It seems highly unlikely that the Jacobites would have purposefully caused the explosion when it gave them no advantage but risked their own people. There's also no evidence of them blowing up or otherwise destroying any other place during the campaign and they had no reason to do so now. Such an action would have been more in keeping with Cumberland's army.

The next day, the army gathered at Crieff, where there was another review. Here it was found that the desertion had not been as bad as previously thought, many of the highlanders having been prone to wandering around the villages in the area, making it impossible to keep track of them all[29]. This can only have deepened Charles's feelings of mistrust regarding the clan chiefs and especially Lord George, a situation which will have been made much worse, if the following anecdote is true.

According to Seward, during the retreat from Stirling, Lord George interrupted Charles at dinner and announced that the retreat was cowardly and shameful and suddenly seemed dead set against it. There was then another council meeting, at which Lord George would only allow people to speak when he called upon them, and he would not allow Charles to speak until everyone else there had expressed an opinion. Reportedly, Charles followed Lord George's wishes and waited until everyone else had spoken, but such erratic and disrespectful behaviour must have deepened the divisions in the command and infuriated the prince[30].

Chapter Twenty-Four

Cumberland in Scotland

Cumberland and his army marched out of Edinburgh on 31 January, only one day after he arrived in the city. The next day he wrote to the Duke of Newcastle from Falkirk, expressing his surprise that the Jacobite army had withdrawn from that town despite their victory there. He found only some wounded soldiers from both sides[1]. The next day he moved on to Stirling, having missed the Jacobite army by only one day.

This next letter to the Duke of Newcastle, written on 2 February, reveals a lot about what Cumberland thought of the Jacobites and, I would argue, the Scots as a whole. Or certainly the highlanders. He believed that the Jacobite army would break up now and go into hiding, where his soldiers would not easily be able to follow. He suggested that orders should be given to kill anyone who had a weapon in their home as that would be indicative of taking part in treason. He didn't seem to consider the fact that many people may have had arms in their homes but remained neutral throughout the conflict, or indeed, been supporters of his own family. So, either he considered all Scots to be Jacobites or at the very least he thought they were disposable in his attempts to stamp out support for the Stuarts[2].

Cumberland pursued the Jacobites north to Crieff in Perth and Kinross. He arrived there three days behind Charles and his army, who had marched out in two columns, moving separately, deeper into the highlands. Charles had left with the highland regiments, heading towards Inverness to drive out Lord Loudoun, the Hanoverian supporter who had arrested Lord Lovat in December. Lord George along with Lord John Drummond took the cavalry and lowland regiments via Perth. The two columns planned to meet again at Inverness[3].

On discovering this, Cumberland wrote to Newcastle again and told him that he believed the rebellion was all but crushed and that Charles was really fleeing back to France. Cumberland also reports that he has been allowing his soldiers some freedom – in other words, he was allowing his men to pillage the towns and estates they passed through[4]. There is no mention of whether they restricted themselves to places which had shown support for the Jacobites, but he does not seem to be particularly discerning in this regard. Perhaps his heavy-handedness was simply a result of his youth, but it cannot have endeared him to the Scots, who were largely ignored by the leaders in London the rest of the time. He does refer specifically to plundering the rebel's homes in the letter dated 10 February, from Perth. He is complaining that some highlanders in his army have refused to carry out such plunder[5]. It was common to harass the families of known Jacobites; women and elderly or incapacitated family members who had stayed behind were considered fair targets.

This was in part straight punishment, but it was also designed to encourage desertion from the Jacobite army. If a man was worried about his wife and other family members at home, it might cause him to abandon the prince and return home to protect his family. It was a sort of psychological warfare, a tactic we saw utilised by the British while the Jacobites were in England and rumours were spread regarding the violence and depravity of the soldiers from the north.

It seems that the Jacobite command were not above using such threats themselves – but on their own men rather than the other side. A letter from Captain Alexander Campbell to Sir Everard Falkner reports news that a number of Camerons and MacDonalds had returned to the area, followed by their clan chiefs with orders from Charles to reassemble them and, should they refuse, to destroy their houses and take their cattle[6]. Of course, this information comes from the enemy rather than the Jacobite command themselves. We know that the British army were not above lying about the Jacobites, but in this case there seems little to gain by doing so.

Chapter Twenty-Five

Inverness

When the Jacobite army left Crieff, Charles marched to Blair Atholl, the home of the Duke of Atholl, where he stayed for a week, hunting and shooting. This seems an odd thing to do while retreating from the British army, without his full strength of men around him. Why give Cumberland the chance to catch him here, exposed with only half of his army? Was he, perhaps, hoping to force a confrontation by using himself as bait? Did he hope that Cumberland would catch up with him here and that the danger to their prince would force the Jacobite army to come and fight for him? If that was his plan, it didn't work; Cumberland heard that Charles was at Blair Castle, hunting, and he did not believe it, deciding instead that it was a story intended to be a distraction while Charles escaped the country[1].

After leaving Blair Castle, Charles met up with Lochiel and others and besieged the Redcoat barracks at Ruthven, forcing the small garrison to surrender. The British soldiers were allowed to leave, and the buildings were put to the torch[2].

From Ruthven, the prince marched to Inverness, arriving on 16 February at Moy Hall, the home of the Mackintosh chiefs. There, he was attended by Lady Anne Mackintosh, who had personally raised a regiment for the prince's cause, which had fought at Falkirk. Lady Anne did this despite the fact that her husband, Angus Mackintosh, was a serving captain in the British army.

While staying at Moy Hall, Charles did not have many guards with him, the army being spread over some considerable distance in order to find accommodation and provisions for them all. Lady Anne was concerned at the lack of guards and feared for the prince's safety, so she recruited Donald Fraser, a local blacksmith, and four servants to act as additional guards. She sent them out to patrol an area beyond Charles's guards, and after nightfall they moved to around two miles out from the hall.

Meanwhile, in Inverness, Lord Loudoun had heard of the prince's arrival and saw an opportunity to strike a blow that may end the rebellion by capturing Charles – not to mention an opportunity to claim the £30,000 reward that the Hanoverians had placed on the Stuart prince's capture. He marched out of Inverness with around 1,500 men[3]. The Dowager Lady Mackintosh, Anna Duff, mother-in-law of the current Lady Anne, heard about Loudoun's plans and sent a young man called Lachlan Mackintosh to try and sneak past the troops before they reached Moy Hall and warn the prince.

An advance party from Loudoun's force was sneaking up to Moy Hall when Donald Fraser and the servants stumbled across them. They immediately fired and began calling the rallying cries of various clans, making as much noise as they could. In the dark, Loudoun's men believed there to be a far larger force than there really was and retreated in a panic, throwing confusion into the ranks. The Macleod piper Donald Ban MacCrimmon was shot and killed and another man was wounded. MacCrimmon was said to have the second sight and had apparently composed a lament that said he would never return home[4]. Despite the initial confusion, Lord Loudoun did manage to restore order in his ranks and waited an hour before deciding that, having lost the element of surprise, there was no point attacking and he withdrew, returning to Inverness.

While all of this was going on, young Lachlan Mackintosh managed to get past all of the soldiers and arrived at Moy House around five in the morning. He woke one of the prince's men, who was sleeping in the kitchen, and warned him that Loudoun was coming. The household was awoken, and Charles fled to the banks of Loch Moy, where he was met by Lochiel and his men. They waited there, prepared to fight if necessary, until receiving the all-clear from Moy Hall.

The following day, hundreds of Loudoun's soldiers deserted, leaving his position in Inverness untenable. He retreated on the ferry across the Moray Firth, leaving Inverness open to the Jacobites[5].

Charles stayed at Moy Hall until 18 February, when he marched on Inverness with two or three thousand men. When he arrived, he drew up in battle formation, expecting Loudoun to come out and fight but instead Charles was shocked to see Lord Loudoun and his men fleeing to boats which would carry them across the Firth. The Jacobite army entered another town without violence. Fort George remained manned with a garrison of around 200 but after a few days' siege, they surrendered to Charles on 25 February. The Jacobites took possession of the supplies within the fort and then destroyed the building.

Charles took up residence at Culloden House, the Lord President having fled with Lord Loudoun. On 24 February, he was joined there by Lord George who spoke of the difficulties his column had faced and then talked about sourcing supplies of meal and having them distributed throughout the highlands, in case the army had to retreat further. Needless to say, Charles did not approve of this plan, and wanted the meal brought to Inverness, where the army was currently in residence[6].

PART FIVE

Culloden

Chapter Twenty-Six

Spring

On 27 February 1745/6 Prince William Augustus, the Duke of Cumberland, marched his army into Aberdeen, where they settled to see out the remainder of the winter. Between the increased activity of the Royal Navy all around the coast of Scotland, and Cumberland's army occupying Aberdeen, it became practically impossible for French ships to land with reinforcements or supplies for the Jacobites. Cumberland, on the other hand, was able to use the navy to move supplies such as food and equipment for his troops[1]. Charles had no such luxury; what provisions he could get had to be sourced from the highlands, where over-land transport was challenging, and the people did not have a lot to spare. He was also running out of money, which made buying supplies difficult, not to mention paying his soldiers.

The weather kept Cumberland in Aberdeen throughout March, while the Jacobites remained in the vicinity of Inverness. In papers from a Mr John Scrogy of Tullich, dated 28 March 1746, Cumberland was advised that the Jacobites had around 4,000 men in the Elgin and River Spey area, 3,000 in Inverness, and a further 1,500 returning from Atholl. This puts their numbers at 8,500, around the same as they had at Falkirk, and suggests that desertion over the winter was not as much of a problem for Charles as the British army command had previously assumed[2].

A few days later, Cumberland wrote to Newcastle, expressing his frustration at being delayed by the weather. He intended to march on Inverness as soon as the River Spey became crossable. He wrote of some Jacobite deserters that had been caught and how they told him that they had had no pay for the last week and that Charles was out of money. This concerned Cumberland, because he believed that, without pay, Charles's army would soon break up, returning home, where it would be much harder to catch them. Cumberland believed that the government would be too lenient in dealing with the rebels when the immediate danger had passed, and that the door would be left open for further uprisings in the future. He believed that there would have to be significant punishment, followed by changes to the law and system of government in the highlands in order to prevent further action in the future[3].

While in Aberdeen, the duke took advantage of the time to drill his men in the practicalities of facing the Jacobite army, especially the highlanders. He understood that the only way to beat them would be by counteracting the panic that they had been able to create before. He needed his soldiers to stay calm and collected on the field of battle. He had already moved the cavalry into reserve and now he introduced some new manoeuvres which were designed specifically with the highlanders in mind. These were practiced over and over again, until they were perfected.

On 7 April, Cumberland and his army marched out of Aberdeen and headed for Inverness[4].

During this time, Lord Loudoun was making a nuisance of himself in Inverness. He sent detachments over the Firth to harass and attack the Jacobite forces there but as soon as they mounted a response, Loudoun's men would flee back across the water, where the prince's men could not follow, due to a lack of boats. Charles needed to deal with Loudoun. They knew that Cumberland would march on them as soon as the weather improved enough to allow his army to travel. If Loudoun and his men were still in the area when Cumberland arrived, they could cross the Firth and attack the Jacobite army from the rear while they faced Cumberland's force, placing the Jacobites between two armies.

According to Johnstone, the prince ordered that all boats of any kind in the area be brought to Findhorn where, on the night between 19 and 20 March, the Duke of Perth led around 1,800 men across the water. Their advance was shielded by thick fog and Loudoun's men did not discover they were under attack until the Jacobites were almost upon them. Loudoun's men threw down their arms and many were taken prisoner, while others, including Loudoun, escaped. However, the editor of Johnstone's memoir states that the events were actually a little different. According to them, the attack was made from Tain, not Findhorn, and that, upon crossing, the Duke of Perth and his men came across a small detachment of Loudoun's forces, a group of about 200 men, who were taken prisoner. After this, Loudoun split his force and retreated, travelling to Skye with the Lord President, Duncan Forbes[5].

127

Early in March, Charles had travelled to Elgin where he became very ill, with a spotted fever. According to O'Sullivan, the prince got up after nine or ten days, against the wishes of the doctor who was tending to him. He returned to Inverness on 21 of March to discover that his army was out of money. The Marquis d'Éguilles had provided some money to pay the troops but it wasn't enough. In addition, they had very little food and, without money, no way of procuring more. In response to the situation, Charles began to consider having his own money printed, something he discussed at length with the engraver, Robert Strange who had joined him in Edinburgh. Strange immediately took on the challenge of designing a Stuart bank note and then engraving the copper plates required and organising the construction of a rolling printing press[6]. Of course, any money printed like this would only have any value if the Stuart Restoration succeeded.

On 25 March, the returning *Le Prince Charles* was pursued by the Royal Navy and ran aground about eighty-five miles north of Inverness. The men, arms, and money on board, intended to support Charles, were all captured by some of Loudoun's men. This would have been a great blow to the prince. Despite their success in defeating Fort Augustus, the Jacobite army were unable to claim Fort William and they eventually gave up the siege at the beginning of April, when all of the army were called back to Inverness. Lord Elcho states that around 4 April 1746, the prince entertained thoughts of marching towards Aberdeen to face Cumberland there, but his army were unpaid and poorly provisioned so Elcho doubted they would follow Charles south. Such concerns became unnecessary when news arrived from Lord John Drummond that Cumberland's army was on the move[7].

Lord John Drummond and his brother, the Duke of Perth, were stationed with around 2,000 men at Speymouth, there to defend the river crossing as best they could. Their first objective was to prevent the British army from crossing and if that wasn't possible, slow the crossing for as long as they could, to give the rest of the Jacobite army time to regather and prepare to face them.

Captain O'Sullivan was sent to report on matters and his judgement was that it would be impossible to prevent the crossing, as the river was low enough that there were multiple places where it could be forded. He believed the best thing they could do under the circumstances was watch the enemy and get what information they could back to Charles in

Inverness. Alexander MacDonald disagreed and believed that defending the river would have been a simple thing[8]. Both agreed that the small force there could not hope to stand against Cumberland's army alone and so they retreated to join the rest of the Jacobite army at Inverness. By 13 April, Cumberland had crossed the Spey and was in Elgin, only around forty miles away.

When the news reached Inverness that the British army had crossed the Spey without opposition, they were stunned, according to Johnstone[9]. He writes that Charles left Inverness on 13 April and travelled straight to the field of battle, where they remained, sleeping outside, on the ground, without tents or food other than biscuits and water. According to Lord Elcho, there were those who advised the prince to retreat until the rest of the army could be gathered together, around 3,000 men being away at the time, but Charles would not listen as he was optimistic about the outcome of the battle[10].

Dawn on 15 April saw the Jacobite army drawn up in battle order on Culloden Moor. There was a dispute here about the best location to fight. O'Sullivan selected this area to the south side of Culloden, with park walls to their right. Lord George felt this ground was too open and flat, that it served the British army, with their cannons and cavalry, better than the Jacobites, and especially the highlanders. Lord George favoured the ground on the other side of the water of Nairn, land that was hilly and boggy and would limit the usefulness of the British cavalry, being difficult for horses to navigate. In light of how the cavalry had behaved at the last two battles, it seems an odd concern to have as the cavalry charge actually worked in the Jacobites' favour previously. In addition to the horses, the boggy, hilly ground would reduce the usefulness of the British army's cannons.

O'Sullivan however, disagreed with Lord George's assessment. This is likely to have been at least to some extent because the suggestion came from Lord George; by this point the prince did not have much trust or love for Murray, and O'Sullivan was one of Charles's group of core advisors. Relations between the two men had never been especially good, but by now the command structure was strained to breaking point. However, he did appear to have good reason for his disagreement. O'Sullivan argued against the area Lord George suggested chiefly because of a ravine that would lie between the front lines of the two armies. On the one hand, this could act as a natural defence between the two, keeping the British army and cavalry from charging the Jacobites – however it would also prevent the Jacobites from charging. O'Sullivan knew that the highlanders in particular, usually took only one shot before discarding their guns and running at the enemy, sword in hand. The ravine would prevent them from doing this and O'Sullivan felt that they would not be as effective with guns only as the regular troops on the British army side would be, since the highlanders had not spent the same time training with firing and reloading quickly[11].

Charles received advice from both men and, despite Lord George having a lot of support, he chose the field suggested by O'Sullivan. The prince also ordered that biscuits be brought from Inverness. Due to some error there, only one biscuit per soldier arrived, even though none of them had eaten since the day before. This was a really bad time to make mistakes with provisions; they were preparing to face Cumberland's army at any moment, the troops needed to be well-fed and rested, in so far as was possible.

Further disagreements amongst the command broke out when Lord George gave the right wing of the frontline to the Athollmen, his own clan. Traditionally, this spot was considered a position of great honour and was usually occupied by the three MacDonald regiments: Clanranald, Glengarry and Keppoch, none of whom were happy about the last-minute change. They took their complaint to the prince, who seemingly asked them to accept it without argument for his sake but didn't appear very happy about it[12]. The MacDonalds took the far left but remained unhappy about the situation.

Charles then sent Lord Elcho out to gather intelligence about the whereabouts and behaviour of Cumberland's army. Lord Elcho observed the British army for some time before returning to Culloden to advise Charles that they were camped at Nairn and did not look as though they intended to move from there that day[13]. Lord George had an idea for how they could use this to their advantage.

At this point in *Dragonfly in Amber* both Jamie and Claire are with the prince, along with the men from Lallybroch. They have run out of ways to prevent the coming battle and know well what the outcome will be. They are desperate to save, not only themselves or even the army, but the highland way of life, which would soon be destroyed. Thinking themselves alone, they discuss a last, desperate attempt to keep the battle from happening, killing Charles Edward Stuart. If the prince died now, Claire reasons, there would no longer be any reason to fight and the army would disperse. I'm not sure that her reasoning was quite sound. After all, Charles was not king, only the heir. Many of the men there, including Lord George Murray, were there because of their loyalty to James rather than Charles and may well have continued to fight. Also, knowing what we do about Cumberland, it is unlikely that he would have allowed them to disperse without violent repercussions.

Jamie considers what Claire says but, in the end, he cannot bring himself to murder someone in cold blood, and especially not the prince, to whom he had sworn his allegiance. Unfortunately, Jamie's uncle, Dougal MacKenzie has overheard their conversation and bursts in upon them. He accuses Claire of being a witch and casting a spell on Jamie to make him do her bidding. The couple try to reason with him, but he attempts to kill Claire and Jamie must kill Dougal instead. Jamie and Claire leave the battlefield and eventually Claire realises that Jamie is taking her back to Craigh na Dun. She doesn't want to leave him, but Jamie has figured out that Claire is pregnant. He fully expects to die on the battlefield and does not want Claire and his child to have to live in hiding and in fear. He makes her promise to live, to go back to her own time, to her first husband, Frank, and to raise their child in peace.

They spend one last night together in a hut on the hillside, below the stones before Claire reluctantly leaves and Jamie returns to the Culloden, prepared to die with his men.

Chapter Twenty-Seven

The Night March

Charles knew that if they waited too long for the battle, his army would not be fit to fight. With no proper food supply and no cover, they would not be able to maintain their strength for long. Accordingly, he wanted to march to Nairn and attack immediately. He called a council of war and asked for advice. According to Lord Elcho, at this time, Lord George made a speech, recommending that they wait until dusk and then march to Nairn overnight, to attack the British camp just before dawn. He argued that the British army relied upon discipline and training, while the highlanders were the opposite. He believed that the chaos and confusion of an attack before the camp had properly woken would even the playing field somewhat[1].

Lord George recommended that the right wing, under his command, march around Nairn and attack the British camp from the rear, while the left wing, under the Duke of Perth, would attack from the front. For this attack to have the element of surprise, which was intended, it was vital that it take place while it was still dark[2]. This would require a swift march over difficult terrain in the dark. It was a lot to ask of men who had neither enough food nor rest.

It was decided to keep the plan a secret from the men until the last minute. Perhaps the prince was worried about word reaching Cumberland and ruining the element of surprise. In the event, the secrecy actually harmed Charles's position as, not long before dusk, many of the men wandered off in search of food or somewhere to spend the night, after it became apparent that Cumberland would not attack that day[3]. Upon this discovery, Lord George argued against going, but Charles was set on the idea, sure that they would win the ensuing battle. There is some suggestion that prior to beginning the march, the prince ordered that a close watch be kept on Lord George in case he made some effort to betray them to Cumberland's army. Even now, the prince did not trust Lord George although he had done nothing to deserve such suspicion.

Lord Elcho tells us that Lord George knew of the suspicions and so did his duty without offering advice[4].

Before setting off on the march, orders were given to maintain absolute silence as far as possible, and when attacking the enemy camp, to pull down tents upon their occupants and stick their sword into any lumps in the bundle. This was clearly an attempt to kill or wound as many of the enemy as possible before they even knew they were under attack. An anonymous document held in the Royal Archives purports to be revised orders that were given, telling the troops to use both guns and swords and that no quarter was to be given[5]. This meant that there would be no prisoners taken, no mercy shown, kill everyone. While it's certainly possible that these were, in fact, Charles's orders at this time, it doesn't sit well with how he had behaved until this point. At every opportunity before now, Charles had shown mercy. Wounded were given treatment, prisoners kept well or released on parole, even the British spy caught near Ashburne had not been executed. None of these seem like the actions of a man who would order 'no quarter'.

The march commenced at between eight and nine on the night of 15 April, with Lord George leading. The terrain was difficult as they did not wish to use the road, in case they were seen, so instead they travelled overland, in the dark. Try as they might to stay together, the army ended up strung out across the countryside, the rear falling farther and farther behind. Multiple times, the van was forced to slow down and wait for the rear to catch up, but even that wasn't enough. At two in the morning, the van was forced to come to a complete halt to wait for the rest of the army to catch up.

Now, at this point there are conflicting accounts of exactly what happened next. Johnstone tells us that when they were within half a league of the British army camp, Lord George ordered a halt and sent word to the prince that they would have to wait until the army could gather together and form proper battle lines before attacking. According to Captain Johnstone, Charles sent word that Lord George should not wait for the rest of the troops but should attack immediately. On hearing this, Lord George supposedly turned around and started marching back to Culloden, directly against the prince's orders. The prince did not realise what was happening and almost stumbled into the enemy camp before he became aware of the retreat[6].

There is, however, an extensive note from the editors of Johnstone's *Memoirs,* giving a rather different account of what took place. They share an excerpt from Home, which says that the Jacobite army was strung out for most of the march, the rear continually losing ground and requesting that the van halt, but that Lord George just ordered the van to slow down. By two in the morning, they were still four miles away from the British army camp and they realised that there was no possibility of making it to Nairn in time for the planned night-time attack. Lord George discussed the problem with the principal officers who were with him and they were not all in agreement – Lord George, amongst others, thought it best to retreat as they had lost the element of surprise. A Mr Hepburn led the argument for continuing on to Nairn, stating that he never expected to find the camp asleep and that it made more sense to continue and attack now than to march back and be attacked when they were exhausted. Home claims that, during this debate, John Hay, who was acting as secretary came up to the front and heard all of this. He then rushed back to where Charles was and told him what was happening. Charles rode for the front of the army, intending to order the attack, but met the van, who were already retreating. Charles is then said to have accused Lord George of betraying him[7].

According to an account given by Lord George himself and quoted in the editor's notes following Home's account, when the van was forced to halt and wait for the rear to catch up, they were a full four miles from Nairn and it was clear that they would only be able to cover, at best, two more miles before daybreak, given how long it had taken them to cover the distance they had already travelled. That meant they would be in view of the British Army camp for two miles as they approached, allowing the enemy to fully prepare to meet them in battle. Lord George states that all of the principal officers who were in the van agreed that a retreat would be the best course of action. O'Sullivan came to the front and advised that, while Prince Charles would like the attack to go ahead, he accepted that Lord George had a better idea of what could be done in time. Lord George decided that it would be best to retreat without awaiting further orders from the prince[8].

Although this would have been unusual in a normal army, the Jacobite army had always operated in this manner, with Lord George making decisions during battles without awaiting orders from the prince.

Also detailed in the editor's note is the account given by John Hay, who was acting as secretary to the prince while Secretary Murray was still recovering from his illness. His account ties in with Home's – that he came up to the van and found Lord George and Mr Hepburn arguing about whether to go on and that he went straight back and informed the prince. Charles rode for the front to make sure that the attack went ahead as planned, but on the way met the van on the way back. The prince is said to have been furious and have accused Lord George of betraying him.

Charles himself remembered riding to the front of the army and being persuaded by Lord George that the best course of action was to return to Culloden and said that he had agreed[9]. It's unlikely that Charles rode to the front and discussed it with Lord George before an order was given, but there's no sense from his statement of events that he felt betrayed by Lord George, as claimed by Hay and Home.

There follows, in the editor's note, an analysis of the situation, which is interesting, but cannot be relied upon due to the very clear bias shown against the prince – they refer to him as an imbecile at one point[10]. While it is indeed difficult to remain dispassionate when studying events of such import, it is essential that a historian does not allow their personal opinions to colour their conclusions.

Lord Elcho gives another version of events. He writes that by the time the van got within three miles of Nairn, it was already beginning to get light. This seems unlikely as, at that time of year, sunrise would probably have fallen sometime between five and six. So, for Lord Elcho to be correct, the stop would have occurred later than any other account suggests. He goes on to state that Lord George called a halt and Lochiel came up to the front to see what was happening. Lord George argued strongly for turning around since they had lost the element of surprise that had been the rationale for the night attack. Lord Elcho states that the prince was very much in favour of the attack going ahead, although he doesn't mention how this information was relayed, as he does not mention the prince coming to the front, nor a messenger going back and forth. He states that while the discussion was still ongoing, the army turned and began to march back and that he has no knowledge of how or why this happened[11].

It may seem odd to spend so much time looking at the various different accounts of what happened on that night march, but it is one of the most important points of the campaign, as everything that happened the following day was influenced by that aborted attempt at a night attack. The troops marched back to Culloden, this time taking the road since they didn't have to avoid being seen. They were exhausted, desperately hungry and no doubt frustrated that their effort had been for naught. Some of the Horse Guards were so exhausted that they peeled off from the main army during the retreat and found a barn to sleep in[12]. It's unlikely that they were the only ones.

By the time they had returned to Culloden, Lord Elcho tells us, no one could think of anything but sleep. Between the night without sleep and the lack of food for the last few days, they were pushed beyond their limit. Many of the men went to the towns and villages nearby and even back to Inverness to look for food and somewhere to rest, while the officers went to Culloden House and lay down to sleep, wherever they could find space. They would not, however, be able to rest for long. Barely two hours after their return to Culloden, a group who had been left to watch the British army came racing into camp with the news that a party of Cumberland's cavalry were two miles away, with the main body of the British army only a couple of miles behind[13].

Chapter Twenty-Eight

The Battle of Culloden

Imagine for a moment that you are a young soldier in the Jacobite army. Food is scarce – it always is during winter in the highlands – so you haven't had quite enough to eat for a while, but the last couple of days have been worse, only a biscuit or two per man. You've been outside, uncovered, since leaving Inverness, three days ago. April in the north of Scotland may be spring, but it's still chilly, especially overnight. Snow at this time of year is not unusual. You have marched all night, covering a distance of eight miles or so over difficult terrain. Your body is nearing the end of its endurance. Imagine settling down to sleep, directly on the ground, with no tent over you and nothing for warmth but the plaid which is your kilt. It's cold enough to see your breath in the early morning air, as you lie there, shivering, trying to ignore the gnawing hunger in your belly. You know that, if not today, then another day very soon, you will be required to fight. The soldiers you will face have been well-fed and far better trained. They are better equipped and more experienced. Even that knowledge isn't enough to keep you awake and you collapse into an exhausted slumber. It feels as if you have only just closed your eyes when you are awoken by the call to arms. Everything is chaos, the drums and pipes are sounding, men are running everywhere. You grab your weapons and race to your position, looking for familiar faces, but many of the men from your regiment wandered off in search of food and you can't see anyone you recognise. You fall in, roughly where you should be, and say a quick prayer, begging God to let you live long enough to see your wife and family again. And then it begins.

16 April 1746 was a cold, wet and windy day. As Cumberland advanced, the Jacobite army scrambled to their places. According to Lord Elcho, at least 2,000 men were missing from the previous day, so the prince was only able to field around 5,000 troops[1]. Because of Cumberland's position, they were unable to occupy the field that had been chosen by O'Sullivan the day before, instead drawing up a

little further to the west, closer to Culloden House. This new ground did offer some advantages. The Jacobite army was able to arrange itself between the walls of Culloden Park and what was known as the Culwhiniac Enclosures, thus giving them walls on either side, theoretically making it more difficult for the British army to outflank them. This would, however, only work as long as the British did not send troops behind the walls, unseen by the Jacobites, to pull down any loose sections.

The front line was strung along between the two lots of walls in this order: the Glangarry MacDonells on the far left, by Culloden Park, followed by the other, smaller, MacDonald regiments, Clanranald, Keppoch, Chisolm, Maclachlan and Monaltrie. Next came Makintosh, Fraser, Appin Stewarts, Lochiel with the Camerons and finally Lord George and his Athollmen at the far right, next to the Culwhiniac Enclosures. In the second line, behind this one, there were: the French picquets to the left, behind the MacDonalds, followed by Perth, Glenbucket, Kilmarnock, Stuart, Ogilvy and Gordon, with the Royal Ecossais at the right, behind the Athollmen. At the rear, in the reserve, were the cavalry; Strathallan's Horse, Scotch Hussars, O'Shea, FitzJames and Lord Elcho[2].

According to O'Sullivan, Lord George began to complain over his men being on the right side, the very thing he had argued in favour of the day before. An insistence which had caused great unhappiness amongst the MacDonalds, who claimed this honour as theirs, going all the way back to the time of Robert the Bruce. This seems like an odd thing for Lord George to complain about. If it is true, then he would appear to be behaving somewhat erratically, which is not something that had been seen from him before. Perhaps it was a sign of his exhaustion and frustration with the situation – he was still in favour of withdrawing into the mountains and leading the Duke of Cumberland away from his supplies and open fields of battle and into mountain passes that would benefit the highland fighting style more[3].

Whether Lord George complained about being on the right or not, the Jacobites held position as Cumberland's army approached until Lord George spotted a horseshoe shaped turf wall which protruded out in front of the wall of the Culwhiniac Enclosures. This would be an obstacle directly between the Athollmen and the approaching British army, impeding the line of their charge. Seemingly without consulting anyone else, Lord George ordered his men to change formation and move forward. This may have been the right move, but the lack of consultation meant that the front line was now disordered and contained gaps which the enemy may have been able to exploit. According to O'Sullivan, he spotted the gaps in the line and went to speak to Lord George, advising him of the problem but Lord George would not acknowledge him and did nothing to restore order. O'Sullivan then called forward the Perth, Glenbucket, and Stuart regiments from the second line to fill in the gaps, all while Cumberland and his men continued to advance.

Unknown to the Jacobites, General Hawley and his cavalry had come up unobserved behind the horseshoe shaped wall that had caused the trouble for Lord George, and from there, they had entered the Culwhiniac Enclosure. From there, out of sight of the Jacobite army, Hawley had begun to pull down walls, making space to move men through and come around the right flank. The first the Jacobites knew of this was when O'Sullivan discovered that they had broken through and formed up behind the Jacobite lines. O'Sullivan sent regiments from the reserves and cavalry to form up and protect the rear from any attack from Hawley[4].

Time passed as the two armies manoeuvred and got into position, before the battle itself commenced. It was raining heavily and, unlike at Falkirk, this time the wind was blowing in the faces of the Jacobites. They were a smaller force, smaller even than they had been the day before, following that ill-fated night march, now surrounded by a larger, better equipped, better trained, better fed army. They were cold and exhausted and hungry. They were almost certainly frightened. They knew that failure meant death, whether on the battlefield or facing the hangman's noose but still, they jeered at the British soldiers and goaded them and shouted their defiance to any God who might be listening.

It's not easy to piece together what happened next. Any battle is a time of chaos and confusion, with every person involved conscious of what's going on in their immediate vicinity, but few able to see beyond that. In the case of this battle, there is the added complication of the divisions between those whose accounts we have to rely upon. Lord George Murray, Colonel O'Sullivan and Lord Elcho all gave detailed accounts but as there was so much hostility between them, all of their experiences must be viewed through that filter.

At some time between noon and one, a group of British soldiers came forward and the Jacobites shot at them. This fire was ineffective and was quickly answered by a barrage from Cumberland's men[5]. They aimed particularly for the area where Charles was mounted, protected by Lord Balmerino and his Horse Guards. Several people around the prince were killed and, when he was spattered with mud and blood from the nearness of the shots, he finally agreed to move a short distance back[6].

Cumberland's troops kept up heavy fire on the Jacobite lines, fire that they had no way to withstand. This fire caused a number of casualties and, according to Lord Elcho, caused some of the front line to throw themselves to the ground, while others ran away[7]. The British troops could see that the Jacobite lines could not hold for long under such fire, and so prepared themselves for the coming charge.

One of the reasons that the highland charge was so effective, was the sight of a wall of troops running forward at great speed, swords raised. In this instance, the Jacobite frontline was at an awkward angle, with one end farther away from the enemy than the other. Added to that, the ground between the two armies was uneven and boggy, not easily traversed at speed. This resulted in a staggered charge, with some areas of the line bunching up into a mob and getting in each other's way[8]. The normal method for the regular troops would have been to take turns firing upon the other side, so that as one soldier was reloading his weapon, another would be firing, keeping up a steady rate of fire. This was less effective against the usual highland charge because of its speed – a lesson that the British army learned after their previous encounters. At Culloden, they did not fire in a volley, but instead all fired at once.

This was not the only lesson they had learned. The front line of the British troops fixed their bayonets and prepared to meet the coming charge. In ordinary circumstances, they would be preparing to use their bayonets to strike the man directly in front of them, however this was not very effective against the highlanders who would be protected by a targe, a small, round wooden shield, usually strapped to the left arm. Instead, Cumberland's army had drilled a new move while waiting in Aberdeen for the weather to improve. Each man in the front line struck with his bayonet into the side of the man attacking the soldier to his right, relying upon the man at his side to do the same for him[9]. It must have taken a great deal of willpower and trust in your brethren to follow such a protocol with an angry highlander running towards you.

According to the account of Captain Johnstone, the front line of the Jacobite army charged but at different times, many of the men hampered by ground that was boggy and waterlogged. The right and centre of the Jacobite line met the British army first, with the left lagging behind. They were 'not twenty paces' from the enemy when some of the left wing broke and fled, swords in hand[10]. The editor of the memoirs notes that the MacDonald clans retreated and that this was as a result of being placed on the left of the field rather than the right. If this is true, then the MacDonalds abandoned their prince and their fellow soldiers all because they were offended; that hardly seems the actions of a clan who deserved the position of honour they were upset over losing. The behaviour of one MacDonald stands out though, MacDonald of Keppoch, who had been away on leave in the run up to this battle. He had travelled at all haste to be with the prince for this engagement and arrived just in time to take his position in the front line. When the other MacDonalds turned and retreated, he continued alone, sword in hand. He was shot and fell to the ground. According to the editors' note, a friend who had followed him said that this wound was not fatal, and he entreated Keppoch to retreat. Instead Keppoch got to his feet and continued his charge, only to be shot once more, this time fatally[11].

The result of the left flank of the Jacobite army collapsing, was that the centre and right were left unsupported and soon afterwards had no choice but to retreat. Johnstone believed that if the right had been able to hold just a little longer and the centre had been properly supported, then the British army may have been the ones to retreat, as the men who fought did so well[12].

Although a great number of the Jacobite front line had been caught in the initial round of fire, there was also intense hand-to-hand fighting, and in fact, the Jacobites managed to overrun the regiments that were operating Cumberland's cannons. The duke called in support from his reserves and they were eventually able to drive the Jacobites back[13].

At this time, the retreat became widespread, and confusion reigned. The remainder of the Jacobite army fled the field, closely pursued by the British cavalry. It was a slaughter, with reports that the British troops took revenge for their humiliation at Prestonpans and Falkirk, acting in ways that were contrary to the conduct usually expected of soldiers in the king's army. The road from Culloden to Inverness was said to be littered with the bodies of Jacobites, cut down as they fled. Orders were given for no quarter, and Cumberland's soldiers bayoneted wounded men where they lay on the battlefield – men who, under ordinary circumstances, should have been taken prisoner and tried. There were reports of wounded Jacobites being manhandled into piles where they were shot by cannons[14]. Johnstone writes that the wounded were left lying on the field from the day of the battle, a Wednesday, until the Friday, at which point Cumberland sent soldiers to dispatch any who had not succumbed to their wounds. Johnstone also tells of a group of fleeing rebels who had taken shelter in a barn. It was surrounded by British soldiers who set it alight and then used their bayonets to force anyone who tried to flee back inside, where they were all burned to death[15].

Seward writes that around one thousand Jacobites were killed on the field, with at least five hundred slaughtered in the following days[16]. This would have represented more than a quarter of the five thousand soldiers who took the field that day.

Watching the *Outlander* television series, one is often brought to emotion. There are many episodes and scenes that are difficult to watch for a variety of reasons, but 'The Battle Joined' (season 3, episode 1) was in a class of its own. We see Jamie, lying wounded, on a pile of bodies, beneath Black Jack Randall, the British army officer who has haunted and shaped his life for the last several years. As Jamie lies there, drifting in and out of consciousness and waiting to die, we are shown flashbacks to the battle. They do wonderfully to give a sense of the noise and confusion on the battlefield; cannon fire throws dirt and soldiers into the air, smoke drifts everywhere from gunfire, obscuring the view, Jacobites and Redcoats fight with swords and knives and in some cases their bare hands. Bodies litter the ground. Jamie and Jack make eye contact through the chaos and of course, this is how their story must end. Their fight is both brutal and beautiful; both skilled swordsmen, both fighting their nemesis. Jack wounds Jamie in the thigh, but it is not enough to save his own life as Jamie drives his sword through Jack's torso and they collapse together.

Afterwards, as Jamie lies there amongst the dead, he can hear British soldiers moving across the field, bayoneting any wounded they come across. Snow begins to fall and Jamie dreams of Claire, peaceful in the knowledge that she and his child are safe, 200 years in the future. He thinks he sees her walking across the battlefield, coming to lead him home. Instead, it's Rupert and a few MacKenzie men, searching for survivors. They carry Jamie away and take him to a barn nearby where other Jacobites are hiding. It's not long before the group there are discovered by some English officers and each one is taken outside and executed. While this is clearly distasteful, it is carried out by the Redcoats as something that is demanded by duty and is no way enjoyed. In this way it does not reflect the experiences written about by people who were there.

One of the officers overhears Jamie speaking to another of the prisoners and realises that here he has the infamous 'Red Jamie', a prisoner that would no doubt be worthy of reward given his role as one of Charles's close advisors. But this officer is brother to John Grey, the young man whom Jamie had caught near his camp prior to meeting the prince at Prestonpans. The young man whom Jamie had spared. John Grey has a debt of honour to spare Jamie's life and his brother honours that debt by securing a cart and sending Jamie home to Lallybroch.

Chapter Twenty-Nine

Flight

Prince Charles managed to escape the battle that day, though there are conflicting accounts of how this happened. Charles himself writes that he was forced from the field by the people around him who could see that the battle was lost and were concerned for his safety. This account is supported by William Home, who recalls that the prince was forced from the field, his horse being led by one of his guards. O'Sullivan writes that Charles intended to die on the field but was eventually persuaded by those around him that his escape was essential to any further hopes of the cause[1]. Johnstone tells us that as soon as the prince saw the battle was lost, he escaped with some of FitzJames' Horse[2]. Lord Elcho reports that as soon as the left wing broke the prince turned his horse and left the field[3]. Elcho points out that Charles made no effort to rally the troops, but it is apparent from his entire account that he found the prince lacking throughout the campaign and was bitter about it.

Lord Elcho writes that he met with Charles and his entourage at Stratherrick, about four miles from Culloden. Here, he states that the prince was cold toward the Scottish officers – but this is a familiar complaint from Lord Elcho now, and one which must be taken with a pinch of salt – and ordered them all to go to Ruthven and await further instructions, but before they had travelled far, Sherridan caught up and said that the prince now ordered the army to disperse and fend for themselves as best they could[4]. However, this account does not agree with those of others who were with the prince.

It seems that no official plan had been made for a rendezvous point in the case of defeat. That's not entirely surprising, given how the battle itself came upon them at short notice, while they were all exhausted from the ill-fated night march. In addition, Charles does not seem to have ever accepted the possibility of defeat. In both of the previous confrontations, the British army had run away from the Jacobites, no doubt deepening in the prince's mind the notion that they would recognise him as their rightful sovereign and refuse to fight against him.

Charles himself travelled to the home of Thomas Fraser in Gorthleck, where he met Lord Lovat for the first time. From there, he went to Fort Augustus where, according to Captain O'Neill, he waited for some time, expecting the army to join him. When there was no sign of this happening, he continued to Castle Invergarry where he rested and had a meal. Still hearing no news of his troops gathering at Fort Augustus, he retired into the mountains. All of the people who were still with him at this time maintain that he wanted to know what had happened to his troops[5]. This undermines Lord Elcho's assertion that he had already told them to disperse.

For the next few days Charles kept on the move, from Invergarry to Glenpean, to the Braes of Morrar, then on to Borrodale, where he once more stayed at Angus MacDonald's house, as he had on his arrival in Scotland, eight months ago. Here, Charles later wrote, he decided that he could best serve the cause by taking ship for France, where he would personally beseech Louis to send the men and resources that he had so long promised and had yet failed to properly deliver. The prince saw that there was nothing more he could do in Scotland without that support and believed that by appealing to Louis in person, he could persuade the French king to do as promised. This is not the image of a defeated prince, who didn't care what happened to his army, as painted by Lord Elcho.

While at Borrodale, Charles received a letter from Lord George Murray, dated 17 April, the day after the battle. This letter reads as though the man who wrote it felt utterly defeated. It is angry and pained and desperately sad. Lord George criticises the decision to begin the rebellion in the first place without the guaranteed support of France. He goes on to vent his frustration at Charles's reliance on advice from O'Sullivan, who we know Lord George clashed with throughout the campaign. He blames O'Sullivan for the ground the battle was fought on – although, they did not end up on the field that O'Sullivan had actually chosen. Lord George then complains that Mr Hay had failed in his duty with regards to the provisions, and as a result the Jacobite army was half-starved when they were forced to fight. In short, Lord George lays the defeat at Culloden at the feet of O'Sullivan and Hay. He ends the letter by resigning his commission though restating his loyalty to the cause[6].

At the time of sending this letter, Lord George was at Ruthven with around two thousand troops, some of whom had not arrived in time for the battle, having been away from the main army. Johnstone writes of arriving in Ruthven on 18 April and finding Lord George along with many other clan chiefs and four or five thousand troops who were all eager to continue the fight. Johnstone tells us that Lord George sent out one of his aides-de-camp to look for the prince, and to advise him that his army awaited his presence. The account continues that they had no word of the prince until 20 April, at which point Lord George's aide returned with word from Charles that each man should see to his own safety as best he could. Johnstone reports great sadness among the highlanders, who dispersed feeling abandoned by their prince[7].

Days later, Charles wrote a letter to the chiefs, which he entrusted to Sherridan to pass on, with a request to keep his departure a secret for as long as possible. In this letter to the chiefs, Charles explains that he is travelling to France with the intention of securing help, which he believes to be the only way he can help now. He acknowledges the fact that the French may have found it convenient to extend the duration of the rebellion so as to distract the British army in Europe and destabilise the country for French gain. Charles considers that by leaving Scotland he is removing that temptation from France, rendering it so that the only way they will gain from the situation is by supporting a full Stuart restoration[8]. It is clear that Charles believed he would return to Scotland with French support and that, for him, the rebellion was not over.

PART SIX

The Aftermath

Chapter Thirty

Charles Travels to France

Travelling from Borrodale to France was neither quick nor easy for Charles. He was the most wanted man in Scotland and, while he still had a great many supporters, there would be those who were desperate to align themselves with the British in an effort to avoid the brutal retaliation that was being carried out across the highlands.

Charles left the mainland and travelled to the Hebrides, a group of islands off the north-west coast of Scotland. The Royal Navy was patrolling these waters, making it difficult to move between the islands without notice. In fact, the prince and his party got stuck on a small island for eight days, without food other than fish that washed up on shore. They eventually arrived on South Uist on 14 May, and stayed in Coradale for three weeks, awaiting news from the mainland about how things stood with his army. Popular stories put Charles and his companions in a small cave on the island, but he actually stayed in a small house in the forest[1]. While there, he received a visit from Hugh MacDonald of Baleshare, who had come with letters and newspapers sent by Lady Margaret MacDoanld at the prince's request.

Baleshare later wrote about his experience with the prince and described how he came out of the mist very close to the house, taking them by surprise. After he was recognised and vouched for, he was taken inside to meet the prince. Charles was dressed in highland wear and both his clothing and his face were patched with soot from the rain coming through the sooty roof of the house. Charles called for food and drink to be served to his guests, despite the fact that they had little to share. They were served brandy and, as they drank together, Baleshare grew bold and offered to tell the prince what he believed to be the greatest barriers against him, which Charles agreed to hear. According to Baleshare's account, he told the prince that it was his religion and arbitrary government. Charles then supposedly replied that the princes of Europe have little or no religion[2] – suggesting that he believed religion to be

148

simply a public act that was required of princes rather than anything they particularly believed in. One can certainly see how Charles could get such a notion from Louis XV, with his many mistresses and broken promises, but I suspect it would have pained James to hear his son speak so. James had essentially refused the throne when taking it meant that he would have to change his religion.

Baleshare goes on to say that they spent three days like this, drinking and talking as friends, and that the prince outdrank everyone else, being the only one not suffering from a terrible hangover at the end of it all. In fact, Charles took care of the others while they nursed their aching heads[3].

Later, Baleshare learned that there were men searching for the prince on South Uist and so went to find him and warn him. Charles was no longer in the small house but was staying outdoors without adequate supplies. Baleshare was shocked by the prince's appearance and wrote to his brother, Donald Roy MacDonald, asking him to send 'necessities' and in particular shirts and blankets, along with the newspapers that Charles had requested[4].

Around this time, Charles received bad news from the mainland. A letter arrived from Secretary Murray, who informed the prince that the clans had lain down their weapons and were no longer to be relied upon[5]. This shouldn't have been particularly surprising, since Charles had told them all to seek their own safety; it would not have been reasonable, or indeed possible, for the army to stay together indefinitely while he went to France, with neither money nor provisions to rely upon and with Cumberland still to be dealt with. However, it would no doubt have been a blow. Perhaps Charles had expected that they would be able to go into hiding and await his return, but such an idea seems naive at best.

At this time, Charles also learned that two French ships, the *Mars* and the *Bellona,* had arrived some weeks before, carrying money and arms. They had been sent prior to the battle at Culloden either to support the prince or to carry him safely to France. Some members of the Jacobite army were in hiding in the area where the ships landed, off the west coast and they came together and brought the cargo ashore. The money would later become known as the Arkaig treasure. None of the Jacobites who gathered knew of Charles's whereabouts and so, unable to get word to the prince, and hounded by the Royal Navy, both ships returned to France, carrying with them some fleeing Jacobites, including the Duke of Perth, Lord John Drummond, Sir Thomas Sherridan (Charles's tutor and confidant), John Hay and John Daniel. The Duke of Perth did not survive the journey[6].

The money that was brought ashore became a matter of legend, one that still sees treasure hunters out looking for it now. Historian Sarah Fraser gives an interesting account of it[7]. Apparently, the money was initially placed in the care of Secretary Murray, who was arrested in June and transported to London[8]. Care of the money then went to Lochiel and the Camerons. Their accounts suggest that some of the gold was distributed to various clan chiefs to reimburse the men who had received no pay for some time in the prince's service. Most of it however was squirreled away in various hiding places, in the hope that Charles would return, and the money could be used to reignite the rebellion. Clues to the various places it could be hidden have surfaced over the years, however no one has found it yet, despite both Charles and James sending people to search for it after all hope of a return had been lost.

By mid-June Charles was still in Scotland, still in hiding, and despite his best efforts, he found himself in trouble. He had reached Loch Boisdale, only to discover that Alexander MacDonald of Boisdale, whom he had been hoping would help him, had been captured. He then discovered that British troops were closing in, with Captain Caroline Scott of Fort William on one side and Major General John Campbell on the other. His only hope for escape was over the sea but he had no boat.

Fortune brought Charles to run into Flora MacDonald, a brave young woman close to the prince's own age. Flora was the stepdaughter of Hugh MacDonald of Armadale, a captain in the local militia, who were aiding in the search for Charles, which meant that she could get the necessary paperwork to allow for travel between the islands. There's some debate about whether Flora acted with or without the knowledge of her stepfather, but either way, she agreed to escort the prince to Skye, as long as he dressed as a maid. She sent Charles to Corrodale to wait while preparations were made.

Charles was taken to Benbecula where he stayed with a tenant of Clanranald. There he met up with Flora MacDonald, amongst others. Here he was also forced to say goodbye to Captain O'Neill who had been with him throughout his flight. On the evening of 27 June, Charles dressed as Flora's maid and set sail for Skye. There is a story that Flora fell asleep during the crossing and that she awoke to find Charles leaning over her, covering her head while the sails were adjusted. Charles is also said to have sung songs during the crossing to keep their spirits up[9].

On Skye, they stayed at Kingsburgh House, where Mrs MacDonald, the lady of the house, thought Charles to be a particularly unattractive woman, as he paced the hall in his disguise. When she discovered who he was, she is said to have lamented to her husband that they would be ruined, to which he replied that it would be in aid of a good cause[10]. Charles spent the night and the next day was sent a maid to help him dress once more in women's clothing. He is reported to have been very jovial about it all, laughing and joking with the maid about needing an apron. His host, Alexander MacDonald, arranged for a suit of highland clothing to be made available to the prince after he had left Kingsburgh House. Charles and Flora then made their way to Portree, from where the prince was taken by boat to another island, Raasay. Charles gifted Flora a locket containing his portrait[11].

Less than a fortnight later, Flora was arrested as one of the boatmen who had sailed them to Skye had been arrested and confessed. Flora maintained that her travelling companion was an Irish maid named Betty Burke. Flora was imprisoned at Dunstaffnage Castle and, briefly, the Tower of London. She was released in 1747 and returned to Scotland[12].

Charles continued to move around the western isles, waiting for an opportunity to travel to France. At the end of August, he received word that Lochiel would meet him at Badenoch and he travelled at night with a small group of protectors. He was described as being dressed in Highland garb and wearing a long red beard. At the beginning of September, they arrived in Ben Alder forest, where they found Lochiel and his cousin, Cluny MacPherson. Lochiel was still suffering from the wound he took at Culloden and had been cared for by Dr Stuart Thriepland.

Cluny was concerned for the prince's comfort while he was forced to hide out. Therefore, he took the prince farther up Ben Alder, where he had built a structure that later became known as Cluny's Cage[13]. It was an ingenious structure, made out of branches, twigs and moss, against the face of the mountain, where smoke from their cooking fire would be disguised. The prince stayed there with Cluny himself, Lochiel, Lochgarry, Dr Archibald Cameron and others. Guards were located all around the area and brought news and supplies to the men hiding there.

By 13 September, news had reached the cage that two French ships had arrived, looking for Charles to take him to safety. They left the safety of the mountain, travelling at night until, on 19 September 1746, Charles boarded the *L'Heureux,* promising to return soon and finish what he had started. The following day, five months after his defeat at Culloden, Prince Charles Edward Stuart left Scotland, accompanied by Lochiel, Dr Archibald Cameron and Colonel John Roy Stuart.

In the fifteen months that he had been in Scotland, Charles had raised an army against all expectations, achieved a string of successes that had turned Britain on its head, won the love and support of many and the criticism of others and then lost it all. He left Scotland, and especially the highlanders, in a worse position than they had been in before he arrived, making it extremely unlikely that they would ever rise again, but I think it would be unfair to lay all of the responsibility for that at his feet. At every turn Charles was let down by people who had promised support to his campaign. He was also let down by the squabbling and infighting in the Jacobite command. While he may not have been the romantic hero that the stories about him like to suggest, neither was he alone in failing the cause.

Chapter Thirty-One

Elsewhere in Scotland

What was going on in the rest of Scotland while Charles was hiding out in the highlands?

Immediately following the victory at Culloden, the Duke of Cumberland made straight for Inverness. The road between the battlefield and that town was strewn with bodies and the following day, he sent out troops to scour the area around the battlefield for any Jacobites who had fled. In his orders, he made reference to the possibly fake Jacobite orders which had said that no quarter should be given[1]. This is a clear indication that he expects his men to execute any Jacobites they should find. While it may have been common practice to chase down and kill men fleeing from the battlefield, this goes further than that practice and was unusual even for the time.

On 19 April, three days after the battle, Cumberland wrote to the Duke of Newcastle with news of what had transpired, having already dispatched a messenger by boat on 16 April. He gives an account of the casualties from the battle, listing two thousand Jacobites dead on the battlefield or in the pursuit as well as 222 French prisoners (who must be treated as prisoners of war) and 326 Jacobite prisoners[2]. He goes on to comment on the fact that few Jacobite wounded were able to leave the field, which lends support to the assertions that the wounded were killed where they lay, rather than taken prisoner, as would have been common practice at the time. Cumberland then explains that he is distinguishing between the French troops as prisoners of war and the people who were born in Britain, whom he regards as rebels[3]. This is an important distinction as the legal requirements for each were different. Prisoners of war were generally required to be treated well and to be allowed to return home when the hostilities had ended. They were also often freed on parole, in this case meaning that they were allowed to return home on the condition that they would not take up arms against their captor again. This is how Charles treated all of the British soldiers that he captured throughout his campaign, with many of them returning to fight under Cumberland at Culloden. Rebels on the other hand, could be shot without trial, a power that Cumberland used (some might say abused) extensively following the battle. He mentioned in this same letter to Newcastle that he had sent a detachment into Fraser lands to kill any rebels they found there[4].

By the end of May, Cumberland had settled in Fort Augustus, despite the fact that it was in a poor state after the Jacobite attack. His men continued to harass anyone suspected of being a Jacobite, burning homes, taking cattle and threatening the families of men who were still in hiding. He did however order that these measures only be used against suspected rebels and did not allow his men indiscriminate plundering[5].

There was some disagreement between leading Hanoverians over how to fully subdue the highlands now that the Jacobite army had dispersed. Lord President Duncan Forbes advised that all leaders of the rebellion who had also been involved in the 1715 uprising should be dealt with swiftly and mercilessly, having previously received leniency which he considered they had abused. But he also urged restraint in dealing with the Jacobites more widely, pointing out that severe punishment of all would only deepen ill feeling towards King George II and sow the seeds of future rebellions[6].

Cumberland had a vastly different opinion, as he wrote of to the Duke of Newcastle[7]. He felt that he had reached the end of what the military could do in the area, but he very firmly believed that without a complete change of governance, there would be another rebellion in the future. He even went so far as to say that everyone in the country had been involved. It's not clear here if he means all Scots, or merely all highlanders, but either way he's displaying a clear bigotry towards these people, many of whom had played no part in the uprising. Cumberland goes on to suggest sending several clans to the Indies, suggesting that they would be happier there (it's not clear what he's basing this assumption on) and that Britain will be more peaceful without them[8]. Given the fact that Cumberland's own grandfather was transplanted into Britain, and that his own family were not native to the isles, it seems particularly unfair for him to speak of sending away clans who had a much longer history with Scotland than he did.

Transportation to the West Indies was an existing punishment at the time and was widely utilised with the private men who were captured, although not amongst the officers. But what Cumberland suggests goes further than sending away enemy combatants, by referring to sending whole clans. In fact, many of the Jacobite prisoners who were not important enough to make a spectacle of were transported to the Colonies, where they became indentured servants. This was akin to slavery although there were some differences. An indentured servant had a set amount of time to serve, often around seven years[9]. After that time had passed, they would be free to build a life for themselves. However, in reality the conditions were so poor that the vast majority of people died before their term was over, either from disease or injury or malnutrition. That's if they even survived the journey; in 1619, a ship carrying 180 indentured servants to Virginia saw 130 of its passengers die during the voyage[10].

In May 1747, *The Gentleman's Magazine* reported that around 1,000 Jacobite prisoners had been transported to the colonies in the aftermath of the uprising[11]. Most of these were men who had surrendered their weapons and given themselves over for imprisonment in the months following Culloden. Such 'mercy' was not shown to any clan chiefs or officers who were captured, as we shall soon discuss.

Throughout the late spring and into early summer, Cumberland's men continued to scour the highlands and islands for any trace of Charles or of the tattered remnants of his army. Catholic and Episcopal churches were burned down[12], not for having taken part in the rebellion, but for their religious beliefs, which gave them a connection to the Stuarts. Church ministers were also put under pressure by Cumberland to inform upon their congregation, with many sending lists to the duke of people from their parish who had either joined the rebellion or supported it in other ways. Other ministers were unhappy about being asked to inform on their parishioners, instead suggesting that their time would be better spent praying for them[13].

It wasn't only churches that were targeted – entire villages were burnt to the ground, their tenants turned out with nothing but the clothes on their backs. We see a clear example of this in the journal of John Ferguson, captain of the Royal Navy sloop, the *Furnace*. On 18 May, he landed a party of soldiers at the Bay of Morar in north-west Scotland. There he reports that they burnt a small village. From there, they moved on to Arisaig, where they came to a house where Charles had lodged, which they burned down along with two or three villages. On 29 May they burned down the house of Kinlochmoidart. They received news that Lord Lovat was hiding at Morar so went in search of him, finding him on 7 June, hiding in a tree trunk. He was arrested to be taken to London for trial and all of the houses in and around Morar were burned[14]. In all of this, only one house is said to have been directly associated with Charles.

There's no evidence of any crimes committed by the people of these villages, no due process, they were simply caught up in the fury of the Hanoverians as they sought to exert control over a country that, as far as they were concerned, had defied them. Such behaviour is entirely in line with the instructions issued by Sir Everard Fawkener on 8 June, which ordered that locals whom the captains suspected of having any knowledge of the whereabouts of any Jacobites who had fled from Culloden should be menaced and even threated with execution[15]. Again, the people that are being referred to here are not accused of or even suspected of being Jacobites. These are largely innocent bystanders, being threatened with murder in an attempt to bully them into giving information that many of them likely just didn't have.

Chapter Thirty-Two

Trial and Execution

In London, the government were busy too. They wanted to make sure that there was no repeat of the situation after the 1715 uprising, when differences in legal systems resulted in considerably fewer executions in Scotland than in England. To counter this, an act was passed that allowed King George II to issue commissions for trying rebels in any part of the country, regardless of where the crime took place. This meant that even the Jacobites who had never crossed the border and only fought in Scotland could be tried in England, where the legal system was much more heavily influenced by the Hanoverians. All of the Jacobites who were caught at any point during or after the uprising were therefore tried in England, with trials taking place in London, York and Carlisle. Donald MacDonald of Kinlochmoidart, one of Charles's earliest supporters, was tried and executed in Carlisle.

Most of the high-ranking prisoners were taken to London and held in the Tower prior to trial and execution. The private men in the Jacobite army did not fare so well. Hundreds of them – mostly men but also a few women – were sent south to await trial and were held on prison hulks, boats that were moored in the Thames or Thames Estuary and on which prisoners were put to work at various tasks. Conditions on these prison hulks were so poor that many prisoners died before trial. Outbreaks of typhus and cholera were common, due to overcrowding and unsanitary conditions[1]. Conditions in prisons such as Newgate were not much better[2].

At the end of June 1746, thirty-four mid-ranking prisoners were indicted for High Treason. These prisoners included the officers of the Manchester Regiment. On 3 July the prisoners were brought before the court to hear the indictment and enter a plea. Three pled guilty, while the rest pled not guilty and were bound over for trial. On 15 July, Francis Towneley, colonel of the Manchester Regiment and the man whom Charles had left as Governor of Carlisle during the flight north the previous December, stood trial. Importantly, he was accused not just of treason by joining the Jacobite army but specifically of having appeared at Carlisle on 10 November 1745 and taking possession of that city in a warlike manner[3]. This accusation is completely untrue as Towneley did not join Charles's army until they were in Preston several weeks later. It also seems pointless. Towneley did take up arms in the Jacobite army and occupied Carlisle until Cumberland's men laid siege to the town in late December. They had ample occasion to charge him with the treason, there was no reason to add this false accusation.

Towneley's lawyer argued that since Towneley held a commission from the King of France he should be considered a member of the French army and therefore treated as a prisoner of war. The court considered that this actually went against Towneley, as a citizen born in Britain and therefore a subject of King George should not be member of an army that was at war with Britain[4]. Initially the jury could not reach an agreement, but they left the court for ten minutes and returned with a unanimous guilty verdict[5].

Between 15 and 22 July, the English prisoners were all tried and all but one was convicted. John Hunter was acquitted as a witness could confirm that he had run away from the Jacobites and had been captured by them and taken prisoner. On 22 July, the convicted prisoners were brought in front of the court for sentencing. All were to be hanged, drawn and quartered, the traditional punishment for treason. This involved the prisoner being hanged until close to death, then they would be cut down and their entrails would be removed. This would be followed by their genitals being cut off and thrown into a fire before finally, they were beheaded[6]. This punishment was described to Jamie in great detail in *Dragonfly in Amber* by the French executioner who worked at L'Hôpital des Anges alongside Claire.

Despite facing such an awful death, the men were reported to have remained stoic until the last. Early on the morning of 30 July, nine of them – Francis Towneley, Thomas Chadwick, James Dawson, George Fletcher, Thomas Deacon, John Berwick, Andrew Blood, Thomas Sydall and David Morgan – were woken, dressed and transported for execution[7]. They were placed on three sledges which were then led to Kennington Common, where a crowd had already gathered to watch the execution. They were transferred to a cart, from which they were to be hanged, while nearby a fire was lit in preparation for burning their body parts. They took some papers from their hats and threw them into the crowd. They also delivered papers to the sheriff and then threw their hats into the crowd. These too contained papers. The papers were reportedly declarations that they believed they died for a just cause and declared their allegiance to King James III[8].

Their faces were covered, nooses were tightened around their necks and the cart was gradually moved away. Unlike a drop hanging such as those we are familiar with from films and television scenes, where the neck is broken by the fall, these men were slowly strangled to death. In fact, Towneley was not yet dead when he was cut down for the next stage of the process and in the end, the executioner had to cut his throat. Towneley's genitals were removed and thrown into the fire, followed by his heart and bowels. After all of that, his head was removed with a cleaver. Each of the men executed that day received the same treatment until, finished, covered in blood, the executioner shouted, 'God save King George', a sentiment which was echoed by the crowd[9]. Well, who would be brave enough not to agree, following such a spectacle?

The heads of Towneley and Fletcher were placed on spikes over Temple Bar, the west gate into the City of London. Syddall and Deacons' heads were placed over the marketplace in Manchester while Berwick and Chadwicks' were sent to Carlisle to be displayed there, a gruesome reminder of the cost of rebellion[10].

The peers of the realm who had been captured escaped such an undignified fate. Lords Balmerino, Kilmarnock, Lovat, Tullibardine and Cromartie were kept in the Tower of London, awaiting trial. Tullibardine, who had been in poor health, died while incarcerated, on 9 July. On 28 July, Balmerino, Kilmarnock and Cromartie were tried in front of their fellow peers, including the duke of Newcastle, whom Cumberland had been writing to all these months.

Kilmarnock and Cromartie pled guilty, while Balmerino entered a not guilty plea on the basis of a technicality. The indictments specified that he was there at the taking of Carlisle, which he was not. Witnesses testified that at some point during the rebellion he had ridden into Carlisle at the head of his horse regiment, with sword drawn. As we saw with Francis Towneley, it didn't matter if the details of the indictment were correct or not. Balmerino was found guilty. All three lords were given the opportunity to address their peers.

Lord Kilmarnock asked for mercy, arguing that he could have escaped after Culloden but instead gave himself up to the King's justice. He said that he had been wrong to join the rebellion and that he regretted it, as well as declaring George the true King. Lord Cromartie also expressed regret over his participation in the rebellion, mentioning his pregnant wife and unborn child and the effect that his death would have on them. Lord Balmerino did not ask for mercy. All three were sentenced to be hanged, drawn and quartered, but had their sentence reduced to beheading.

They were returned to the Tower to await a date of execution. The Privy Council – a group of nobles who served as advisors to the monarch – had advised the King to show mercy to one of the three, something which George was inclined to do. The brutality of the defeat and pursual of the Jacobites during and after the battle of Culloden were causing people to feel some sympathy towards the Jacobites and George needed to turn that around[11]. But which of the three should he pardon? It clearly couldn't be Balmerino since he remained unrepentant for his part in the uprising, so it had to be either Kilmarnock or Cromartie. The Duke of Hamilton petitioned on behalf of Lord Kilmarnock, but it seems that he had few friends at court.

Lord Cromartie's pregnant wife on the other hand, made a strong impression on the King. She petitioned George and was initially dismissed but she fainted at his feet and was assisted by Prince Frederick, the Prince of Wales and his wife, who took pity on the young pregnant woman[12]. This was no doubt aided by the fact that Lady Cromartie's father was Prince Frederick's private secretary[13]. Either way, the petition was successful, and Cromartie's sentence was commuted to life in exile in Devon, his titles and lands stripped from him and his heirs[14].

Lords Kilmarnock and Balmerino were sentenced to die on 18 August. On the day of their execution the two men were escorted from the Tower together. As they were led outside, they were met by the sheriffs, who are reported to have said 'God bless King George,' as was traditional. Kilmarnock bowed while Lord Balmerino replied 'God bless King James'[15]. Defiant to the end.

The lords were taken to a house beside the scaffold where their sentence would be carried out. Inside the house they were given space and time to compose themselves, pray, and say their farewells to friends and family. During this time, Balmerino requested an audience with Kilmarnock and there asked him if he was aware of any order given by Charles that no quarter be given to the British army at Culloden. Kilmarnock replied that he had not heard of Charles giving such an order but that, after his capture, he became aware of an order signed by Lord George Murray giving such instructions[16]. Balmerino then bade Kilmarnock farewell stating that he wished he could face this penalty alone for both of them[17].

Kilmarnock was taken to the scaffold first, where he refrained from addressing the crowd. He prayed, ending with a petition to God for the wellbeing of King George II and his family. The executioner was reported to have been so moved by this that he asked for forgiveness and burst into tears, whereupon Kilmarnock gave him a small bag with money in it and said that he would drop his handkerchief as a signal that he was ready for the fatal blow. He then took some time in tucking his hair up out of the way and removing his jacket and then his waistcoat in order to bare his neck. He placed his head upon the block, took two minutes for silent prayer, and then dropped his handkerchief as agreed. The executioner removed Kilmarnock's head with one clean blow. The head was caught in some red baize material and both it and his body were removed to prepare the scaffold to receive Balmerino[18].

Throughout the wait, Balmerino retained his cheerful air and when he was called to the scaffold, he saluted his friends and bade them farewell without any sense of regret. He mounted the scaffold confidently and paraded around the area, examining his coffin and its inscription as well as the execution block. He was dressed in the same blue uniform he had worn at Culloden. He read out a speech to the crowd, in which he spoke of his allegiance to the Stuarts and then he extolled the virtues of Charles and refuted the claim that the prince had ordered that no quarter be given at Culloden. He closed with a prayer for the wellbeing of King James and his sons[19].

Balmerino then paid the executioner and apologised for not having more money to offer but he added his coat and waistcoat to the price. He replaced his wig with a plaid (tartan) cap, in defiance of the law that had recently been passed banning its use, declaring that he died a Scot. He is said to have taken the axe from the executioner and tested the sharpness of the blade with his thumb before handing it back and advising the man where to make the killing strike. He said a final farewell, declared that he had confidence in God and that his conscience was clear, and then gave the signal for the executioner that he was ready.

Unfortunately, the executioner was not ready, and being surprised by the quickness of the signal, he fumbled the first blow and failed to take Balmerino's head off. While one account says the blow rendered Balmerino insensible, another states that after the first blow Balermino tried to turn his head towards the executioner. Either way, it took three strikes with the axe before Lord Balmerino was dead[20]. It hardly seems a fitting end for a man who met his fate with such equanimity.

Meanwhile, Simon Fraser, Lord Lovat (and Jamie's grandfather in the *Outlander* series) had his trial delayed until March 1747 and during that time he petitioned the Duke of Cumberland for mercy, reminding him of all the times he had been of service to the crown and the fact that he had been close to the royal family when Cumberland himself was a baby[21]. None of his protestations did him any good though and eventually Lovat was tried, found guilty and sentenced to death, like his compatriots.

On the morning of the execution, he was reported to have awoken early and requested his wig, so that the barber would have plenty of time to comb it out and make sure that it was presentable. Like Lords Kilmarnock and Balmerino before him, he was escorted from the tower to a house close to the scaffold where he was given time to compose himself and say his farewells.

When he was taken to the scaffold, a chair was placed for him to rest on prior to the execution – he was in poor health and eighty years old on the day of his execution. He quoted briefly from both Ovid and Horace[22]. He then prayed and removed his hat, wig and coat, giving them to a friend to be returned to his body when it was all over. One of his attendants that day was a Mr James Fraser, perhaps the same one who had attempted to kidnap Lord President Forbes. Not our Jamie though – in *Voyager* Jamie was still in hiding in 1747. Lovat placed his head on the block and after a short prayer gave the signal to the executioner, who took his head off with one swift blow[23]. Lord Lovat was the last person to be publicly beheaded in Britain and the last peer of the realm to be executed.

There is a popular story that so many people had turned out to see the Old Fox meet his end that a stand of seats collapsed, killing a number of spectators and injuring far more. Lovat is said to have laughed at this event and to have still been laughing as the fatal blow was struck, thus he was the origin of the phrase 'to laugh your head off'[24].

After his death, there followed a mystery about the whereabouts of his body. It was taken from the scaffold back to the Tower for interment and the official records show that his body was buried beneath a chapel floor in the Tower of London, although clan tradition has long held that some of his kinsmen intercepted his body and transported it home to be buried on Fraser lands. A headless body was found in a casket in Wardlaw Mausoleum, near Inverness and was initially thought to belong to the clan chief, however, after an investigation by anthropologists, led by Dame Sue Black, it was determined that these remains belonged to a young woman[25].

Across England, hundreds of other Jacobites were tried with many of the low-ranking ones being sentenced to transportation to the West Indies. More than ninety however were executed, most by hanging, for their part in the uprising. For some of the people tried, this came as a result of simply being heard to toast Charles's health or wish him well, rather than take any active part in supporting the Jacobites. The Hanoverians wanted to make sure that they fully suppressed any hint of a future restoration.

Lord Lovat may have been the last man to be publicly beheaded, but he was not the last Jacobite to be executed. That dubious honour goes to Dr Archibald Cameron. One of the first men to join Prince Charles when he landed in Scotland and brother to Donald Cameron of Lochiel, Dr Archibald Cameron was one of the prince's inner circle. While there is some debate as to the part he played in the uprising, with some people claiming that he was just acting as physician to his brother while others suggest that he was a personal assistant to Charles, there is no doubt that he became important to the prince as he was one of the few who stayed in Cluny's Cage and joined the prince in his flight to France[26].

Once in France, Dr Cameron remained close to the prince, reportedly visiting him regularly in his Paris apartment, as well as receiving a pension from the French government and a commission from the Spanish government as a result of his service to the Jacobite cause. He is reported to have secretly returned to Scotland in September of 1749 to recover some of the Arkaig gold for the use of Charles and is alleged to have taken 6,000 Louis d'ors (French gold coins) with the agreement of MacPherson of Cluny[27].

Dr Cameron returned to Scotland in 1753, to secure more of the gold for the prince. He was lodging at Brenachyle near Loch Katrine when he was betrayed by a Hanoverian spy known as Pickle[28]. He was arrested and held at Edinburgh Castle before being shipped south to the Tower of London. He was sentenced to death by hanging, drawing and quartering but this was partially commuted. He posed an awkward question – as the younger brother of the Cameron chief, he was not a commoner, subject to hanging, however, he was not a lord himself, since he was a younger brother and therefore was not a peer of the realm, entitled to die by beheading[29].

On the day of the execution, Dr Cameron bade farewell to his wife, who had travelled from France to be with him in his final days, then was taken to the place of execution. There would be no crowds as there had been for his compatriots who had been executed years before. The sheriff offered him all the time he needed to make his peace, but the doctor simply said a few prayers with the clergyman who attended and then announced that he was ready[30]. He was hanged for twenty minutes before being cut down. He was not quartered, but his heart was removed and burnt[31].

Diana Gabaldon's *Voyager* tells us how Jamie hides in a cave near Lallybroch while the Redcoats search the countryside for him. He lives like this for years, visiting his family once a month, until events make it clear that he is putting them in danger. In order to protect his family and tenants, he stages his own capture, allowing them to collect the reward money for him as well as establishing themselves as loyal subjects of the crown, undeserving of further harassment.

Jamie escapes execution and instead is imprisoned in Ardsmuir prison, where he becomes a leader to the inmates. Conditions are awful, with the men crowded together, given poor rations and nothing but a blanket for a bed. They often share the space with rats and disease is rife. Lord John Grey, the young man whom Jamie spared before the battle of Prestonpans, is assigned as the new governor of the prison and he establishes a working relationship with Jamie which blossoms into a friendship. Lord John does what he can to improve conditions for the prisoners until eventually Ardsmuir is renovated as a barracks. Most of the prisoners are transported to the colonies to complete their sentences, but Lord John arranges for Jamie to be placed at Helwater, an estate in the Lake District, where he becomes an indentured servant, working as a groom. While there, he performs a great service for the family and they are able to secure a pardon for him, which eventually allows him to return home to Lallybroch.

Chapter Thirty-Three

The Highlands

For the thousands of people who lived in Scotland, and especially the highlands, but had not taken part in the rebellion, life would also never be the same again. The campaign had brought its own difficulties to the area. They had been forced to find food and shelter for not just one army but two, and many towns and villages were forced to pay taxes to Charles to support his campaign and then again to King George's tax collectors who didn't care that the money was already gone. Other towns faced fines from the Jacobites for standing against them. See for example, the situation in Paisley, a town in Renfrewshire which had been forced to pay a fine of £500 to Charles and his army when they passed through in December 1745, on the mad flight from England[1]. The town later brought a court case to recover the costs but were ultimately unsuccessful.

Many towns and villages in the highlands were burned down in retribution by Cumberland's forces, driving these people south to Edinburgh and Glasgow where they often lived in poverty and squalor, through no fault of their own.

The government and the Hanoverian royal family wanted to make sure that this would be the final Jacobite uprising and so they set about dismantling the way of life that they considered a crucible for rebellion. A number of Acts of Parliament were passed to enable this.

The Heritable Jurisdictions Act 1746

This was probably the most important piece of legislation in undermining the power of the clan chiefs. Prior to this, the clan chiefs had legal power to adjudicate both criminal and civil cases involving members of the clan. There's a lovely example of this in *Outlander* when Claire witnesses the clan coming before Calum for judgement on their disputes. There was no royal jurisdiction in Scotland, except in cases of treason. All other issues were dealt with locally by the clan chiefs or their representatives.

The Heritable Jurisdictions Act removed this right, extending crown jurisdiction throughout Scotland. It acknowledged these rights as a form of property and therefore compensation was paid to the clan chiefs who had taken no part in the uprising. Those who had been with Charles were attainted for High Treason and were stripped of their lands and titles. The powers that had been possessed by the Scottish lords were transferred to sheriffs who would be appointed by the crown. The Act also removed the hereditary justiciarship from the Duke of Argyle, who received £25,000 in compensation for this[2]. The power was transferred to the High Court of Justiciary. In total, £152,000 was paid in compensation to the various lords who lost their powers under the act.

The other important thing covered by this act was the abolition of a clan chief's right to call his clan to arms. Prior to the Wars of the Three Kingdoms in 1644, Scotland did not maintain a standing army, instead relying upon each clan chief to raise able-bodied men to fight if and when required. Even after 1644, when a Scottish army was established, it was a small force and there was still very much the expectation that the crown could call upon the lords to raise their clan to support that army. This was the tradition that allowed the Jacobite chiefs to build an army for Charles. Many of the men who were brought out to fight quite likely didn't care much one way or the other who sat on the throne. After all, the King was hundreds of miles away and rarely even visited Scotland. The clan chief had much more influence over their day-to-day lives than the monarch did, and so they did as they were told, whatever their personal opinions. Removing this right from the chiefs meant that there could never again be a rising on the scale of this one.

The Act of Proscription 1746

The other key piece of legislation used was the Act of Proscription. On the one hand, this act reaffirmed the existing Disarming Act which required all highlanders to give up their arms. British soldiers went from house to house and removed any weapons that could be found[3]. This is likely to have caused difficulty in a part of the country where hunting for food to feed your family had not yet died out. After the date which the act came into force – 1 August 1746 – it was illegal for any highlander to bear arms. Anyone found with a weapon could face fines, imprisonment or, for a second offence, transportation to the colonies for a period of seven years. This section of the Act related specifically to highlanders, listing the geographic areas which it would affect as 'within the shire of Dunbartain, on the north side of the water of Leven, Stirling on the north side of the river of Forth, Perth, Kincardine, Aberdeen, Inverness, Nairn, Cromarty, Argyle, Forfar, Bamff, Sutherland, Caithness, Elgine and Ross'[4]. So, we can see this is a direct punishment of the people the crown considered responsible for the rebellion.

The act defined a weapon as 'broad sword or target, poignard, whinger, or durk, side pistol, gun, or other warlike weapon'[5]. Some of these terms are unfamiliar today. A broad sword is self-explanatory, a target, also known as a targe, was a small shield often worn by highlanders in battle, a poignard was a long, lightweight dagger, a whinger was a kind of short sword that was also used as a knife at meals, a durk – or dirk – was a long-bladed dagger that was traditionally worn in the highlands, and also often doubled as an eating knife at mealtimes. And we know about pistols and guns. So, the act banned anything that could be used as a weapon, but also items that would be used in day-to-day life. Dirks would be used to cut food at mealtimes but also for tasks such as skinning rabbits or gathering foraged food, stripping bark from wood to make kindling and many other non-aggressive uses. These were tools of everyday life, not just weapons of war.

The ban also applied to anyone living in the defined areas – not just people who had taken part in the rebellion or were known to have Jacobite sympathies. Under this law, any highlander who kept a broad sword that had been handed down through generations of their family, or had a dagger or gun used for providing food for their family could ultimately face seven years as an indentured servant in the colonies – a sentence that, as discussed earlier, few survived. To say that this law was heavy-handed would be an understatement.

The other part of the Act applied to the whole of Scotland but was, again, aimed at the highlanders. It banned the wearing of anything considered highland dress, defined as: 'plaid, philibeg, or little kilt, trowse, shoulder belts, or any part whatsoever of what peculiarly belongs to the highland garb; and that no TARTAN, or partly-coloured plaid or stuff shall be used for great coats, or for upper coats'[6]. The punishment for being caught wearing any of these items after the effective date of the legislation was initially being jailed for six months, without parole and, for a second offence, transportation to the colonies for a period of seven years. Bear in mind that many of those affected were not particularly well-off. The highlands were a subsistence culture, where you had what you need but very little else. These were not people who had a wardrobe full of clothes they could switch to, or the resources to replace their clothing just because the government and the crown had decided that the clothing was too closely linked with rebels to be allowed. For many, the choice would have been to go undressed or risk wearing clothing that could see them imprisoned or transported – even if worn in the privacy of their own homes.

While one could argue that there was a justification for the requirement for highlanders to disarm, in that the weapons could pose a threat to the peace and safety of the kingdom, no such argument can be made against the wearing of highland dress. This was nothing but an attack on an entire culture as a punishment for the actions of a fraction of them.

The Act of Proscription did two other important things, which snuck below the radar a little. It required that all teachers in any school in Scotland must be registered with the crown, even (especially) private schools. These teachers were required to take oaths of loyalty to the crown and to lead prayers within the school that specifically prayed for King George by name, as well as praying for the health of his heirs and the entire royal family. The penalty for failing to do so was six months imprisonment and, for a second offence, transportation to the colonies in America for life[7]. Just take a moment to consider that. A life sentence for the crime of not praying for the health and wellbeing of the king and his family. Passing laws such as this may be one of the reasons people rebelled in the first place.

The final thing the Act did was to indemnify anyone who was acting on behalf of the state, or out of loyalty to King George, for any wrongdoing or actions that they took which were contrary to normal laws[8]. In other words, it excused the deeds of Cumberland and his soldiers, as well as anyone else who could make a convincing argument that they were acting in loyalty to the crown or opposition of the Jacobites, from any culpability. The families of the Jacobite soldiers who were hunted down and murdered after Culloden, the families who were harassed, the innocent people who had their cattle stolen, their homes invaded, their villages burnt to the ground…there would be no legal remedy or recompense for any of them.

The interesting thing about this provision is that it actually acknowledges the fact that Cumberland and his men went too far, that they exceeded the law, for if they hadn't there would be no need to indemnify them. This makes it clear that, even if some of the stories about what the British soldiers did after Culloden are exaggerated, not all of them were. The crown and the government were clearly concerned over liability for the British Army's actions in the course of their duty.

Military Building

Another effect of the 1745 rising was the decision to rebuild and strengthen the forts in the highlands with the intention of keeping a permanent army presence in the area. The focus was on the three forts along the length of the Great Glen, spanning from Fort William on the west coast, to Fort George, near Inverness on the east coast.

Fort William was not taken by the Jacobites during the 1745 rebellion and became the base of operations for the hunt for Charles as that summer wore on.

Fort Augustus, positioned near the south end of Loch Ness, had been taken by the Jacobite army after a short siege and although the building was still standing, it had been gutted. The Duke of Cumberland stayed there for a time in the days following the battle of Culloden, after moving on from Inverness. It was subsequently strengthened and remained an active barracks until 1818, by which time the highlands had been completely pacified and highlanders were far more likely to be found fighting for the British Army than against them. On being decommissioned, it was sold to the Lovat family who later passed it to the Benedictine order, who built an abbey and a school there, until it became too costly to stay. In 1998 the land reverted to the Lovat family who then sold it.

Fort George, at Inverness, stood against the Jacobites after Lord Loudoun fled, under the command of Major George Grant[9]. The garrison surrendered after a siege that lasted around a week, on 25 February 1745/6. The Jacobite army took all of the arms, ammunition and provisions contained within the fort and then destroyed the building. Following the battle of Culloden, the decision was made to rebuild, although a dispute with Inverness Town Council over the partial loss of use of the harbour for the fort meant that it was relocated to nearby Ardersier Point on the estates of the Cawdor Clan, who were loyal to King George[10]. The fort was designed by Lieutenant-General William Skinner, who went on to become the Chief Military Engineer in Britain and took twelve years to complete. The largest construction job ever to take place in the highlands – which is saying something considering the number of castles in the highlands – it required many of the materials to be brought in by sea and took the work of 1,000 men to complete[11].

By the time the fort was completed, the Jacobite threat was over, and it has never seen military action, instead becoming a training base which is still in use to this day. Fort George became home to several highland regiments over the course of its long history but is perhaps most closely associated with the Seaforth Highlanders. Between a changing economic landscape, legislation which limited their roles in the clan, and a desire to prove loyalty to the crown, limiting any further damage to their homes and people, many clan chiefs set about raising military regiments which would fight as part of the British army.

In 1778 Kenneth MacKenzie, the Earl of Seaforth, formed the 72nd Highlanders (the Duke of Albany's Own) who trained at Fort George before spending much of their time fighting overseas. They were joined in 1793 by the 78th Highland Infantry (The Ross-shire Buffs) raised by MacKenzie's grandson, Francis MacKenzie, first Baron Seaforth. In 1881, a military reorganisation saw the two regiments amalgamated into what would be known as the Seaforth Highlanders and Fort George was assigned as their depot[12]. They would remain there for the next eighty-three years.

Fort George is still an active military base but parts of it are open to the public and are managed by Historic Environment Scotland.

Roads

At the same time as building and strengthening the forts in the highlands, the infrastructure of roads was being upgraded. The project of creating a network of military roads in the highlands had begun following the 1715 uprising. In 1724, Major-General George Wade (the same George

Wade who would later command British forces at Newcastle upon Tyne and consistently missed facing Charles's army while they were in England) was sent north to evaluate the military conditions and make recommendations as to how the government could work to suppress future rebellions[13].

General Wade advised the government that another rebellion was almost guaranteed and suggested keeping heavily manned forts, connected by wide, straight roads that would allow for the movement of men and artillery through country that was especially difficult to travel. The highlands had few roads at this time, and the roads that were there were narrow and not suited to the movement of large numbers of men or heavy artillery. The three forts already discussed were built or updated and a road was built linking them, right across the heart of the highlands, from Fort William to Inverness. Wade made it his goal to build a road that was sixteen feet wide, where possible, well-graded, properly drained, and surfaced well enough to endure the movement of large numbers of troops as well as carts and artillery[14]. In some places he had to compromise on these goals, but he achieved a lot considering the challenges of the terrain.

Construction took place between April and October each year, the winter weather being too harsh for such activities. Wade used crews of one hundred men at a time, overseen by seven officers[15]. Between 1726 and 1731 Wade oversaw the construction of the road from Fort William to Inverness and roads from Dunkeld to Inverness, Crieff to Dalnorcardoch and Dalwhinie and Ruthven to Fort Augustus. This last contained a significant feat of engineering at the time, the Corrieyairack Pass, a road that climbed 2,500 feet, over the course of eighteen switchbacks[16]. It must have been a source of some distress to Wade that the first army to make use of this road was Charles's Jacobite army in 1745, marching from Glenfinnan to Perth[17].

After the 1745 uprising, the government decided that they needed more roads in the highlands if they were going to be sure of preventing another uprising and the job passed to Major William Caulfield. Although not as well-known as his predecessor, Caulfield actually built many more miles of road than Wade – over 800 miles to Wade's 250. He undertook his own feat of engineering in creating 'the Devil's Staircase' climbing 850 feet from Glencoe[18]. Caulfield was also responsible for the road from Dumbarton to Inveraray, which is still largely followed by the modern A82 and A83. At the peak of this road, a stone and bench were erected, urging travellers to 'rest and be thankful' which is what the area came to be known as.

By the time of Caulfield's death in 1767, the Jacobite threat had been largely suppressed and the road building project came to an end. As the need for the roads for military purposes passed, the responsibility for the roads passed to local authorities and various private entities. Some, unsuitable for travellers and poorly maintained, were abandoned and have largely disappeared, while others became the base of the road system in use today[19]. Some stretches of the original military roads are in use now as footpaths for hillwalkers and mountain bikers, such as the Devil's Staircase which forms part of the West Highland Way.

Ordnance Survey Maps

Anyone who has taken part in any sort of hillwalking or orienteering will be familiar with the Ordnance Survey Map, but few people know that it began as a result of the 1745 rebellion. There's a clue in the name, as the defence ministry in the 1700s was called the Board of Ordnance[20]. Following the uprising, the government realised that they knew less about the Scottish Highlands than they did some areas of Europe, and that to properly pacify the area – and prepare for the possibility of a further uprising – they needed to understand the terrain. So, a young engineer named William Roy was sent to begin an undertaking that would not be complete for eight years. Groups of around eight people would measure angles with survey compasses and used chains of around fifty feet long to measure distances between landmarks[21]. Other details were sketched in by eye.

This was the most detailed survey of the highlands that had been carried out to date. Roy went on to geodetically connect the observatories in London and Paris to resolve a dispute about their relative positions. As part of this task, he commissioned the most accurate theodolite that could be built. In 1791, the year after Roy's death, the Board of Ordnance bought another theodolite and began the mammoth task of producing a detailed map of the whole of Britain and the Ordnance Survey Map as we know it was born[22].

The Highland Clearances

It is commonly thought the Highland Clearances were caused by the fallout of the 1745 rebellion. In truth, it was far more complex than any one issue and had multiple causes and contributing factors, however it seems likely that the actions taken by the government in the aftermath of 1745 played a part. Even before the rebellion, the economic landscape of the highlands had been slowly changing, with clan chiefs becoming more like landlords than protectors and looking for ways to maximise the income from their lands. This trend continued after the uprising and was contributed to by the government's handling of the estates that had been stripped from the clan chiefs who had joined the uprising. These estates were reorganised with an eye towards commercialisation and increasing profits rather than supporting the people of the area[23].

The legislation that came into place following the uprising was focussed on destroying the clan culture of the highlands and although it had already been slipping away, this surely hastened its demise. Clan chiefs had most of their rights stripped from them, relegating them to the role of landlords and undermining the ties they had previously had with their communities. Indeed, this was the purpose of the legislation and it succeeded, contributing to a shift towards a culture that valued profit over people.

From the 1780s, landowners began to realise that they could earn more money from their land by using it to graze sheep rather than in supporting crofts. Some of them began to relocate their tenants to the coast, where they could take advantage of the fishing and kelping opportunities. Others just evicted their tenants with no care for where they would go. The most notorious example of this was carried out on the Sutherland estates by the Countess of Sutherland and her husband Lord Stafford. The estate was extensive, the largest in private ownership in Europe at the time[24]. Between 1807 and 1821 several thousand people were evicted from their homes and moved to the coastal areas of the estate. They were expected to cultivate barren land and take up fishing, although the area they had been moved to lent itself to neither. They were also given tiny crofts that were insufficient to support the families expected to live there. There were also instances of those being forced to move being mistreated, especially by Patrick Sellar, an advisor to the Sutherland family. He was known to throw people out of their homes with no regard to circumstances and then to destroy the houses so that they could not return[25].

Other landowners took a gentler approach and moved people only gradually, but regardless of how it was done, many thousands of people were relocated. At the same time, people were emigrating to the colonies, hoping to find a better life overseas.

During the late 1700s there was also mass recruitment of highland men to fight in the British Army. It was not lost on the government that many of the highlanders they had faced in the rebellion were skilled and ferocious warriors and, with proper training, they could be a great asset to the crown. The outbreak of the Seven Years' War in 1756 increased the demand for soldiers and recruitment of highlanders got underway in earnest. It is estimated that by the time of the French Wars, between 37,000 and 48,000 British troops were highlanders. From a population of around 250,000 to 300,000 that is a significant proportion[26].

Whether it was as a result of the 1745 uprising or the other factors that contributed to the clearances that began in the 1750s and continued for a century, life in the highlands would never be the same again.

Epilogue

Prince Charles Edward Stuart arrived in Brittany on the north coast of France on 30 September 1746. Louis XV invited him to Versailles, something he hadn't done during the year and a half which Charles had spent waiting for him to decide to invade England. Charles was desperate to return to Britain and begged Louis to invade. The French king offered 6,000 troops to reclaim Scotland, but Charles had his heart set on London. France could not now afford a full-scale invasion and so they remained at a stalemate[1].

Charles lived in Paris, in great style, running up debts for Louis' government to pay. He surrounded himself with hard-drinking men and had a number of mistresses. His brother Henry, the Duke of York, came to visit him and was shocked at the way he lived. Upon returning to Rome Henry entered the priesthood. Charles saw this as evidence that his father and brother had both given up on a restoration and took it as a great betrayal. He never saw his father again[2].

In 1748 France signed the Treaty of Aix-la-Chapelle, which ended the War of the Austrian Succession after eight long years of fighting across Europe. It also stated that neither James III nor his children could live in France. Charles publicly refused to go, embarrassing Louis, until eventually he was arrested outside the opera. He spent three days in prison before eventually agreeing to leave. His relationship with France would never recover.

Charles spent some time in Avignon before returning to Paris in disguise and living under a number of pseudonyms. He had a string of tempestuous love affairs, none of which seemed to make him happy. He converted to Anglicanism during a secret trip to London in 1750, hoping that would increase support for him in Britain[3].

In 1756, war once more broke out between France and England and in 1759, the French began to plan an invasion and invited Charles to join their plans, intending to put Charles on the throne after defeating George

II[4]. England learned of the planned invasion and the Royal Navy created a blockade and destroyed the French fleet. The invasion had failed.

King James III and VIII died on 1 January 1766. Charles travelled to Rome and installed himself in the Palazzo del Re where he had grown up. Pope Clement allowed him to live there and paid him a pension but never recognised him as King. This meant that he had no chance of support from the other Catholic Kings of Europe. Any hope he had of a restoration was effectively over. Charles died from a stroke on 31 January 1788[5].

Outlander may romanticise these events a little for the sake of good fiction, but it doesn't require much altering to do so. Jamie and Claire could have been like so many of the people of the time, fighting for a cause they believed in, trying to change the course of the future in hopes of creating a better world.

Unlike so many of the people who were caught up in the rebellion, Jamie and Claire both survived Culloden and everything that came after. It may have been the end of the Jacobite cause, but it was not the end of their adventures.

The End

Appendix One

Jacobite Timeline

Year	Event
1685	King Charles II died and was succeeded by his younger brother, James II and VII, a Catholic.
1688	James's second wife, Mary of Modena, gave birth to a son, James Francis Edward Stuart, giving rise to a fear of a Catholic line of succession.
1688	Powerful Protestants in government invited William of Orange to invade England, which he did in November.
1688	Fearing for his and his family's lives, James II and VII fled to France.
1689	The British parliament declared that, by leaving the country, James had abdicated the throne and invited his daughter Mary and her husband, William of Orange, to become joint Monarchs of Scotland, England and Ireland. This was known as the 'Glorious Revolution'.
1689	The first Jacobite uprising in both Scotland and Ireland. The Irish Jacobites were defeated but the Scottish Jacobites prevailed over the British forces.
1691	King William offered pardons to any Scottish Jacobites who would swear allegiance to him.
1692	The massacre of the Glencoe MacDonalds in retribution for their part in the uprising.
1694	Death of Queen Mary. William remained as King.
1701	Parliament passed the Act of Settlement, passing succession to the throne to the Hanovers, should William and then Anne (Mary's younger sister, still a Stuart) die without heirs.

Year	Event
1701	James II died, succeeded by his son, James Francis Edward Stuart, the Jacobite King James III and VIII.
1702	William of Orange died and was succeeded by Queen Anne, James II and VII's second daughter.
1707	Parliament passed the Act of Union, uniting the kingdoms of England and Scotland, leading to an increase in support for the deposed Stuarts in Scotland.
1714	Queen Anne, the last Stuart monarch to reign in Great Britain, died without an heir. As a result of the Act of Settlement, the throne passed to Georg, Elector of Hanover.
1715	Second Jacobite uprising in Scotland, led by the Earl of Mar. Joined by James III and VIII.
1716	James III and VIII departed again for France when it became clear that they could not win.
1720	Prince Charles Edward Stuart was born.
1727	King George died and was succeeded by his son, King George II.
1744	Charles left Rome and travelled to France with the intention of invading England with the support of King Louis XV of France.
1745	Charles arrived in Scotland, landing on the Isle of Eriskay.
1745	The Jacobite forces took possession of Edinburgh and won a battle at Prestonpans.
1745	The Jacobite army marched into England and took control of Carlisle.
1745	Charles and his army got as far as Derby before being turned back by British forces. They were pursued north as they retreated to Scotland to await French reinforcements.
1746	The Jacobites captured Inverness and won another battle with the British at Falkirk.
1746	The Jacobites met British soldiers, led by the Duke of Cumberland, at Culloden. The Jacobites were roundly defeated and hunted down throughout the highlands.

Year	Event
1746	Charles escaped to Skye with the help of Flora MacDonald and subsequently returned to France.
1746	Parliament passed the Act of Proscription, seeking to disarm the highlanders and banning the wearing of tartan or other highland dress, except for the army.
1746	Parliament passed the Heritable Jurisdictions Act, removing power from the clan chiefs in the highlands.
1766	Death of James III and VIII.
1788	Death of Charles Edward Stuart.
1807	Death of Henry, Duke of York (Charles's younger brother) and the end of the male Stuart line.

Appendix Two

Major Players and Clan Affiliations

Donald Cameron of Lochiel – one of Charles's earliest supporters, despite initially advising him to return to France until he could raise troops and money – Clan Cameron.

James Drummond, Duke of Perth – joined the rebellion in September and was appointed Lieutenant-General alongside Lord George Murray – Clan Drummond.

Arthur Elphinstone, Lord Balmerino – another early supporter, Lord Balmerino was captured at Culloden and executed – Clan Elphinstone.

Simon Fraser, Lord Lovat – known for playing both sides, Lord Lovat joined the rebellion late in the campaign – Clan Fraser.

Sir John MacDonald – one of the Seven Men of Moidart, who arrived in Scotland with the prince, John MacDonald was an Irishman who had fought for France.

Alexander MacDonald of Keppoch – another early supporter of the prince, Keppoch died heroically at Culloden – Clan MacDonald of Keppoch.

Donald MacDonald of Kinlochmoidart – Charles stayed with Kinlochmoidart before raising his standard at Glenfinnan – Clan MacDonald of Kinlochmoidart.

George MacKenzie, Earl of Cromartie – joined the uprising only after Charles had invaded England and received a pardon after Culloden – Clan MacKenzie.

Ewen MacPherson of Cluny – originally serving on the Hanoverian side, Cluny was 'taken prisoner' by the Jacobites, and shortly became an officer. Known for helping Charles hide after he fled from Culloden – Clan MacPherson.

John Murray of Broughton – served Charles as Secretary, running all civilian elements of the campaign. After Culloden he turned state's evidence, earning the enmity of many of his compatriots – Clan Murray.

William Murray, Duke of Atholl, Marquis of Tullibardine – one of the Seven Men of Moidart, he arrived in Scotland with Charles and had the honour of unfurling the standard at Glenfinnan – Clan Murray of Atholl.

Lord George Murray – younger brother of the Duke of Atholl. One of the most influential men of the campaign, Commander of the Jacobite Army – Clan Murray of Atholl.

John O'Sullivan – Adjutant-General to the Jacobite forces in 1745 and one of the Seven Men of Moidart, often disagreed with Lord George Murray.

Thomas Sherridan – one of the Seven Men of Moidart and Charles's tutor from when he was a boy.

David Wemyss, Lord Elcho – joined the prince at Edinburgh and became one of the war council, commanded the cavalry Lifeguard – Clan Wemyss.

Acknowledgements

When I first contemplated writing this book, in early 2020, I had no idea what the following year would look like. I couldn't have imagined tackling a project like this and having my movements so restricted. I found myself working on this through a global pandemic which meant that I was unable to visit as many of the sites discussed in these pages as I had planned to do, and I was forced to rely upon other people's scholarship and the materials available on the internet far more than I had planned.

I owe a debt of gratitude to the many people who have been working tirelessly over the years to digitise and make available materials held in archives across the country. In particular, at The National Library for Scotland, The National Archives, The National Trust for Scotland, the National Galleries of Scotland and Historic Environment Scotland.

Personal thanks must go to Vanessa at the West Highland Museum in Fort William, who answered my emails with patience and kindness, during a difficult time.

Thank you to my Commissioning Editor at Pen and Sword, Claire Hopkins, who was a source of support from the very beginning, and to Chris Evan Brown, who first spoke to me about writing this book. A whole team of people worked on this book and all deserve praise and thanks.

The beautiful cover art was created by Cat Hellisen and I can't thank her enough for it. You can see more of her artwork at www.cathellisen.com.

I am writing this in March 2021, as we begin to see the light at the end of the tunnel that has been covid. It has been, without a doubt, one of the most challenging years of my life, as I have no doubt is true for many of you reading this. I am very lucky in that I have a lot of support from family and friends but this last year a few particular friends have been a constant source of love and support, without which I would not have stayed sane long enough to write this book. For listening to me witter on at length about *Outlander* and the Jacobites, sending me links to interesting articles about that time period, and generally keeping me together, my heartfelt thanks go to Beth Faulds, Natalie Fergie, Sammy H.K. Smith, Charlotte Bond and Gareth Hunter. You are the very best of people.

As always, my mum was an early reader and put up with lengthy phone calls as I worked my way through the tangles of history and more than once talked me down when I was stressing about not being a good enough writer to handle this topic.

And finally, this book would not exist without the support of my family. My children put up with me spending most of my free time hidden away in my office, researching and writing or filling dinner table conversation with stories of Bonnie Prince Charlie and the dashing James Fraser. I would not have been able to do any of this around homeschooling and pandemic life without the constant support of my husband, who dealt with more than his share of bedtimes and weekend trips to the park while I was buried in the past. He has championed my writing since the first time I sat in front of the keyboard and none of my books would exist without him.

Bibliography

Websites

https://www.scotsman.com/arts-and-culture/british-spy-map-18th-century-jacobite-threat-revealed-240412

https://www.westhighlandmuseum.org.uk/collection.jsp?collection=jacobite&item=3#collection-items

http://www.bbc.co.uk/arts/robertburns/works/charlie_hes_my_darling/

http://www.rampantscotland.com/songs/blsongs_cope.htm

http://www.bbc.co.uk/doctorwho/classic/episodeguide/highlanders/detail.shtml

https://nationalarchives.gov.uk/documents/education/timeline-final.pdf

https://www.scottishhistory.org/articles/massacre-of-glencoe/

https://www.jacobites.net/skye-boat-song.html

http://januarymagazine.com/profiles/gabaldon.html

http://www.bbc.co.uk/doctorwho/classic/episodeguide/highlanders/detail.shtml

https://www.britannica.com/topic/Jacobite-British-history

http://www.waulk.org/index.asp?pageid=176756

https://www.scotlandinfo.eu/history-of-cloth-making-and-waulking/

https://www.youtube.com/watch?v=yvnmgcAoOSc&feature=youtu.be

http://greatscottishclans.com/clans/mackenzie.php

https://www.castleleod.org.uk

http://clanfraser.org/timeline/1700s/

https://www.shca.ed.ac.uk/Research/witches/

https://www.realmarykingsclose.com/blog/scotland-witch-prickers/

https://engole.info/john-kincaid-witch-finder/

https://www.undiscoveredscotland.co.uk/usbiography/s/jamesfrancisedwardstuart.html

http://en.chateauversailles.fr/discover/history/great-characters/cardinal-fleury

https://www.british-history.ac.uk/london-record-soc/vol22/pp1-11

https://www.historyofroyalwomen.com/marie-louise-de-la-tour-dauvergne/real-woman-outlander-marie-louise-de-la-tour-dauvergne/

https://outlander.fandom.com/wiki/Outlander_Wiki

https://www.nationalarchives.gov.uk/education/resources/jacobite-1745/jacobite-declaration-war/

http://www.visitdunkeld.com/perth-prince-charles.htm

https://www.bankofengland.co.uk/monetary-policy/inflation/inflation-calculator

https://www.undiscoveredscotland.co.uk/usbiography/m/georgemurray.html

https://www.scotsman.com/whats-on/arts-and-entertainment/when-jacobites-took-over-palace-holyroodhouse-844650

https://www.royal.uk/royal-residences-palace-holyroodhouse

https://randomscottishhistory.com/2018/03/10/chapter-40-edinburgh-in-1745-pp-322-329/

https://www.royal.uk/james-vii-and-ii-r1685-1689

https://www.futurelearn.com/info/courses/the-highland-clans/0/steps/71140

https://www.britishbattles.com/jacobite-rebellion/battle-of-prestonpans/

http://www.battlefieldsofbritain.co.uk/battle_prestonpans_1745.html

http://clanmaxwellsociety.com/_history/JMofKirk.php

https://www.electricscotland.com/history/charles/37.htm

https://www.nms.ac.uk/explore-our-collections/stories/art-and-design/the-rise-and-fall-of-hamilton-palace/

https://www.bbc.co.uk/news/uk-scotland-highlands-islands-42741206

https://www.stirlingcastle.scot/discover/about-the-castle/

https://falkirklocalhistory.club/events/battle-of-falkirk-muir-1746/

http://www.douglashistory.co.uk/history/Battles/Falkirk_1746.html#.YClT9DJxflU

https://blair-castle.co.uk/scottish-highland-castle/the-castle/history-of-the-castle/

https://www.historicenvironment.scot/visit-a-place/places/ruthven-barracks/history/

https://www.undiscoveredscotland.co.uk/usbiography/mac/annemackintosh.html

https://www.scottishhistory.org/on-this-day/rout-of-moy/

http://old.scotwars.com/battle_of_moy.htm

https://en.m.wikipedia.org/wiki/Order_of_battle

https://www.nts.org.uk/visit/places/culloden/the-battle-of-culloden

https://www.britishbattles.com/jacobite-rebellion/battle-of-culloden/

http://www.tartansauthority.com/highland-dress/highland-weapons/
ancient-weapons/the-targemaker/

https://www.denofgeek.com/tv/outlander-season-3-does-the-battle-of-
culloden-live-up-to-expectations/

https://www.thecultureconcept.com/outlander-series-3-episode-1-
battle-of-culloden-boston

https://www.sarahfraser.co.uk/jacobite-gold/

https://www.undiscoveredscotland.co.uk/usbiography/mac/
floramacdonald.html

http://www.rampantscotland.com/famous/blfamflora.htm

https://www.historic-uk.com/HistoryUK/HistoryofScotland/Flora-
Macdonald/

https://ibw21.org/reparations/slavery-vs-indentured-servitude-which-
aids-racism/

http://portal.historicenvironment.scot/designation/GDL00243

https://media.nationalarchives.gov.uk/index.php/prison-hulks/

http://www.kenscott.com/prisons/prisonerexp.htm

https://www.oldpolicecellsmuseum.org.uk/content/history/
transportation-3/life_aboard_the_prison_hulks

https://www.thurrock.gov.uk/thurrock-historical-figures/jacobites-
culloden-and-tilbury-fort

https://www.historic-uk.com/DestinationsUK/Newgate-Prison/

https://allthatsinteresting.com/hanged-drawn-quartered

http://www.cracroftspeerage.co.uk/cromartie1703.htm

https://dailysirwalter.blogspot.com/2010/08/execution-of-earl-
kilmarnock-and-lord.html#:~:text=Execution%20of%20Earl%20
Kilmarnock%20and%20Lord%20Balmerino%20On,impending%20
death%20on%20behalf%20of%20the%20Jacobite%20cause

http://www.britishexecutions.co.uk/execution-content.php?key=2037

http://www.britishexecutions.co.uk/execution-content.
php?key=2040&termRef=Lord%20Lovat

https://thecrownchronicles.co.uk/history/history-posts/body-jacobite-
chief-simon-fraser-lord-lovat-exhumed/

https://www.theguardian.com/science/2018/jan/19/headless-body-is-
not-scottish-clan-chief-simon-fraser-experts

https://www.sarahfraser.co.uk/death-of-a-highland-chief/

https://www.scotsman.com/whats-on/arts-and-entertainment/story-last-jacobite-be-hanged-1470851

http://www.britishexecutions.co.uk/execution-content.php?key=2119

https://www.scotsman.com/heritage-and-retro/heritage/scottish-town-owed-ps100000-jacobites-275-year-old-debt-3079238?fbclid=IwAR0dOi67brf82ebYy8gzhu1kmyUxBxIuIy4lxN90g4qQjf0Mp6Hjh7wwdYI

https://petergshilstonsblog.blogspot.com/2013/01/the-1745-jacobite-revolt-aftermath.html

https://www.legislation.gov.uk/apgb/Geo2/20/43

http://self.gutenberg.org/articles/eng/Heritable_Jurisdictions_(Scotland)_Act_1746

https://www.britannica.com/place/United-Kingdom/Walpoles-loss-of-power#ref483271

https://www.historicenvironment.scot/visit-a-place/places/fort-george/history/

https://www.nam.ac.uk/explore/72nd-regiment-foot-duke-albanys-own-highlanders

https://www.scotlandinfo.eu/general-wade-military-roads-scotland/

http://www.scotshistoryonline.co.uk/bridges/html/mil-roads.htm

https://www.sabre-roads.org.uk/wiki/index.php?title=Wade%27s_Military_Roads

http://homeatfirst.com/DEVILSTAIR.HTM#:~:text=The%20Devil%E2%80%99s%20Staircase%20looks%20south%20across%20Glen%20Coe,,bracken,%20and%20heather,%20lined%20with%20tendrils%20of%20watercourses

https://www.womenshistory.org/articles/women-and-beer-forgotten-pairing

https://www.smithsonianmag.com/history/women-used-dominate-beer-industry-until-witch-accusations-started-pouring-180977171/

https://www.nam.ac.uk/explore/black-watch-royal-highlanders

https://www.history1700s.com/index.php/articles/19-medical-history/84-smallpox-scourge-of-the-18th-century.html

https://www.sciencealert.com/centuries-long-timeline-of-smallpox-records-shows-how-a-fatal-disease-is-eliminated

http://jmla.mlanet.org/ojs/jmla/article/view/932/1082

https://www.healthline.com/health/congestive-heart-failure#treatment

https://military.wikia.org/wiki/Caroline_Frederick_Scott

https://www.scotsman.com/arts-and-culture/who-was-most-notorious-redcoat-1745-rebellion-329345

https://archives.collections.ed.ac.uk/repositories/2/archival_objects/143020

https://stewartsociety.org/history-of-the-stewarts.cfm?section=famous-stewarts&subcatid=19&histid=176

https://www.bbc.com/news/uk-scotland-highlands-islands-12996911

https://sites.google.com/site/culduie/theconfessionsoffloramacdonald

http://www.castlesfortsbattles.co.uk/highland/fort_william_fort.html

http://www.outlanderlocations.com/locations/blackness-castle/

https://www.bamburghcastle.com/castle/

http://hopetoun.co.uk/estate/outlander-at-hopetoun/

https://www.scotsmagazine.com/articles/culross/

http://scottishhistorysociety.com/the-highland-clearances/#:~:text=The%20Highland%20Clearances%201%20Brief%20account%20of%20events.,3%20Key%20Figures.%20...%204%20Suggested%20reading

https://www.totallytimelines.com/charles-edward-stuart-young-pretender-1720-1788/#:~:text=Charles%20Edward%20Stuart%20converted%20to%20Anglicanism%20during%20a,sought%20the%20backing%20of%20Frederick%20II%20of%20Prussia

Articles

Butler, James Davie, *British Convicts Shipped to American Colonies*, American Historical Review 2 (October 1896), pp.12-33.

Cowan, Edward J., and Henderson, Lizanne, 'The last of the Witches? The Survival of Scottish Witch Belief', Goodare, Julian, ed., *The Scottish Witch-hunt in Context,* (Manchester University Press, Manchester, 2002).

Dennison, E.P., 'Women: 1 to 1700', in M. Lynch, ed., *The Oxford Companion to Scottish History* (Oxford: Oxford University Press, 2001).

Dingwall, Helen M., 'Illness, Disease and Pain', in Foyster, Elizabeth and Whatley, Christopher A., *A History of Everyday Life in Scotland, 1600-1800,* (Edinburgh University Press, Edinburgh, 2011).

Dodgshon, Robert A., 'Everyday Structures, Rhythms and Spaces of the Scottish Countryside', in Foyster, Elizabeth and Whatley, Christopher A., *A History of Everyday Life in Scotland, 1600-1800,* (Edinburgh University Press, Edinburgh, 2011).

Durie, Alastair, 'Transport and Travel', in Foyster, Elizabeth and Whatley, Christopher A., *A History of Everyday Life in Scotland, 1600-1800,* (Edinburgh University Press, Edinburgh, 2011).

Ewen, E., 'The early modern family' in T. M. Devine and J. Wormald, eds., *The Oxford Handbook of Modern Scottish History* (Oxford: Oxford University Press, 2012).

Foyster, Elizabeth, 'Sensory Experiences: Smells, Sounds and Touch', in Foyster, Elizabeth and Whatley, Christopher A., *A History of Everyday Life in Scotland, 1600-1800,* (Edinburgh University Press, Edinburgh, 2011).

Goodare, Julian, 'The Scottish Witchcraft Panic of 1597', Goodare, Julian, ed., *The Scottish Witch-hunt in Context,* (Manchester University Press, Manchester, 2002).

Goodare, Julian, 'Witch-hunting and the Scottish State', Goodare, Julian, ed., *The Scottish Witch-hunt in Context,* (Manchester University Press, Manchester, 2002).

Greenburg, Stephen J, MSLS, PhD, AHIP, 'Claire Fraser, RN, MD, OMG: history of medicine in the Outlander novels and series', *Journal of the Medical Library Association,* 2020.

Harris, Bob, 'Communicating', in Foyster, Elizabeth and Whatley, Christopher A., *A History of Everyday Life in Scotland, 1600-1800,* (Edinburgh University Press, Edinburgh, 2011).

Historic Environment Scotland, *Statement of Significance: Fort George,* 2016.

Historic Environment Scotland, *Statement of Significance: Blackness Castle,* 2018.

Historic Environment Scotland, *Statement of Significance: Linlithgow Palace, Peel and Park,* 2017.

Historic Environment Scotland, *Statement of Significance: Doune Castle,* 2020.

Hutton, Ronald, 'The Global Context of the Scottish Witch-Hunt', in Goodare, Julian, ed., *The Scottish Witch-hunt in Context,* (Manchester University Press, Manchester, 2002).

Levack, Brian P., 'The Decline and End of Scottish Witch-Hunting', Goodare, Julian, ed., *The Scottish Witch-hunt in Context,* (Manchester University Press, Manchester, 2002).

MacDonald, Stuart, 'In Search of the Devil in Fife Witchcraft Cases, 1560-1705', Goodare, Julian, ed., *The Scottish Witch-hunt in Context,* (Manchester University Press, Manchester, 2002).

MacInnes, A. I., 'Scottish Gaeldom, 1638-1651: The Vernacular Response to the Covenanting Dynamic', in J. Dwyer, R. A. Mason and A. Murdoch, eds., *New Perspectives on the Politics and Culture of Early Modern Scotland,* (Edinburgh, 1981).

Martin, Lauren, 'The Devil and the Domestic: Witchcraft, Quarrels and Women's Work in Scotland', Goodare, Julian, ed., *The Scottish Witch-hunt in Context,* (Manchester University Press, Manchester, 2002).

Miller, Joyce, 'Devices and Directions: Folk Healing Aspects of Witchcraft Practice in Seventeenth-Century Scotland', Goodare, Julian, ed., *The Scottish Witch-hunt in Context,* (Manchester University Press, Manchester, 2002).

Miller, Joyce, 'Beliefs, Religions, Fears and Neuroses', in Foyster, Elizabeth and Whatley, Christopher A., *A History of Everyday Life in Scotland, 1600-1800,* (Edinburgh University Press, Edinburgh, 2011).

McKean, Charles, 'Improvement and Modernisation in Everyday Enlightenment Scotland', in Foyster, Elizabeth and Whatley, Christopher A., *A History of Everyday Life in Scotland, 1600-1800,* (Edinburgh University Press, Edinburgh, 2011).

Nenadic, Stana, 'Necessities: Food and Clothing in the Long Eighteenth Century', in Foyster, Elizabeth and Whatley, Christopher A., *A History of Everyday Life in Scotland, 1600-1800,* (Edinburgh University Press, Edinburgh, 2011).

Sharpe, James, 'Witch-Hunting and Witch Historiography: Some Anglo-Scottish Comparisons,' Goodare, Julian, ed., *The Scottish Witch-hunt in Context,* (Manchester University Press, Manchester, 2002).

Symonds, Deborah, A., 'Death, Birth and Marriage' in Foyster, Elizabeth and Whatley, Christopher A., *A History of Everyday Life in Scotland, 1600-1800,* (Edinburgh University Press, Edinburgh, 2011).

Whatley, Christopher A., 'Order and Disorder', in Foyster, Elizabeth and Whatley, Christopher A., *A History of Everyday Life in Scotland, 1600-1800,* (Edinburgh University Press, Edinburgh, 2011).

Whatley, Christopher, A., 'Work, Time and Pastimes', in Foyster, Elizabeth and Whatley, Christopher A., *A History of Everyday Life in Scotland, 1600-1800,* (Edinburgh University Press, Edinburgh, 2011).

Wasser, Michael, 'The Western Witch-Hunt of 1697-1700: the Last Major Witch-Hunt in Scotland', Goodare, Julian, ed., *The Scottish Witch-hunt in Context,* (Manchester University Press, Manchester, 2002).

Yeoman, Louise, 'Hunting the Rich Witch in Scotland: High Status Witchcraft Suspects and their Persecutors, 1590-1650', Goodare, Julian, ed., *The Scottish Witch-hunt in Context,* (Manchester University Press, Manchester, 2002).

Manuscripts

The Royal Archives
Cumberland Papers, including the Captured Stuart Papers CP/MAIN/1-69. Stuart Papers SP/MAIN/235-307.

National Archives
NA Printed handbill from Lord John Drummond, Scottish Commander, 2 December 1745 (SP 54/26/90B).

NA Extract from an intelligence report for the Admiralty given by ship master, Samuel Jones whose ship was captured off the Scillies by French privateers from Nantes, 12 October 1745 (SP 42/29/111).

National Library of Scotland
Bell, Robert Fitzroy, ed., *Memorials of John Murray of Broughton,* Edinburgh, 1898.

Great Britain Royal Commission on Historical Manuscripts, *The Manuscripts of Lord Kenyon,* 1894.

Books
Blaikie, W.B., *Origins of the 'Forty-Five,* (Edinburgh, 1916).

Byrom, Elizabeth, *The Journal of Elizabeth Byrom in 1745,* (London, Forgotten Books, 2018).

Devine, T.N., and Wormald, J., eds., *The Oxford Handbook of Modern Scottish History* (Oxford: Oxford University Press, 2012).

Devine, T.M., *The Scottish Clearances: A History of the Dispossessed,* (Penguin Books, London, 2019).

Duffy, Christoper, *The '45, Bonnie Prince Charlie and the Untold Story of the Jacobite Rising*, (Phoenix Books, London, 2007).

Dwyer, J, Mason, R. A. and Murdoch, A., eds., *New Perspectives on the Politics and Culture of Early Modern Scotland*, (Edinburgh, 1981).

Ekirch, A. Roger, *Bound for America: The Transportation of British Convicts to the Colonies, 1718-1775*, (Clarendon Press, Oxford, 1990).

Elcho, David, Lord, ed. Evan Charteris, *A Short Account of the Affairs of Scotland in the Years 1744, 1745, 1746*, (David Douglas, Edinburgh, 1907).

Fraser, Sarah, *The Last Highlander: Scotland's Most Notorious Clan Chief, Rebel & Double Agent*, (Harper Collins, London, 2012).

Foyster, Elizabeth and Whatley, Christopher A., *A History of Everyday Life in Scotland, 1600-1800*, (Edinburgh University Press, Edinburgh, 2011).

Gabaldon, Diana, *Outlander*, (Cornerstone Digital, 2011).

Gabaldon, Diana, *Dragonfly in Amber*, (Cornerstone Digital, 2011).

Gabaldon, Diana, *Voyager*, (Cornerstone Digital, 2011).

Goodare, Julian, ed., *The Scottish Witch-hunt in Context*, (Manchester University Press, Manchester, 2002).

Johnstone, James, *Memoirs of the Rebellion in 1745 and 1746*, 2nd edition (Longman, London, 1821).

King James VI, *Daemonologie, in Forme of a Dialogue, Divided into Three Bookes*, ed. Harrison, G.B., (New York, 1966).

Lynch, M., ed., *The Oxford Companion to Scottish History* (Oxford, Oxford University Press, 2001).

Macrie, Thomas, *Memoirs of Sir Andrew Agnew*, (Johnstone & Hunter, 1850).

McLynn, Frank, *Charles Edward Stuart: A Tragedy in Many Acts*, (London, Routledge, 1988).

Mitchison, R., *Lordship to Patronage, Scotland 1603–1745* (Edinburgh: Edinburgh University Press, 1983).

Parkinson, Richard, ed., *The Journal of Elizabeth Byrom in 1745*, (Manchester, 1857).

Pittock, Murray, *Culloden*, (Oxford University Press, Oxford, 2016).

Riding, Jacqueline, *Jacobites: A New History of the '45 Rebellion*, (Bloomsbury, London, 2017).

Seward, Desmond, *The King Over the Water: A Complete History of the Jacobites*, (Birlinn, Edinburgh, 2019).

Endnotes

Introduction

1. http://www.bbc.co.uk/arts/robertburns/works/charlie_hes_my_darling/.
2. http://www.rampantscotland.com/songs/blsongs_cope.htm.
3. https://www.jacobites.net/skye-boat-song.html.
4. http://januarymagazine.com/profiles/gabaldon.html.
5. http://www.bbc.co.uk/doctorwho/classic/episodeguide/highlanders/detail.shtml.
6. Riding, Jacqueline, *Jacobites: A New History of the '45 Rebellion,* (Bloomsbury, London, 2016) p.338.
7. https://www.britannica.com/topic/Jacobite-British-history.
8. Seward, Desmond, *The King Over the Water: A Complete History of the Jacobites,* (Birlinn, Edinburgh, 2019).
9. https://www.scottishhistory.org/articles/massacre-of-glencoe/.
10. Seward, 2019, p.160.

Chapter One: The MacKenzies and the Frasers – What Was Clan Life Really Like?

1. Gabaldon, Diana, *Outlander,* (Cornerstone Digital, 2011).
2. Devine, T.M., *The Scottish Clearances: A History of the Dispossessed,* (Penguin Books, London, 2019) pp.26-36.
3. As quoted in A. I. Macinnes, 'Scottish Gaeldom, 1638-1651: The Vernacular Response to the Covenanting Dynamic', in J. Dwyer, R. A. Mason and A. Murdoch, eds., *New Perspectives on the Politics and Culture of Early Modern Scotland,* (Edinburgh, 1981) p.84.
4. Dodgshon, Robert A., 'Everyday Structures, Rhythms and Spaces of the Scottish Countryside', in Foyster, Elizabeth and Whatley,

Christopher A., *A History of Everyday Life in Scotland, 1600-1800,* (Edinburgh University Press, Edinburgh, 2011).

5. Devine, 2019.
6. Dodgshon, 2011, pp.37-38
7. McKean, Charles, 'Improvement and Modernisation in Everyday Enlightenment Scotland,' in Foyster and Whatley, 2011, p.57.
8. http://www.waulk.org/index.asp?pageid=176756.
9. Devine, 2019, p.28.
10. http://greatscottishclans.com/clans/mackenzie.php.
11. Devine, 2019, p.31.
12. https://www.castleleod.org.uk/history/the-people-who-lived-here/.
13. Riding, 2016, p.97.
14. Riding, 2016, p.484.
15. https://www.castleleod.org.uk/stories/the-jacobite-rising-of-1745/.
16. https://www.undiscoveredscotland.co.uk/usbiography/f/simonfraser.html.
17. 'Letter from the Associators to Cardinal Fleury', translated in Blaikie, W.B., *Origins of the 'Forty-Five,* (Edinburgh, 1916).
18. Riding, 2016, p.338.
19. http://clanfraser.org/timeline/1700s/.

Chapter Two: Claire the Hostage – How Were Women Treated in the Highlands?

1. E. P. Dennison, 'Women: 1 to 1700', in M. Lynch, ed., The Oxford Companion to Scottish History (Oxford: Oxford University Press, 2001), pp.645-646.
2. E. Ewen, "The early modern family" in T. M. Devine and J. Wormald, eds., *The Oxford Handbook of Modern Scottish History* (Oxford: Oxford University Press, 2012).
3. Ewen, 2012, p.275.
4. Miller, Joyce, Lecture, *Witchcraft in Medieval and Early Modern Scotland,* Hosted by the University of Edinburgh Feminist Society, 03/11/2020.
5. Symonds, Deborah, A., 'Death, Birth and Marriage' in Foyster, Elizabeth and Whatley, Christopher A., *A History of Everyday Life in Scotland, 1600-1800,* (Edinburgh University Press, Edinburgh, 2011) p.98.

6. Mitchison, R., *Lordship to Patronage, Scotland 1603–1745* (Edinburgh: Edinburgh University Press, 1983) pp.86–8.
7. Symonds, 2011, p.99.
8. Whatley, Christopher, A., 'Work, Time and Pastimes', in Foyster, Elizabeth and Whatley, Christopher A., *A History of Everyday Life in Scotland, 1600-1800,* (Edinburgh University Press, Edinburgh, 2011) p.280.
9. Whatley, 2011, p.28.
10. https://www.womenshistory.org/articles/women-and-beer-forgotten-pairing.
11. https://www.smithsonianmag.com/history/women-used-dominate-beer-industry-until-witch-accusations-started-pouring-180977171/.
12. *Ibid.*
13. https://www.undiscoveredscotland.co.uk/usbiography/mac/annemackintosh.html.
14. https://www.nam.ac.uk/explore/black-watch-royal-highlanders.
15. Riding, 2016, p.338.

Chapter Three: A Twentieth Century Nurse Practicing Eighteenth Century Medicine

1. Gabaldon, *Outlander,* 2011.
2. Gabaldon, *Dragonfly in Amber,* 2011.
3. https://www.sciencealert.com/centuries-long-timeline-of-smallpox-records-shows-how-a-fatal-disease-is-eliminated.
4. Gabaldon, *Dragonfly in Amber,* 2011.
5. http://jmla.mlanet.org/ojs/jmla/article/view/932/1082.
6. https://www.healthline.com/health/congestive-heart-failure#treatment.

Chapter Four: Witches or Time Travellers?

1. Gabaldon, *Outlander*, 2011.
2. Outlander, Season One, Episode 11, *The Devil's Mark*, Starz, first aired 18/04/2015.

3. Macdonald, Stuart, 'The Devil in Fife Witchcraft Cases', in Goodare, Julian, ed., *The Scottish Witch-hunt in Context*, (Manchester University Press, Manchester, 2002).
4. Martin, Lauren, 'Witchcraft, Quarrels and Women's Work', in Goodare, Julian, ed., *The Scottish Witch-Hunt in Context*, (Manchester University Press, Manchester, 2002) p.81.
5. *Ibid*, p.86.
6. King James VI, *Daemonologie, in Forme of a Dialogue, Divided into Three Bookes,* ed. Harrison, G.B., (New York, 1966).
7. https://engole.info/john-kincaid-witch-finder/.

Chapter Five: Who Were the Redcoats?

1. https://military.wikia.org/wiki/Red_coat_(British_army).
2. https://military.wikia.org/wiki/Caroline_Frederick_Scott.
3. https://www.scotsman.com/arts-and-culture/who-was-most-notorious-redcoat-1745-rebellion-329345.
4. https://archives.collections.ed.ac.uk/repositories/2/archival_objects/143020.
5. https://stewartsociety.org/history-of-the-stewarts.cfm?section=famous-stewarts&subcatid=19&histid=176, https://www.scotsman.com/arts-and-culture/who-was-most-notorious-redcoat-1745-rebellion-329345.
6. https://www.bbc.com/news/uk-scotland-highlands-islands-12996911.
7. https://sites.google.com/site/culduie/theconfessionsofflora macdonald.
8. https://www.scotsman.com/arts-and-culture/who-was-most-notorious-redcoat-1745-rebellion-329345.
9. https://www.soirbheas.org/wp-content/uploads/2020/04/presentation-The-8-Sheuglie-Grants-involved-in-the-45.pdf.
10. https://www.scotsman.com/arts-and-culture/who-was-most-notorious-redcoat-1745-rebellion-329345.
11. http://www.danielnpaul.com/BritishScalpProclamation-1749.html#:~:text=In%201745,%20he%20was%20placed%20in%20charge%20of,final%20battle%20came%20April%2016,%201746,%20at%20Culloden.
12. *Ibid.*

Chapter Six: Outlander Locations

1. Gabaldon, *Outlander*, 2011.
2. *Ibid.*
3. http://www.castlesfortsbattles.co.uk/highland/fort_william_fort.html.
4. Historic Environment Scotland, *Statement of Significance: Blackness Castle*, 2018.
5. *Ibid.*
6. http://www.outlanderlocations.com/locations/blackness-castle/.
7. Gabaldon, *Outlander*, 2011.
8. https://www.historicenvironment.scot/visit-a-place/places/linlithgow-palace/history/.
9. Historic Environment Scotland, *Statement of Significance: Linlithgow Palace, Peel and Park*, 2017.
10. https://thirdeyetraveller.com/linlithgow-palace-outlander-scenes/.
11. Historic Environment Scotland, *Statement o Significance: Linlithgow Palace, Peel and Park*, 2017.
12. https://www.bamburghcastle.com/castle/.
13. *Ibid.*
14. *Ibid.*
15. *Ibid.*
16. https://outlander.fandom.com/wiki/Castle_Leoch.
17. *Ibid.*
18. *Ibid.*
19. https://www.castleleod.org.uk/history/the-castles-story/.
20. https://www.castleleod.org.uk/history/the-people-who-lived-here/.
21. *Ibid.*
22. Historic Environment Scotland, *Statement of Significance: Doune Castle*, 2020.
23. *Ibid.*
24. *Ibid.*
25. Gabaldon, *Outlander*, 2011.
26. Gabaldon, *Dragonfly in Amber*, 2011.
27. https://outlander.fandom.com/wiki/Lallybroch.
28. Gabaldon, *Dragonfly in Amber*, 2011.
29. http://hopetoun.co.uk/estate/outlander-at-hopetoun/.
30. https://www.scotsmagazine.com/articles/culross/.
31. *Ibid.*

Chapter Seven: Charlie's Early life and Claim to the Throne

1. https://www.undiscoveredscotland.co.uk/usbiography/s/jamesfrancisedwardstuart.html.
2. Seward, 2019, p.117.
3. Seward, 2019.
4. Seward, 2019, p.220.
5. Riding, 2016, p.7.
6. Riding, 2016, p.11.

Chapter Eight: Charles in France: Jamie and Claire Come to Visit

1. Gabaldon, Diana, *Dragonfly in Amber,* (Cornerstone Digital, 2011).
2. Riding, 2016, p.16.
3. Riding, 2016, p.20.
4. Seward, 2019, p.224-225.
5. Riding, 2016, p.23.
6. Riding, 2016, p.25-29.
7. Royal Archives Stuart Papers/Main/256/126-126a Earl Marischal to Charles, Dunkirk, 13 March 1744 NS as quoted in Riding, 2016.
8. Royal Archives Stuart Papers/Main/258/133 James to Sempill, Rome, 14 August 1744 NS as quoted in Riding, 2016, p.34.
9. Bell, Robert Fitzroy ed., *Memorials of John Murray of Broughton,* Edinburgh, 1898.
10. Royal Archives Stuart Papers/Main/258/139 Charles to James, Paris 17 August 1744 N.S.
11. Riding, 2016, pp.39-41.

Chapter Nine: Charles Arrives in Scotland

1. Gabaldon, *Dragonfly in Amber,* 2011.
2. Royal Archives Stuart Papers/MAIN/265/73 as quoted in Riding, 2016, p.55.
3. Royal Archives Stuart Papers/MAIN/265/129 Charles to James, 'Navar' 12 June 1745 NS as quoted in Riding, 2016, pp.59-60.
4. Riding, 2016, pp.62-65.

5. Riding, 2016, pp.77-78.
6. Seward, 2019, p.235.
7. Riding, 2016, p.82.
8. Riding, 2016, p.98.
9. Riding, 2016, pp.98-101.

Chapter Ten: Edinburgh

1. https://www.bankofengland.co.uk/monetary-policy/inflation/inflation-calculator.
2. http://www.visitdunkeld.com/perth-prince-charles.htm.
3. http://www.visitdunkeld.com/perth-prince-charles.htm.
4. https://www.undiscoveredscotland.co.uk/usbiography/m/georgemurray.html.
5. 'Lord George Murray to Duke James, Tullibardine "Six at night" 3 September 1745 O.S.' in Stewart-Murray and Anderson, Atholl Chronicles, Vol. 3, pp.19-20, as quoted in Riding, 2016, p.122.
6. Riding, 2016, pp122-123.
7. 'Copy of the Prince's Summons to the City of Edinburgh to Surrender' in *LM,* Vol. 1, p.249, as quoted in Riding, 2016, p.116.
8. Riding, 2016, pp.133-134.
9. https://www.royal.uk/royal-residences-palace-holyroodhouse.
10. https://randomscottishhistory.com/2018/03/10/chapter-40-edinburgh-in-1745-pp-322-329/.
11. https://randomscottishhistory.com/2018/03/10/chapter-40-edinburgh-in-1745-pp-322-329/.
12. https://www.scotsman.com/whats-on/arts-and-entertainment/when-jacobites-took-over-palace-holyroodhouse-844650.
13. https://www.scotsman.com/whats-on/arts-and-entertainment/when-jacobites-took-over-palace-holyroodhouse-844650.

Chapter Eleven: Prestonpans

1. Riding, 2016, pp.152-153.
2. Johnstone, James, *Memoirs of the Rebellion in 1745 and 1746,* 2nd edition (Longman, London, 1821).
3. Riding, 2016, p.154.

4. http://www.battlefieldsofbritain.co.uk/battle_prestonpans_1745.html.
5. Riding, 2016, p.155.
6. https://www.britishbattles.com/jacobite-rebellion/battle-of-prestonpans/.
7. http://www.battlefieldsofbritain.co.uk/battle_prestonpans_1745.html.
8. Seward, 2019, p.239.
9. Riding, 2016, p.152.
10. Riding, 2016, p.159.
11. Seward, 2019, p.250.

Chapter Twelve: Building an Army

1. Proclamation, Holyroodhouse 24 September 1745 O.S., British Library C.115.i.3.(63).
2. Elcho, David, Lord, ed. Evan Charteris, *A Short Account of the Affairs of Scotland in the Years 1744, 1745, 1746,* (David Douglas, Edinburgh, 1907).
3. Kirkconnell, James Maxwell of, *Narrative of Charles Prince of Wales' Expedition to Scotland in the year of 1745, Edinburgh, 1861.*
4. Riding, 2016, p.177.
5. As quoted in Riding, 2016, p.179 and Seward, 2019, p.243.
6. Lord Elcho, *A Short Account,* p.306.
7. Proclamation, Holyroodhouse 2 October 1745 O.S., British Library C.115.i.3.(64).
8. Riding, 2016, p.184.
9. Seward, 2019, p.241.
10. Seward, 2019, p.246.

Chapter Thirteen: Heading South

1. Lord Elcho, *A Short Account,* p.304.
2. Bell, Robert Fitzroy, ed., *Memorials of John Murray of Broughton,* Edinburgh, 1898, pp.231-232.
3. Johnstone, *Memoirs of the Rebellion,* p.53.
4. *Ibid.*
5. Riding, 2016, p.200.
6. *Ibid.*

Chapter Fourteen: Carlisle

1. Johnstone, *Memoirs of the Rebellion,* p.56.
2. Riding, 2016, p.213.
3. NA SP 36/73/3f. 40 Charles to the Mayor of Carlisle, 'Two in the afternoon' 10 November 1745 O.S. as quoted in Riding, 2016, pp.214-215.
4. Riding, 2016, pp.217-219.
5. Seward, 2019, p.248.
6. https://www.electricscotland.com/history/charles/37.htm.
7. Riding, 2016, p.220.
8. Bell, *Murray of Broughton,* p.243.
9. Johnstone, *Memoirs of the Rebellion,* p.60.

Chapter Fifteen: Travelling South Again

1. RA Captured Stuart Papers CP/MAIN/7/416 Order to the High Constable of Penrith, Penrith 2 November 1745 O.S. as quoted in Riding, 2016, p.230.
2. Riding, 2016, p.232.
3. https://www.historic-uk.com/HistoryUK/HistoryofScotland/The-Stewart-Stuart-Monarchy-of-Scotland/.
4. Seward, 2019, p.160.
5. Seward, 2019, p.159.
6. Seward, 2019, p.161.
7. Lord Elcho, *A Short Account,* pp.328-329.

Chapter Sixteen: Manchester

1. Riding, 2016, p.240.
2. Riding, 2016, pp.240-241.
3. Johnstone, *Memoirs of the Rebellion,* pp.65-66.
4. Riding, 2016, p.246.
5. 'Brief for the defendant in the suit of the King v William Fowden', in HMRC, *The Manuscripts of Lord Kenyon,* 1894, pp.478-476.
6. Parkinson, Richard, ed. *The Journal of Elizabeth Byrom in 1745,* (Manchester, 1857), p.12.

7. Riding, 2016, p.251.
8. Seward, 2019, p.250.

Chapter Seventeen: The British Forces

1. RACP/MAIN/5/174 Ligonier to Cumberland, London 24 September 1745 O.S. as quoted in Riding, 2016, p.192.
2. Riding, 2016, pp.192-193.
3. RACP/MAIN/6/101 Cumberland to Harrington, Vilvoorde 21 October 1745 N.S. [10 October O.S.].
4. RACP/MAIN/6/161 Proclamation by Field Marshal Wade, Newcastle, 30 October 1745 O.S.
5. NA SP/36/74/19 Resolutions from General Wade's Council of War regarding Carlisle.
6. RACP/MAIN/7/117 George II 'instructions' to Cumberland, Court of St James's, 25 November 1745 O.S.
7. BL Add MS 32705 ff.399-400, Richmond to Newcastle, Lichfield 30 November 1745 O.S. as quoted in Riding, 2016, p.256.

Chapter Eighteen: On the Continent

1. Riding, 2016, p.204.
2. NA SP 36/73/3 ff. 74-75, Copy of a letter from Henry to Charles, Bagneux 26 November 1745 N.S. as quoted in Riding, 2016, p.206.
3. RA Captured Stuart Papers CP/MAIN/7/454 Lord John Drummond's Declaration, Montrose 2 December 1745 O.S. as quoted in Riding, 2016, pp.260-261.

Chapter Nineteen: Derby

1. Riding, 2016, p.264.
2. Riding, 2016, pp.265-266.
3. Seward, 2019, p.250.
4. Riding, 2016, p.295.
5. Johnstone, *Memoirs of the Rebellion,* pp.68-69.

6. Lord Elcho, *A Short Account,* pp.336-341.
7. Johnstone, *Memoirs of the Rebellion,* p.70.
8. Seward, 2019, pp.250-251.
9. Starz, *Outlander,* season 2, episode 11.
10. Riding, 2016, pp.302-303.
11. Lord Elcho, *A Short Account,* p.341.
12. Johnstone, *Memoirs of the Rebellion,* p.73.
13. Pittock, M., *Culloden,* (Oxford University Press, Oxford, 2016) p.33.

Chapter Twenty: The Race North

1. RA CP/MAIN/7/324 Cumberland to Newcastle, Packington 6 December 1745 O.S.
2. Riding, 2016, p.309.
3. Parkinson, *The Journal of Elizabeth Byrom,* pp.15-18.
4. RA CP/MAIN/7/352 Furnivall to Cumberland, Congleton Sunday noon, 8 December 1745 O.S.
5. Riding, 2016, p.311.
6. RA CP/MAIN/7/346 Cabinet Meeting Minutes, Whitehall 8 December 1745 O.S.
7. RA CP/MAIN/8/6 Cumberland to Newcastle, Macclesfield 11 December 1745 O.S.
8. RA CP/MAIN/8/24 Cumberland to Newcastle, Macclesfield 12 December 1745 O.S.
9. RA CP/MAIN/8/11 Wade to Cumberland, Leeds 12 December 1745 O.S.
10. RA CP/MAIN/8/44 Cumberland to Newcastle, Preston 15 December 1745 O.S.
11. Johnstone, *Memoirs of the Rebellion,* pp.86-90.
12. Riding, 2016, p.321.
13. Johnstone, *Memoirs of the Rebellion,* pp.92-93.

Chapter Twenty-One: Carlisle Again

1. Johnstone, *Memoirs of the Rebellion,* pp.94-95.
2. RA CP/MAIN/8/89 Cumberland to Newcastle, 'Blickhall' near Carlisle 22 December 1745 O.S.

3. Riding, 2016, p.328.
4. Riding, 2016, p.329.
5. RA CP/MAIN/8/138 Newcastle to Cumberland, Whitehall 28 December 1745 O.S.

Chapter Twenty-Two: Glasgow

1. Johnstone, *Memoirs of the Rebellion,* pp.99-100.
2. Riding, 2016, pp.331-332.
3. Johnstone, *Memoirs of the Rebellion,* pp.103-104.
4. Riding, 2016, p.332.
5. https://www.nms.ac.uk/explore-our-collections/stories/art-and-design/the-rise-and-fall-of-hamilton-palace/.
6. Riding, 2016, p.335.
7. Riding, 2016, p.336.
8. Lord Elcho, *A Short Account,* pp.355-356.
9. Riding, 2016, p.338.
10. Duffy, Christoper, *The '45, Bonnie Prince Charlie and Untold Story of the Jacobite Rising,* (London, Phoenix Books, 2007) p.356.
11. Fraser, Sarah, *The Last Highlander: Scotland's Most Notorious Clan Chief, Rebel & Double Agent.* (HarperCollins, London, 2012) pp.291–292.
12. Fraser, 2012, p.302.
13. Riding, 2016, pp.338-339.

Chapter Twenty-Three: Falkirk

1. Riding, 2016, p.342.
2. Johnstone, *Memoirs of the Rebellion,* pp.110-111.
3. Riding, 2016, p.343.
4. Johnstone, *Memoirs of the Rebellion,* p.117.
5. Johnstone, *Memoirs of the Rebellion,* pp.117-119.
6. Home, *The History of the Rebellion,* p.116 as quoted in Riding, 2016, p.364.
7. Johnstone, *Memoirs of the Rebellion,* p.121.
8. *Ibid,* p. 122.

9. http://www.douglashistory.co.uk/history/Battles/Falkirk_1746.html#.
    YClT9DJxfIU.
10. Riding, 2016, p.348.
11. RA CP/MAIN/9/99 Hawley to Cumberland, Linlithgow 17 January
    1745/6 O.S.
12. Johnstone, *Memoirs of the Rebellion,* pp.126-127.
13. Riding, 2016, p.350.
14. Johnstone, *Memoirs of the Rebellion,* p.124.
15. RA Captured Stuart Papers, CP/MAIN/9/245 George Colville [to ?],
    Blair Castle 19 January 1745/6 O.S., as quoted in Riding, 2016, p.351.
16. http://www.douglashistory.co.uk/history/Battles/Falkirk_1746.
    html#.YCrLhjJxfIU.
17. Riding, 2016, p.350-351.
18. Seward, 2019, p.266.
19. Lord Elcho, *A Short Account,* p.381.
20. Johnstone, *Memoirs of the Rebellion,* p.119.
21. Riding, 2016, p.354.
22. *Ibid.*
23. RA CP/MAIN/10/28 Cumberland to Newcastle, Holyroodhouse 30
    January 1745/6 O.S.
24. Riding, 2016, p.357.
25. Riding, 2016, pp.357-358.
26. Johnstone, *Memoirs of the Rebellion,* p.142, editor's notes.
27. Riding, 2016, pp.358-359.
28. Riding, 2016, p.360.
29. *Ibid.*
30. Seward, 2019, p.266.

Chapter Twenty-Four: Cumberland in Scotland

1. RA CP/MAIN/10/37 Cumberland to Newcastle, Falkirk 1 February
    1745/6 O.S.
2. RA CP/MAIN/10/43 Cumberland to Newcastle, Stirling 2 February
    1745/6 O.S.
3. Riding, 2016, p.361.
4. RA CP/MAIN/10/74 Cumberland to Newcastle, Crieff 5 February
    1745/6 O.S.

5. RA CP/MAIN/10/168 Cumberland to Newcastle, Perth 10 February 1745/6 O.S.
6. RA CP/MAIN/10/266 Captain Alexander Campbell to Fawkener, Fort William 17 February 1745/6 O.S.

Chapter Twenty-Five: Inverness

1. RA CP/MAIN/10/168 Cumberland to Newcastle, Perth 10 February 1745/6 O.S.
2. Riding, 2016, p.371.
3. http://old.scotwars.com/battle_of_moy.htm.
4. *Ibid.*
5. *Ibid.*
6. Riding, 2016, pp.343-344.

Chapter Twenty-Six: Spring

1. Riding, 2016, p.378.
2. RA CP/MAIN/13/25 Intelligence from several hands, Strathbogie, 28 March 1746 O.S.
3. RA CP/MAIN/13/88 Cumberland to Newcastle, Aberdeen 31 March 1746 O.S.
4. Riding, 2016, pp.380-381.
5. Johnstone, *Memoirs of the Rebellion,* pp.161-162.
6. Riding, 2016, pp.384-385.
7. Lord Elcho, *A Short Account,* p.419.
8. Riding, 2016, p.390.
9. Johnstone, *Memoirs of the Rebellion,* p.169.
10. Lord Elcho, *A Short Account,* p.422.
11. Riding, 2016, p.395.
12. Riding, 2016, p.396.
13. Lord Elcho, *A Short Account,* p.426.

Chapter Twenty-Seven: The Night March

1. Lord Elcho, *A Short Account,* p.426.
2. Riding, 2016, p.397.

3. Lord Elcho, *A Short Account,* p.427.
4. Riding, 2016, p.398.
5. Riding, 2016, pp.398-399.
6. Johnstone, *Memoirs of the Rebellion,* pp.172-175.
7. Johnstone, *Memoirs of the Rebellion,* editor's notes, pp.178-179.
8. *Ibid*, pp.180-181.
9. *Ibid*, p.182.
10. *Ibid.*
11. Lord Elcho, *A Short Account,* p.428.
12. Riding, 2016, p.409.
13. Lord Elcho, *A Short Account,* pp.428-429.

Chapter Twenty-Eight: The Battle of Culloden

1. Lord Elcho, *A Short Account,* p.430.
2. Riding, 2016, p.414.
3. *Ibid*, p.417.
4. Riding, 2016, pp.418-422.
5. Lord Elcho, *A Short Account,* p.431.
6. Seward, 2019, p.272.
7. Lord Elcho, *A Short Account, p.*431.
8. Riding, 2016. p.424.
9. *Ibid.*
10. Johnstone, *Memoirs of the Rebellion,* p.192.
11. Johnstone, *Memoirs of the Rebellion,* editors' note, p.193.
12. Johnstone, *Memoirs of the Rebellion,* p.196.
13. Riding, 2016, p.425.
14. Seward, 2019, p.275.
15. Johnstone, *Memoirs of the Rebellion,* p.197.
16. Seward, 2019, p.275.

Chapter Twenty-Nine: Flight

1. Riding, 2016, pp.429-430.
2. Johnstone, *Memoirs of the Rebellion,* p.198.
3. Lord Elcho, *A Short Account,* p.434.

4. *Ibid*, pp.434-436.
5. Riding, 2016, p.432.
6. RA SP/MAIN/273/96 Letter from Lord George Murray to Charles [copy], Ruthven 17 April 1746 O.S.
7. Johnstone, *Memoirs of the Rebellion,* pp.198-202.
8. RA SP/MAIN/273/117 'The Prince's letter to ye Chifs, in parting from Scotland' 28 April 1746 as quoted in Riding, 2016, pp.438-439.

Chapter Thirty: Charles Travels to France

1. Riding, 2016, p.453.
2. 'Hugh MacDonald of Baleshare's Account' in *LM,* Vol. 2, pp.95-103 as quoted in Riding, 2016, pp.453-455.
3. Seward, 2019, p.28.
4. Riding, 2016, p.456.
5. *Ibid.*
6. *Ibid*, p.457.
7. https://www.sarahfraser.co.uk/jacobite-gold/.
8. Riding, 2016, p.457.
9. *Ibid*, p.467.
10. *Ibid.*
11. https://www.historic-uk.com/HistoryUK/HistoryofScotland/Flora-Macdonald/.
12. *Ibid.*
13. Riding, 2016, p.492.

Chapter Thirty-One: Elsewhere in Scotland

1. Riding, 2016, p.442.
2. RA CP/MAIN/14/58 Cumberland to Newcastle, Inverness 19 April 1746 O.S.
3. *Ibid.*
4. *Ibid.*
5. Riding, 2016, p.459.
6. *Ibid*, p.460.

7. RA CP/MAIN/15/221 Cumberland to Newcastle, Fort Augustus 27 May 1746 O.S.

8. *Ibid.*

9. Butler, James Davie, *British Convicts Shipped to American Colonies*, American Historical Review 2 (October 1896), pp.12-33.

10. https://ibw21.org/reparations/slavery-vs-indentured-servitude-which-aids-racism/.

11. Butler, *British Convicts Shipped to American Colonies,* p.16.

12. RA CP/MAIN/14/354 Ancram to Fawkener, Aberdeen 9 May 1746 O.S.

13. Riding, 2016, p.461.

14. RACP/MAIN/16/59 Captain John Ferguson's Journal, 'Tobbermury' 11 June 1746 O.S.

15. RA CP/MAIN/16/8 Fawkener to the commanding officers of His Majesty's ships, Fort Augustus 8 June 1746 O.S.

Chapter Thirty-Two: Trial and Execution

1. https://www.oldpolicecellsmuseum.org.uk/content/history/transportation-3/life_aboard_the_prison_hulks.

2. https://www.historic-uk.com/DestinationsUK/Newgate-Prison/.

3. Riding, 2016, p.473.

4. *Ibid*, p.474.

5. *Ibid.*

6. https://allthatsinteresting.com/hanged-drawn-quartered.

7. Riding, 2016, pp.474-475.

8. *Ibid.*

9. *Ibid*, p.476.

10. *Ibid.*

11. *Ibid*, p.483.

12. https://www.castleleod.org.uk/stories/the-jacobite-rising-of-1745/.

13. Riding, 2016, p.484.

14. https://www.castleleod.org.uk/stories/the-jacobite-rising-of-1745/.

15. Riding, 2016, p.485.

16. https://dailysirwalter.blogspot.com/2010/08/execution-of-earl-kilmarnock-and-lord.html#:~:text=Execution%20of%20

Earl%20Kilmarnock%20and%20Lord%20Balmerino%20
On,impending%20death%20on%20behalf%20of%20the%20
Jacobite%20cause.

17. http://www.britishexecutions.co.uk/execution-content.
    php?key=2037.
18. *Ibid.*
19. Riding, 2016, p.488.
20. Ibid, p.489.
21. http://www.britishexecutions.co.uk/execution-content.
    php?key=2040&termRef=Lord%20Lovat.
22. *Ibid.*
23. *Ibid.*
24. http://clanfraser.org/clan-chiefs/.
25. https://www.theguardian.com/science/2018/jan/19/headless-body-
    is-not-scottish-clan-chief-simon-fraser-experts.
26. https://www.scotsman.com/whats-on/arts-and-entertainment/story-
    last-jacobite-be-hanged-1470851.
27. *Ibid.*
28. https://www.sarahfraser.co.uk/jacobite-gold/.
29. *Ibid.*
30. http://www.britishexecutions.co.uk/execution-content.
    php?key=2119.
31. *Ibid.*

Chapter Thirty-Three: The Highlands

1. https://www.scotsman.com/heritage-and-retro/heritage/scottish-town-
   owed-ps100000-jacobites-275-year-old-debt-3079238?fbclid=Iw
   AR0dOi67brf82ebYy8gzhu1kmyUxBxIuIy4lxN90g4qQjf0Mp6
   Hjh7wwdYI.
2. Macrie,Thomas,*MemoirsofSirAndrewAgnew*,(Johnstone&Hunter,
   1850) p.8.
3. https://petergshilstonsblog.blogspot.com/2013/01/the-1745-jacobite-
   revolt-aftermath.html.
4. TextoftheActasquotedon:http://www.tartansauthority.com/tartan/
   the-growth-of-tartan/the-act-of-proscription-1747/.
5. *Ibid.*

6. *Ibid.*
7. *Ibid.*
8. *Ibid.*
9. Riding, 2016, p.374.
10. Historic Environment Scotland, Statement of Significance, Fort George, last reviewed 2016, p.3.
11. *Ibid.*
12. *Ibid.*
13. https://www.scotlandinfo.eu/general-wade-military-roads-scotland/.
14. *Ibid.*
15. http://www.scotshistoryonline.co.uk/bridges/html/mil-roads.htm.
16. https://www.scotlandinfo.eu/general-wade-military-roads-scotland/.
17. https://www.sabre-roads.org.uk/wiki/index.php?title=Corrieyairack_Pass.
18. http://homeatfirst.com/DEVILSTAIR.HTM#:~:text=The%20Devil%E2%80%99s%20Staircase%20looks%20south%20across%20Glen%20Coe,,bracken,%20and%20heather,%20lined%20with%20tendrils%20of%20watercourses.
19. https://www.scotlandinfo.eu/general-wade-military-roads-scotland/.
20. https://www.ordnancesurvey.co.uk/about/history.
21. *Ibid.*
22. *Ibid.*
23. http://scottishhistorysociety.com/the-highland-clearances/#:~:text=The%20Highland%20Clearances%201%20Brief%20account%20of%20events.,3%20Key%20Figures.%20...%204%20Suggested%20reading.
24. Devine,T.M.,*TheScottishClearances:AHistoryoftheDispossessed,* (Penguin Random House, London, 2019) pp.226-228.
25. Devine, 2019, p.227.
26. Ibid, p.254.

Epilogue

1. Seward, 2019, p.285.
2. *Ibid*, p.286.
3. https://www.totallytimelines.com/charles-edward-stuart-young-pretender-1720-1788/#:~:text=Charles%20Edward%20

Stuart%20converted%20to%20Anglicanism%20during%20
a,sought%20the%20backing%20of%20Frederick%20II%20
of%20Prussia.

4. Seward, 2019, p.299.
5. *Ibid*, p.327.